QUENTIN TARANTINO

To Mum and Dad

Quentin Tarantino

The Cinema of Cool

by Jeff Dawson

APPLAUSE
NEW YORK • LONDON

An Applause Original

QUENTIN TARANTINO: THE CINEMA OF COOL
by Jeff Dawson

Library of Congress Card No. 95-79935

ISBN: 1-55783-227-7

APPLAUSE BOOKS
211 W. 71st St.
New York, NY 10023
Phone: (212) 595-4735   Fax: (212) 721-2856

Cover picture © Stephen Lovell Davis/Retna Pictures

Contents

Foreword

Quentin introduced me to a new world of words, a place where people communicate with phrases that are so fresh and full of surprises they never fail to make you smile. He can elevate a seemingly normal conversation into a fascinating exchange with a poetry only he is capable of giving. His observation of behaviour and communication is completely unique, yet you never feel it is arty or self-conscious . . . it just works.

Strange, dark, humorous, twisted, sweet, surprising and never failing to engage you in a way you have not experienced before, he seems to have some uncanny knack of tapping into the DNA of his characters. If I didn't know better, I'd say Quentin was on acid.

He is the first writer I have ever read where I would skip the visual stage direction and just read the dialogue. Before Quentin, script reading was a different process for me – all about shading and colouring environments and staging visuals in support of the characters – but with Quentin I read from one line of dialogue to the next, constantly smiling. And, no matter how dark or twisted the characters may appear, they always have an inherent sense of humour. The pure balls he has in combining the most conflicting emotions you could ever conjure up. Outrageous and daring, he not only gets away with it, it's brilliant.

Quentin and I come from different worlds, different continents, but our common denominator is our passion for film. I see my films as canvasses where I fill in the various colours, emotional and visual, but Quentin's ear for dialogue gave me a whole new focal point. I now see people through different eyes. Having spent my early years as a painter, for me it was as big a revelation as Francis Bacon's vision of people and their inner souls. The darkness, the twisted sense of humour and the surprises – all the qualities I attribute to Quentin.

I am a bad reader. Normally a script takes me two to three sittings, but I read *Reservoir Dogs* and *True Romance* back to back at 4 a.m. after a 16-hour plane ride (I also read *Pulp Fiction* on a plane some months later, laughing out loud the whole flight). When I had finished, I picked up the phone and said, 'I want to do both these movies.'

Quentin is a mirror of the characters in his movies – outrageous and unpredictable with a boundless energy – normally something in Hollywood

I would attribute to drugs. This is not the case. His overwhelming enthusiasm for movies has made everyone excited . . . and now everyone wants a piece of him.

As a spinner of great yarns, that unique voice made my last two films very happy experiences. It could be his arrogance or lack of cynicism, but the man has the courage of his convictions, listening to others but never swayed by their opinions. In a town where everyone needs to validate their point of view, this is both comical and admirable. Quentin will expound his theories to anyone who'll listen.

What is so often misunderstood is that it isn't only pop references that pour from his characters' mouths. He has the ability to establish figures with full 3-D foibles, quirks and histories within a few lines of dialogue. His work on *Crimson Tide*, for example, made every character into a real person, each very fresh and very different. Who would have ever have thought of an executive officer on a nuclear submarine having an in-depth conversation about Lipizzaner horses? Yet it worked brilliantly – so much so that it became the book-end for the movie.

True Romance portrayed very different players, the kind of characters Quentin is famous for. For me it was Alabama's story, seen through her eyes – dreamy and strange. Clarence, meanwhile, is Quentin – dark, twisted, sharp and very sweet.

Quentin would have made a very different *True Romance* – tougher, edgy, less dreamlike, less self-conscious – but I stuck religiously to his script, as did the cast. Nobody wanted to alter anything, just reproduce what was on the page because it was so good. So good that, as a romantic at heart, I fell in love with Clarence and Alabama and wanted to see them fulfil their dream. Quentin had shattered that dream with Clarence's death. Though I shot both endings, my weakness for romanticism let Clarence and Alabama live happily ever after.

For someone who had always been a hired gun for the studios, the low pressures of a small budget, the creative freedom given to me by producer Sammy Hadida and, above all, Quentin's wonderful script made *True Romance* my best movie experience to date.

My only true disappointment with Quentin is that I feel I have now lost him to his own material. Much as I would love him to write something else that I could direct, I think this time has gone, his life now dedicated to writing and directing his own material and occasionally acting in the films of others. For me it is a selfish loss.

To the world of movies, 'Quentin, give us more . . .'

Tony Scott
May 1995

ACKNOWLEDGEMENTS

Naturally, this book would not exist without the kind help of others, chiefly, of course, Quentin Tarantino, who was very generous with his time specifically for this project. It was a privilege to be granted such access to someone who is not only incredibly busy but has a multitude of journalists beating at his door, and I am extremely grateful.

Huge thanks also to Bumble Ward for helping me at every turn, Tony Scott for kindly penning the Foreword and to *everyone* who gave their time, especially Roger Avary, Lawrence Bender, Craig Hamann, Samuel L. Jackson, Cathryn Jaymes, Lance Lawson, Sally Menke, the William Morris agency, Don Murphy, Eric Stoltz, Oliver Stone, David Wasco and Sandy Reynolds-Wasco, and Connie Zastoupil.

And last, but by no means least, can I express my immense gratitude to everybody else who kindly helped along the way – Emma Cochrane, Rod Lurie, Kevin Murphy, Mark Salisbury, Julie Smith – and, above all, Barry McIlheney, Philip Thomas and *Empire* magazine.

Some of the interviews in this book I initially conducted for *Empire* – *Reservoir Dogs* (Steve Buscemi, Eddie Bunker, Harvey Keitel, Michael Madsen, Tim Roth, Quentin Tarantino) and *True Romance* (Patricia Arquette, Dennis Hopper, Tony Scott, Christian Slater, Quentin Tarantino, Christopher Walken). They appear courtesy and copyright *Empire*/EMAP Metro and I am indebted to them for kindly granting permission to use them here . . .

Preface

Marcellus: Something is rotten in the state of Denmark.

Hamlet, Act I, Scene iv

Just what is it with Cannes? Imagine a sort of posh Brighton dumped on the French Riviera, stripped of its pier and amusement arcades and a good 600-franc taxi ride from Nice airport.

Throw into the picture a multitude of films, 3000 journalists, 1500 unaccredited press, there on the off-chance of muscling in on the action, as many film industry people again, 10,000 rubberneckers cluttering up the narrow streets and an army of monkey-suited 'helpful' staff, whose job, it seems, is to tell you 'non' and then smile triumphantly, and you have, in a nutshell, Le Festival International du Film.

In May 1992 I sat in a flea-pit cinema in a back street of that town, one of the picture houses where they show the out-of-competition films. The fare on offer was a low-budget American gangster film by an unknown first-timer. It had been a big hit at the earlier Sundance festival in the States, a gig specifically for independent movies, though this was hardly enough on a sweltering afternoon to convince sanctimonious European journalists to come and take a look at this thing they called *Reservoir Dogs*, even though most of them had put in requests to interview Harvey Keitel, whose presence on the Côte d'Azur had caused no small degree of interest. They were more concerned with the fact that Keitel was about to head off to New Zealand to make a film with Jane Campion. I was curious because of fellow Brit Tim Roth. As for the director – not really. He just had a weird name.

And so, with a stinking Gallic hangover, tired and emotional (always the best way to see a film), I sweated away with a rump of dedicated hacks. We numbered just five, but midway through the film – at precisely the point where Marvin The Cop gets his *ad hoc* reconstructive surgery – our number had reduced by one, a Belgian woman having muttered her way towards the door.

Two years later and Quentin Tarantino, the man who had so irked the Flanders moll, was being referred to as some kind of cinematic genius. In fact, in May 1994, when a 'secret' sneak preview of *Pulp Fiction* was held, two days

ix

ahead of its official Festival première – in that same cinema, ironically – you literally had to fight your way in. And when Tarantino strode forward to collect Cannes' coveted Palme d'Or for a film which was certainly no less shocking than *Reservoir Dogs*, it was a celebration by the very establishment (and an arthouse crowd at that) which had previously had its nose put out of joint.

By the end of March 1995 Tarantino could prefix his name with the words 'Academy Award winner'. There could be no doubt that a powerful film-making force had arrived.

Reservoir Dogs. Bloody? Yes. Violent? Most certainly. But, dripping with style, wit and, above all, a fantastically foul-mouthed humour, it was, without question, one of the most stunning, original and innovative débuts for years. With a continuation of these hallmarks into his other work – whether as director, writer, producer and even actor in films like *True Romance*, *Sleep with Me*, *Natural Born Killers*, *Destiny Turns On The Radio*, *Four Rooms*, *Desperado*, *From Dusk Till Dawn* and, of course, the magnificent *Pulp Fiction*, Tarantino's output, thus far, by virtue of its celebration of junk culture, movie minutiae and sheer entertainment has tapped into the cinema-going psyche, crossing over in a unique way between movie aficionados and those uncluttered by such references.

Tarantino, still young in movie-making terms, has shown that if your script is good, then woe betide those who dare stand in your way. You *don't* have to go the film school route – get some bread (where possible), the advice of some seasoned pros and the rest will follow.

'If you build it,' as the ghosts of baseball past whispered in *Field of Dreams*, 'they will come.'

Of course, there are those who dismiss the idea of a book about someone whose CV is still slight.

However, in my experience as a so-called film journalist – and at this point I must declare once again my debt to the good folks at *Empire*, Britain's biggest-selling movie magazine, for giving this project their wholesome and, indeed, nourishing support – no absolute beginner has generated so much media interest, so many magazine front covers, with music and lifestyle titles as eager to buy into the sounds and the imagery as much as the visuals.

'Part of the distortion of nature,' as Oliver Stone told me, or simply a genuine heartfelt response to a major new talent? We shall see.

Who knows, twenty years down the line they may be conducting some kind of Brando-esque debate, speculating on how such a bright spark got so washed up. Well someone else can have a crack at that. This book is the story so far.

Let's go to work . . .

Jeff Dawson
April 1995

Chapter 1

Johnny Destiny

Saturday, 15 October 1994. The wee small hours of the morning – still the dog end of Friday night in real terms. The Pink Motel, Sun Valley, California – a garish pink slab of priceless 1950s Americana where they rent rooms by the hour and ask no questions. The faded puce paint is cracked, the paths are overgrown and, in the dark recesses of the almost physical blackness of desert night-time, a colony of stray cats, mangy and diseased, dart in and out of the rocks and undergrowth, making a permanently shifting backdrop. Even Norman Bates would have turned his nose up at this place.

A goods train, its wagons stretching back for what seems like forever, creaks past on the adjacent track; a warning bell on the road crossing clangs away to no one in particular. Just when your ears have readjusted to the vast expanse of nothing, the rusting hulk of a huge-finned auto-mobile – the kind where you can fit six people across the front seat, a remnant of the gas-guzzling days – trundles past in the dark, on its way back from, or maybe to, some late-night revelry. The desert silence allows you to hear its motor a good half-mile away, the purring engine dropping down a tone or two as the driver slows to allow his passengers an inquisitive peek at the motel, rising again as they decide on better options to a drink at this watering hole. And then the silence resumes.

Real-life *film noir*.

From the empty expanses to the east, stretching way off to the San Gabriel Mountains, a cold wind howls in, whipping up the sand, momentarily obscuring the buzzing Miller Lite sign in the diner win-dow, and a skinny white kitten, its swollen eyes half-closed through some infection or other, takes shelter behind the front wheel of a bat-tered Plymouth Roadrunner on the motel forecourt. You suddenly wish you'd heeded those warnings about the desert's dramatic night-time drop in temperature – don't be fooled by the palm trees.

Quentin Tarantino, dressed in a crumpled black suit and scarlet dress

1

shirt, strolls nonchalantly into the yard, momentarily silhouetted against the submerged spotlights of the motel swimming-pool, which cast an eerie yellow-greenish rippling glow over their surroundings. Seemingly oblivious to the cold, he looks perfectly at home – this, after all, could pass off as a sister establishment to Jack Rabbit Slim's. And anyway, he has other things on his mind.

'I can't believe it, the lines were right around the fuckin' block,' he yells, barely able to contain his enthusiasm. 'I never thought I'd see the day when that many people would turn out to see my movie . . . They could have fuckin' done anything. They could have seen *Exit to Eden*. They could be watching TV at home. They could be going to a concert or to dinner and whatever, but instead they decided to go see my movie . . . It's fucking *great*.'

Pulp Fiction, you see, amid scenes of quite hysterical, unprecedented hullabaloo in Los Angeles and across the rest of America, has opened tonight and Tarantino, fresh from a night-time cruise around the streets of his own LA neighbourhood – a half-hour drive away, through the canyons that spear the Hollywood Hills – has finally reached his moment of truth.

It seems like an eternity – five months, in fact – since the film's quite stunning revelation at Cannes, back in May, and the hype, beginning with the film's shock victory at that festival, has been building ever since, fuelled in no small part by Tarantino himself, who has devoted nearly all of the subsequent time, right up to this very week, in fact, on an exhausting global promotional tour, thumping the tub on behalf of his baby.

Surf through LA's 70-plus TV channels and you won't go five minutes without a glimpse of the ubiquitous Tarantino or, indeed, his leading man and new-found pal John Travolta, in the throes of a fame he hasn't known since the days of *Grease* way back in 1978.

Pick up a magazine or paper and *Pulp Fiction* is the subject *du jour*, the critics standing as one.

'A work of blazing originality. It places Quentin Tarantino in the front ranks of American filmmakers,' screams the *New York Times* . . . 'The most exhilarating piece of filmmaking to come along in years,' shouts *Entertainment Weekly* . . . 'Indisputably great,' proclaims *Rolling Stone*.

In fact, such has been the euphoria that Miramax, the film's distributor, has dispensed with protocol altogether and in today's *Los Angeles Times*, the first edition of which you'll be able to pick up in a couple of hours, there will be a double-page ad for the film which merely carries a full reprint of *Entertainment Weekly*'s 500-word, grade 'A' review.

David Letterman last week, Jay Leno next – America's two top TV talk shows – Tarantino is the hot ticket in town and today is Judgement Day.

Tarantino is like a kid on Christmas morning. From the moment that the big LA theatres put on special screenings at 9.45 a.m., Friday, to cater for the excess demand, it merely confirmed what he had hitherto hoped for. And his incognito visit tonight to Mann's Chinese Theatre – probably the world's most famous cinema – dressed in dark glasses and with a baseball hat pulled down tightly onto his head, confirms that he has got it right. Within 48 hours, *Pulp Fiction* will have amassed $9.16 million – an extraordinary figure for an independent film – putting it straight to number one at the American box office on its opening weekend, knocking Warner Brothers' big studio glossy starring vehicle, *The Specialist*, right off its perch. David has landed the stone four square between Goliath's eyes. Within ten days it will have notched up more than $21 million (it cost only $8.5 million to make) and maintained its premier slot. By the morning of 28 March, Tarantino himself will have walked off with an Oscar.

'One of the coolest things that happened was there was a one-thirty in the morning screening at the Chinese Theatre,' he enthuses, hurriedly. 'I was just driving up. I saw this line all the way down the sidewalk going down through the parking lot, waiting for the show. The movie's two and a half hours long, so it means that they're not gonna get out of there until almost *four* and it's like – fuck, they're lining up down the block to do that. I saw it and I go, fuuuuck, it's *great*. I did a tour of all the big houses and tomorrow I'm gonna like go to the Valley and to the South Bay, where I'm from, to see how it's doing down there.'

'I've seen the movie all over the fucking world and everything, but it's like it's just a whole different thing when the movie's playing in a movie theatre filled with people. That's a whole different vibe to what you're gonna get at any other place. I can't believe it, I talked to the cinematographer James Carter, he shot *One False Move*. He was going on about the audience reaction to that. But he never *saw* it with an audience.

He saw it with a cast and crew screening, and so I said, "You haven't seen the movie. You haven't *seen* the movie. You watch it with an audience. I saw it at the Film Forum and it just fucking blew everybody away." '

And *Pulp Fiction* is getting the right results.

'Just the sheer satisfaction of watching *Pulp* with an audience,' he enthuses, allowing himself a self-congratulatory smirk. 'The adrenaline shot sequence, for example, is hard to beat. I don't even have a fear of needles, so it never worked into the equation until I saw people diving under the seats. It's *really* cool . . .'

Probably having wolfed down too many E numbers as a kid and jacked up by the kind of adrenaline rush that only *Pulp Fiction*'s Mia Wallace has so far survived, Tarantino is extremely animated, punctuating his Gatling gun delivery with an almost lyrical profanity. Talking a mile a minute in a high register Californian – not unlike that of Mickey Dolenz of The Monkees – words like 'man' and 'cool' (words that non-Americans should *never* contemplate using) are liberally peppered throughout the conversation.

The celebrations, however, must be restricted to verbal acknowledgement of the accolades, for tonight Tarantino is working – acting – in a film he signed on to play the lead role in just two days before he unexpectedly scooped the Palme d'Or.

We are here on the set of *Destiny Turns On The Radio*, director Jack Baran's surreal tale of Las Vegas, loot and lovers on the run – a low-budget independent movie from a first-time script by Robert Ramsey and Matthew Stone. A sort of hard-boiled *noir* meets the *Twilight Zone*.

Dylan McDermott is Julian, an escaped convict on the run; Nancy Travis is his former love Lucille, trapped into a no-hope singing career and a loveless relationship in Las Vegas; James Le Gros is Harry, Julian's former partner in crime, who still holds the stash from a bank heist they pulled together. Typically, Julian must rescue Lucille, grab his share of the dough and then flee with her to Mexico. Well, that's the plan, only an ethereal, fateful stranger – Johnny Destiny – has appeared on the scene and, as his name implies, has begun to orchestrate proceedings.

Quentin Tarantino is Johnny Destiny ('A god,' according to Baran, 'with a small g').

4

Rysher Entertainment/Jim Sheldon

Quentin Tarantino as Johnny Destiny in *Destiny Turns On The Radio*:
'Life's just too short to do movie after movie after movie.'

The Pink Motel, on this occasion, has become The Marilyn Motel – a huge neon image of Monroe in *The Seven Year Itch*, hitching her skirt in stroboscopic rhythm, acting as a beacon for miles around. And, for four nights only, the motel's closed to the public, the notice on the manager's grubby office door having been flipped from 'The genius is in' to 'The genius is out', though this hasn't prevented a wayward prostitute up from Sunset Boulevard sneaking under the wire to ply her trade with a John in room number 4.

It's another take on the sleazy underbelly of America that Tarantino celebrates, though ultimately it proved to be a box office bomb.

'It has this really magical, comic book, *Breathless* [the film], Vegas loose thing about it,' he gabbles, forgetting that there is no actual rule against pausing for breath between sentences. 'Way before I read the script, I remember Kit Carson (one of his favourite screenwriters) talking to me about it and he was describing the character that I would eventually end up playing – Destiny – and he goes, "People get it all wrong. People think that Destiny is what is supposed to happen. In actual fact Destiny is what is *not* supposed to happen."

'Elvis was not supposed to change the face of music, alright. Elvis was supposed to be a truck driver. It was Destiny that brought him into Sun Records. Destiny is what is *not* supposed to happen. Bud Abbott was not supposed to be part of this wonderful comedy team. He was supposed to be a pimp. That's what he was when he met Lou Costello, he was a pimp, alright, but without him Lou Costello couldn't have made it.'

Tarantino wasn't supposed to become one of modern America's most exciting filmmakers, but somehow he got dealt a good hand. And now, fêted by all and sundry, he is being congratulated by the cast and crew who, one by one, come and shake him by the hand, plant a kiss on his cheek, whatever.

Tarantino humbly receives their plaudits and tries not to let his arrival disturb the filming of tonight's scene, the climax of the movie in which Julian and Lucille must make a choice – surrender to the cops or take a chance on their mysterious friend Destiny who, as befits such a curious story, has entered this earth via a heavenly portal at the bottom of the Marilyn Motel swimming pool.

McDermott and Travis stand in the motel yard, trapped in the glare of a police car spotlight. In exasperation they yell at each other, embrace and then, just as the cops yell 'freeze' and they prepare for the worst, a voice reaches them from across the pool, informing that they have an option to surrendering.

'Julian, you can always come with me,' calls Tarantino's Destiny, as he slowly begins to strip down to his shirt and underpants and return

from whence he came. Folding his clothes neatly in a pile on the pool-
side he makes it obvious to the fugitives that all they need to do is dive
into the water – trust Destiny and follow him to his own dimension.

That, though, won't happen just yet, because, first of all, there are a
few logistical problems to take care of.

'As I'm undressing, I'm gonna be hopping around and shit,' he
informs the cameraman as his marks are established for the big leap into
the deep end, an act which does not inspire Tarantino, a nervous swim-
mer, with confidence.

'There's a light down there and I'm gonna hit it,' he points out to the
assistant director who, in turn, asks the regulation industry frogman to
adjust the offending piece of equipment.

'The film that killed Quentin Tarantino,' guffaws cinematographer
James Carter. 'Now wouldn't that be something?'

But we're still not set. The script editor reminds the crew that, according to the letter of her instruction, 'the pool should pulsate', and so a few
dry ice capsules are tossed into the water. Within a few seconds, the
pool has become a bubbling golden cauldron, smoke hovering above the
surface.

'Do it like you're stepping onto an elevator,' instructs Baran, fairly
minimal in his choreography, and a couple of minutes later, after a quick
rehearsal, Tarantino's ready to take his first plunge.

'Surf's up . . . Don't think it hasn't been fun,' he yells to McDermott
and Travis, taking a tidy feet-first jump which, despite his size (six feet
two inches, 190 pounds), doesn't create that much of a splash.

As he climbs out of the pool, a couple of girls from wardrobe fling
towels and blankets about him to keep out the biting cold and, even
though, thoughtfully, the crew have made sure that the water has had
the chill taken slightly off it, he's soon shivering before an industrial
heater, the travails of low-budget filmmaking requiring him to stay in
his wet things for the next take, while a dresser flaps his red shirt in
front of another heater so that on camera, at least, it doesn't look like it's
already been soaked.

The first take was good, they do a couple more for insurance, altering
the dialogue slightly each time, and, after his fourth dip, involving
exactly the same in-and-out procedure as the first, it's in the bag and the
cast and crew dash off for tonight's first dinner break, gathering eagerly

behind the catering chuck wagon in no discernible pecking order.

But then, after some more takes of McDermott and Travis in close-up, the unthinkable happens – it starts to rain – and, with the time approaching five o'clock and the sun threatening to appear above the yard arm, it's time to call it a day, or morning . . .

The following night, Saturday, and we're back, this time to finish off the rest of the scene, Tarantino reading out his part of the dialogue while Nancy Travis and Dylan McDermott, having decided to take a chance on Johnny Destiny, follow him into the water. Because they are being filmed with an underwater camera and as the purse strings are tight, they must get it right first time, which they do, sort of, only the director's notion of them having a passionate embrace as they sink to the bottom is not really fulfilled, given that everyone seems to have forgotten that – as with the witch hunts of yore – people actually float. And so, as they flap about on the surface, everyone, the actors included, burst into raucous laughter. It'll do though.

During a lull in proceedings, Tarantino manages to wangle a break so that he can sneak off to his room and catch John Travolta on *Saturday Night Live* on the TV – a good show in a waning series in which Travolta, the celebrity host of that night's show, does an amusing impression of Marlon Brando, who'd shocked America with a dishevelled, mumbling appearance on *Larry King Live* earlier that week. Travolta takes the whole thing off to a tee and a clearly-amused Tarantino returns to the set grinning like a Cheshire cat that has just been bequeathed a cream franchise.

With a lot of hanging around to do, a small gaggle of actors and crew, Tarantino included, huddle round one of the heaters. One enterprising individual whips out a bag of marshmallows and soon everyone grabs a fork, a skewer, a stick, whatever, and gets toasting.

'How d'ya like 'em done,' quips Tarantino knowingly. 'Crisp or bloody as hell?' And, as the night wears on he can, for a moment, forget about the media pressure and be one of the guys. With the production soon to move up to Las Vegas for a week or so, he expounds his theories on the card game baccarat, gambling ('One time I was driving through Vegas and I just decided to stay and I took the room fee and put it on red') and how down-to-earth Vegas will always be better than refined Monte Carlo.

'Can you imagine,' Tarantino chuckles, 'Omar Sharif winning and going (loudly) *"Fuckin' yeah."* '

There is also, of course, the subject of movies.

Dylan McDermott, perhaps unwisely, asks Tarantino a question about French director Jean-Pierre Melville, a big influence on Tarantino, and it's like a red rag to a bull. Within five minutes we've segued, via Jean-Luc Godard's *À Bout de Souffle* (Jack Baran worked on the American remake) into John Woo's *Hard Target* (the 'only cool Jean-Claude Van Damme movie and it's *not* because of him'), *The Killer* ('It has the greatest dramatic impact'), *Hard Boiled* ('Oh man, that fuckin' opening') and his favourite of them all, *A Better Tomorrow Part Two* ('Oh *man*').

Tarantino, up for a bit of partying when they get a night off, tries to persuade everyone to come along to a nearby 'supper club where they play like this really cool 40s music' but it's not long before the inevitable *Pulp Fiction* questions begin and he's soon explaining in detail his use of stock library film footage for the traffic scene glimpsed through the rear window of the cab in which Bruce Willis's Butch does his runner from the big fight.

'It's filmed on Wilshire,' he tells them. 'You can see there's a movie theatre. *"The Hustler*, starring Paul Newman and Jackie Gleason." '

You sense that being there just as an actor, with no responsibilities beyond pleasing the director, is almost a welcome relief after the pressures of *Pulp Fiction*.

'I mean, the pressure's on when it's your time to do it,' he insists, 'but like during the rest of the time when I'm not working, it's kick-back.'

He didn't *have* to take this part and though he would never admit it, might have chosen not to do so in retrospect, had he known just how much responsibilty he'd have to take for *Pulp Fiction*'s aftermath. But he liked the script, one he'd first heard of nearly seven years ago and one that had become almost legendary within his own film fraternity. And besides, he wanted people not to forget that, before everything blew up with *Reservoir Dogs*, he was, first and foremost, an actor.

'I'm getting all these acting offers which are really cool because I don't have to read for them and that's what I always wanted to do. It's

9

actually really cool after doing something like *Pulp*, which was an epic kind of thing.'

Epic it most certainly was, not so much the scope of the film but the sheer effort to mount the thing – write it, take it through pre-production, shoot it, post-production, Cannes and then, importantly, three straight months of media promotion.

'The press is all part of it,' says Tarantino, 'but now that it's officially opened, I'm done. It's great, but it was all totally exhausting.'

So, for the moment, he can kick back for a bit and enjoy a few novelties. Three days ago he had his first screen kiss, with Lisa Jane Persky ('If Bonnie would have come home in *Pulp Fiction* I probably would have kissed her'). Persky has even been amusing the crew with a fake 'Quentin' tattoo she has on her ankle.

'The kiss was that good,' she quips.

And the day before yesterday he had his first nude scene, rising stark bollock naked on a cloud from above that pool again ('It's not really a nude scene. You don't see anything . . . you'd *better* not see anything, hahaha'). But, in the swirling maelstrom that is *Pulp Fiction*, it's all a trying time.

'It's not that people are jealous,' he insists. 'But different friends of mine, when the press quote them, they never use specific examples. Let's put it like this. What gets more annoying than anything else is the fact that they're looking at me in the middle of a tornado and saying that they're worried about me as opposed to talking to the press about how *fucking* well I'm handling it. You know what I mean? I haven't let it go to my head, but I don't get credit for that, I get their concern because they don't think *they* could handle it. I mean, even Alex [Rockwell] has said things and they all mean the best and all but they put themselves in my position and think about how they'd be freaking out – but I'm *not* freaking out. It's like Roger Avary [his *Pulp Fiction* collaborator] will pontificate on how I'm dealing with things, but I think the thing that comes out when you read these quotes is that Roger's not talking about me, he's talking about himself. *He*'s having problems with this stuff and he's just using me as the vessel to explore it.

'Look, you can't live a normal life when you're making a movie,' he urges, almost apologetically. 'Everything, it's like *everything*. The dentist – oh, I ain't got fucking time for it. Paying my bills – oh, I ain't got fucking time for it. Cleaning my room – oh, I ain't got fucking time for it. Alright, you know, it's *fun*. It's fun being involved in something that big that the rest doesn't matter, but now I don't got time for this – I just want to hang out with my friends, sleep late, learn another language. Life's just too short to do movie after movie after movie. It's like getting married just to get married. I wanna be in love and say, "This is the woman."

'How I feel right now,' declares Tarantino in deadly earnest. 'I never want to make another movie again . . .'

Chapter 2

Counter Culture

At the beginning of 1992, no one had heard of Quentin Tarantino. By the end of it, he was being hailed as the hip new messiah of filmmaking. In the wake of *Pulp Fiction* two years on, the media and the film industry itself had gone into gibbering overdrive.

Dennis Hopper – 'Quentin Tarantino. He's the Mark Twain of the 90s'; Owen Gleiberman, chief film critic, *Entertainment Weekly* – 'He's the greatest American screenwriter since Preston Sturges'; Jon Ronson, *Independent On Sunday* – 'Not since *Citizen Kane* has one man appeared from relative obscurity to redefine the art of filmmaking.'

Today, it is a rare thing indeed to find a style magazine *without* the words Quentin Tarantino plastered somewhere across the cover as if his very name has suddenly become an instant branding for all things cool.

Why?

How on earth did a film geek from nowhere, with no formal training and with no back catalogue, suddenly become *fêted* as the next big thing?

The media interest in a rookie director has been unprecedented. Forget the acting assignments, he's only made two films, for God's sake – *Reservoir Dogs* and *Pulp Fiction*. There followed a third, which he wrote (*True Romance*), a fourth (*Natural Born Killers*), which he also penned but, with no small measure of acrimony, has since chosen to disown, a fifth (*Four Rooms*) to which his contribution is a one-quarter episode and a sixth self-penned movie (*From Dusk Till Dawn*).

'I've never seen, in my lifetime, this degree of reaction for a young filmmaker,' says Oliver Stone, who directed *Natural Born Killers*, ironically a parody of media lionization. 'Never have I seen this in my memory. Yeah, there are fads. They go crazy for one film and that film does not just generally stand up over time because the fad dies, but I've never seen this. It's unbalanced. It's unnatural.'

Unbalanced? Unnatural? Just what *is* all the fuss about?

Who the hell is Quentin Tarantino and why has a man whose fare is about as politically incorrect as you could possibly get in the touchy-feely 1990s managed to garner such a cult following?

Certainly, in a world where new heroes are needed and, more often than not, torn down when they no longer serve their purpose, the Cinderella rise of Tarantino – film geek video store clerk turned hard-boiled director, as the handy showbiz anecdote would have it – has certainly made good copy. The circumstances too have helped. Consider that there has been a 100 per cent rise in cinema attendances over the last ten years and a staggering 800 per cent rise in video sales and the icons of film are now on an equal footing with the their counterparts in the world of music, a position they haven't enjoyed since the advent of rock and roll in the late 1950s.

The first rock star director? Tarantino, unlike any other whose craft has come from behind rather than in front of the camera, now enjoys that kind of status – literally going on global tours, from festival to festival, lecture to lecture, with a devoted following that turns these happenings into tantamount gigs. When he visited London in January 1995 to give a lecture at the National Film Theatre, he was greeted with a reception that in film terms was the equivalent of Beatlemania, fans waiting anxiously for ten hours to get in.

'We had 3000 applications for tickets from members alone,' said NFT spokesman Brian Robinson. 'From early December the phones didn't stop ringing. Every other call was from people asking for Tarantino tickets. We've been having these on-stage interviews since 1981 and Robert Redford didn't attract this intensity of following. Nor did Warren Beatty or Gloria Swanson.'

His script for *Pulp Fiction*, published in paperback in October 1994, became the biggest selling screenplay in British publishing history, gaining a place on the top ten bestsellers' list and being reviewed as if it were a work of literature.

In just about every cultural capital, he is petitioned to attend a film festival mounted in his honour.

'It's really funny because all these festivals want me to go to their things but they can't show a retrospective of my work because I haven't *done* anything,' laughs Tarantino at the irony of it all. 'A friend said to me, "What they should do is show a festival of films that I've always wanted to see but have never got around to, or just pick movies that you've always wanted to see and *say* they're your favourites," except you'd have those embarrassing moments when the lights come up, "Oh, that wasn't very good, was it . . . sorry guys." '

For a film geek, it's the ultimate tribute and, though in another era it would have been considered rather gauche, Tarantino's about as hip as you can get right now, though he is still a little perturbed by the adulation.

'Not because I didn't think the material was worth it but because I didn't think it would be *embraced* . . .'

Domestically speaking, Tarantino certainly doesn't live like the high priest of hip. His home, where he's been for several years, is in an apartment block buffered against a busy West Hollywood street by a high hedgerow and a small courtyard, an area that's reasonably fashionable but not nearly in the league that he could certainly afford. Maybe he just hasn't got around to it.

On a Saturday morning in January 1995, at 11 a.m., he's not yet up, which is hardly a crime – he was working the previous night on the taping of the sitcom *All American Girl*, the comedy vehicle for his friend Margaret Cho. Filmed live before a studio audience after a week of rehearsals, Tarantino plays Cho's boyfriend, brought home to meet the family for the first time ('I told Margaret, "I've got to do your show 'cause I don't like any of your boyfriends yet. I'm gonna be the best boyfriend you ever had" ').

He's done it as a favour and somehow managed to squeeze it in between editing duties on his segment of *Four Rooms* and a trip to the UK. Titled *Pulp Sitcom* and broadcast in February 1994, the episode was a parody of *Pulp Fiction*, a piece of light relief from the grind – Tarantino's character turning out to have a criminal past and the story loaded with jokes from the film (the glowing briefcase, the Samurai sword, even the good old Gimp).

'They hit damn near every big touchstone from *Pulp Fiction* in the course of the episode,' explains Tarantino later on. 'So it's pretty cool.'

There is no answer at Tarantino's door. As is strangely common in Los Angeles, there is no doorbell, but even a loud rapping of knuckles does not have the desired effect. And then, just as you begin to scrawl a note asking him to call you later on, the door creaks open and Tarantino, dishevelled and still in a T-shirt and track bottoms, invites you in, apologizing profusely for being in the land of nod. Step over some flowers that have been left on the doorstep, courtesy of a well-wisher for tonight's Golden Globes, for which he will win the award for Best Screenplay, and you are inside.

The place is a mess. Not dirty, just untidy. There are piles of magazines and records and boxes everywhere, commanding every inch of floorspace. From the looks of it, Tarantino is now in that curious league of celebrity where people simply send him things – a pristine mountain bike, which looks like it won't be used for the foreseeable future, is propped up against the wall and a spanking new pair of trainers sits neatly perched on top of its box. On the table lie other various bits of debris – magazines, mail, a Howard Hawks book, a set of keys and, amusingly, Sam Jackson's 'bad motherfucker' wallet from *Pulp Fiction*. Tarantino now uses it as his own, though, as his friends joke, his wallet doesn't always come easily out of his pocket. Dominating the room is an enormous widescreen television and teetering on top of it, along with a pile of other videos, is one by Sonic Youth (*1991: The Year Punk Broke*) and another marked '*Four Rooms*/Finger Chop/Effects'.

Tarantino sticks some Maria McKee, one of his favourite artists, on the sound system and cranks up the volume to full blast while he gets ready for a trip to grab some breakfast at the local diner. In a back room there are shelves packed with videos. Rather incongruously, they are diligently filed (one is reminded of the character in Barry Levinson's *Diner*, who alphabetized his record collection) – you can see where the priorities lie.

In the hallway, too, is a cupboard neatly stacked with his well-documented board games, ones based on film and TV shows: *Land of the Giants*, *Baretta* and, of course, *Welcome Back Kotter*, the show that starred John Travolta. It was the playing of that board game, in this very apartment, by Tarantino and Travolta that convinced Travolta to take a chance on this film geek and do *Pulp Fiction*.

On the mantelpiece are various dolls – GI Joes, with *and* without realistic hair and gripping hands, and a model of Boy George in his full Karma Chameleon attire.

Huge framed posters dominate the walls – a Japanese *True Romance* publicity sheet and, above the couch, one for Jean-Luc Godard's *Bande À Part* from which he and Lawrence Bender derived the name for their production company, A Band Apart.

It is a shrine to pop, nay junk, culture. A den of slack as they would call it in *Reality Bites*. And though such utter clutter is probably a good indication of what actually goes on between the Tarantino ears, it is not the kind of environment you'd associate with someone who could cope with the intricate plotting of *Pulp Fiction* or, for that matter, win an Oscar for Best Screenplay.

That he has not become enveloped by the trappings of fame suggests that success is still new to him and Tarantino still enjoys – and plays up – the rags-to-riches story.

He has, though, by his own admission, been more calculating than that, firmly in control not only of his own destiny but also of his public image. His popularity is a direct result of the many hundred man hours he's spent indulging the media.

'It's somewhat the case,' concurs Tarantino. 'I mean I've never played the role of a first-time filmmaker. I mean, I might have had questions and everything but basically I pretty much know how I want my career to go and more than anything else from following other directors' careers.'

So where *did* it all begin . . . ?

The apocryphal story, of course, has it that one minute Tarantino was slaving away behind the counter in a video shop and the next minute he was directing his very first film – *Reservoir Dogs*. Rarely are stories that simple.

There are numerous accounts, too, of a rough upbringing (as *Premiere* magazine claimed) – a teenage mother, half Cherokee/half hillbilly, who grew up in the 'swamp of backwater ignorance' of the American South, raising her Huck Finn son in moonshine Appalachia and relocating to Los Angeles in search of work, leaving the high-school drop-out to fend for himself on the mean streets of South Central.

Rarely are these stories accurate – Quentin Tarantino is no working-class hero.

So let's start from the beginning. Quentin Tarantino was born on 27 March 1963 in Knoxville, Tennessee.

His mother, Connie Zastoupil, is, indeed, a native of that state, but was raised in Cleveland, Ohio, before going to high school in Los Angeles, the town she's always considered home.

'I never really lived there [Tennessee],' she explains. 'I *am* half Cherokee, but you wouldn't know it, that's just sensationalism – I did not walk across the United States in moccasins. The only reason I was in Tennessee when Quentin was born was because I was in college there. For some reason I had this romantic notion that I should go to college in the state in which I was born.'

Nonetheless, Connie *was* only sixteen when she became pregnant. A gifted student, she had graduated from high school at fifteen and only got married to become an emancipated minor. 'It wasn't a sordid little teenage pregnancy, it was actually more of a liberated thing.'

The marriage, however, didn't work out.

'His father did not even know that Quentin was born,' says Connie. 'After we separated I found out I was pregnant and never even contacted him.'

While she was pregnant and mulling over names, Connie got hooked on the TV series *Gunsmoke* and, in particular, the character played by Burt Reynolds – Quint Asper.

'But I wanted a more formal name than Quint,' she explains, 'and then I was reading a Faulkner book, *The Sound and the Fury*. The heroine's name was Quentin, so I decided that my child was going to be named Quentin whether it was a male or a female. I was also looking for a limited number of nicknames, the shortest would be "Quent", which I promptly shortened to "Q" (the name by which most of his friends refer to him).'

When Tarantino was aged two, Connie moved back to Los Angeles where she re-married, to Curt Zastoupil, a local musician. Curt adopted Quentin at age two and a half, giving him his surname. In fact, it was only when he had left school and decided to become an actor that Quentin Zastoupil reverted back to to the more stage-friendly moniker of Tarantino, the name of his biological father.

While his mother began to carve out a successful career for herself in the health-care industry, the family made their home in the area of Los Angeles known as The South Bay – 'a fairly affluent area,' according to Connie – first in El Segundo and then Torrance.

Courtesy of Connie Zastoupil

Connie and Quentin: 'We went to the movies all the time.'

A middle-class upbringing for an only child?

'Upper middle-class,' corrects Connie.

With Connie out during the day and Curt working nights, the young Tarantino would spend many hours in the company of his adopted father and his artistic friends, the only child among adults.

He also accrued many hours in front of the TV, filling his down time with shows like *The Partridge Family* and *Kung Fu*. In *Pulp Fiction*, young Butch Coolidge, also from Knoxville, child of a single parent, sits with his nose virtually pressed up against the TV screen watching Clutch Cargo, the 1950s cartoon character with the live-action lips. We can take it that this is a self-reference, a nod to the TV shows Tarantino watched in his youth and which crop up regularly in all his work.

In the true spirit of liberal parent modernity, Tarantino the youngster was allowed to watch pretty much what he damn well pleased when it came to the cinema, too (the censorship restrictions in the States allow juniors accompanied by adults to watch what would be considered restricted 18-certificate films in the UK).

'We went to the movies all the time, it was one of our favourite means of recreation,' says Connie, recalling their early visits. 'I have to say *I* was a child when I was taking him to the movies . . . *Carnal Knowledge* when he was about five . . . *Deliverance*. There was a funny incident in the middle of *Carnal Knowledge* where Art Garfunkel is trying to talk to Candice Bergen into intimacy and he's saying, "Come on. Let's do it, let's do it." And, of course, Quentin pipes up in the theatre, "What's he wanna do, mom?" And that did bring down the house.'

It is no surprise, then, that movies have always been in Tarantino's blood. And so, while his contemporaries were enjoying the likes of *Dumbo* and *The Jungle Book*, Tarantino was already on to much stronger stuff.

'*Deliverance* scared the living shit out of me,' he says. 'I saw it at Tarzana 6 in a double feature with *The Wild Bunch*. I was in fourth grade.'

Poor old Ned Beatty 'squealing like a pig' while some genetically disadvantaged hick informs Jon Voight that his buddy sure has a 'purdy mouth'. Hardly good clean family fodder?

Tarantino grins.

'Did I understand Ned Beatty was being sodomized?' he chuckles. 'No, but I knew he wasn't having any fun.'

Pulp Fiction, of course, has its own '*Deliverance*' scene, which would tend to fuel the arguments of those who suggest that such graphic images *can* corrupt young minds after all.

'I can't watch movies with her now because she talks all the way through,' says Tarantino of his mother. 'She really liked *Wild Orchid*, she thought *Wild Orchid* was a great movie.'

'Well, that's an exaggeration, but I do like Zalman King and he knows better than to argue with me,' retorts Connie.

It is then that the history gets a little out of hand, with fantastic stories about the times his mother would make visits to her folks back in Tennessee, depositing him with his father, who, in the finest Appalachian tradition, made a bit of cash on the side delivering moonshine. As the stories have it, grandpa would sometimes abandon his grandson while on his clandestine missions. More often than not this would take the form of plonking him on the ground next to a speaker at a drive-in cinema (grandpa was fond of biker movies) and leaving him to his own devices.

Unfortunately, all this stuff, whether fuelled by Tarantino or simply a fabrication of the press, is simply made up ('I have no idea who the hell they're talking about because my father has been dead since I was a baby,' says Connie). One of Tarantino's main detractors, Don Murphy, a figure who will emerge as a sort of nemesis, has accused Tarantino of basing the entire Tennessee episode on the genuine hillbilly upbringing of his producing partner and former friend of Tarantino's, Jane Hamsher.

The 'Li'l Abner' episode, as his mother refers to it, certainly makes for a far more interesting story, that's for sure, but has little grounding in reality.

'You know, Quentin wants to have a controversial background,' says Connie, 'though I'm not saying he didn't have controversy *after* he left home, because he lived in some less than desirable areas as he was struggling to make it . . .'

When Quentin was eight, Connie and Curt divorced. Connie resisted the temptation to overly indulge Quentin as he grew up fatherless.

'I spoiled him in some ways and in others I was very strict,' says Connie. 'Though he was not a latch key kid.'

Over the coming years, Quentin's interest in film and TV developed, to the point where Connie would be alarmed by the particularly foul-mouthed tirades coming from his bedroom.

'I'd say, "Quentin", and he'd say, "It's not me, mom, it's GI Joe," ' remembers Connie of Tarantino acting out various scenarios with his plastic characters.

However, though he was a bright kid with an IQ of 160, Tarantino began to have problems at school. He was hyperactive and disruptive, so his teachers suggested calming him by putting him on medication, a move Connie resisted. Although he could happily while away his time

Courtesy of Connie Zastoupil

'I hated school. School completely bored me.'

religiously logging and compiling lists of all the films he'd seen, such attentiveness did not extend to lessons (apart from history, which was, apparently, 'cool').

'I hated school,' Tarantino recalled in *Vanity Fair*. 'School completely bored me. I wanted to be an actor. Anything that I'm not good at I don't like and I couldn't focus on school. I never got math. Spelling, I never got spelling (everyone associated with Tarantino still remarks on his appalling grasp of it). I was good at reading and I was good at history. History was like a movie. But a lot of things that people seemed to learn really easily it took me years to learn. I didn't learn how to ride a bike until the fifth grade. I didn't know how to swim until I was in junior high school. I didn't learn how to tell the time until the sixth grade. I could do the 30s and the o'clocks, but when it got anything more intricate than that, I was perplexed . . . To this day I can't tell the time that well. And when everyone's telling you you're dumb and you can't do what everyone can do when they're seven, you start to wonder.'

'Quentin's strength comes from his ability to write although he really has no ability to *physically* write,' says Roger Avary, who was to become Tarantino's key writing collaborator. 'Quentin writes phonetically. He's a completely self-taught person. It's a bit of a mess.'

Connie remembers, too, the time when she grounded him for a whole summer for having stolen a paperback book from K-Mart (Elmore Leonard's *The Switch*, apparently), though this hardly elevates Tarantino to the status of rebellious youth. But with time on his hands, Tarantino began to channel his ambitions.

'I can't remember a time when I *didn't* want to be an actor. I wanted to be an actor since I was five. I've never understood when I've talked to teenagers or whatever, it's like, "What do you want to do with your life?" and they're trying to figure it out. I've known what I was trying to do since I was in first grade, that I wanted to be an actor and so that's why I quit school, to start studying acting.'

There were big arguments, first, however. Tarantino was already unhappy about being educated at a private, fee-paying Christian school and had begun to frequently play truant.

'I could send him off every day and have him hanging out on street corners or I could let him quit and I thought I'd actually have more control over him if I let him stay at home,' concedes Connie.

And so, at the age of sixteen, with his mother's reluctant consent, Tarantino dropped out of high school, on the condition that he got a job ('I wanted him to see that life without an education would not be a picnic'), though it was always the plan that he would resume education and try to go to college.

Tarantino, perhaps typically, landed his very first job as an usher in a porno cinema, the Pussycat Theatre in Torrance.

'This was a con that he did on his mother,' she laughs. 'He said, "Can I be an usher in a theatre?" and I said, "Okay." Well it didn't occur to me to ask what *kind* of theatre, and it didn't occur to me that a porno theatre would hire such a young kid. The way I found out was I found a book of matches that said Pussycat Theatre. He was still a teenager, but it was like it wasn't that he hadn't seen what he'd seen. It was at the point where the horse was out the barn door.'

'Most teenagers would think, "Cool, I'm in a porno theatre," ' Tarantino says, 'but I didn't like porno. I liked movies. They were very cheesy and very sleazy.'

Around this time, Tarantino enrolled in the acting classes of James Best. Best, as Tarantino is always quick to point out, was the star of Sam Fuller's *Verboten!* and *Shock Corridor*. He is, however, better known as Roscoe P. Coltrane, the sheriff in TV's *Dukes of Hazzard*.

Best's philosophy was simple. In a town where the principal employment for actors was in television, there simply was no need to bother with studying either the craft of theatre or the more detailed Method aspects of film acting. Where landing jobs relied purely on passing fast turnaround auditions, technique relied very much on looking natural before the camera.

'To do this job you got to be a great actor. You got to be naturalistic. You got to be naturalistic as *hell*. If you ain't a great actor, you're a *bad* actor and bad acting is bullshit in this job.'

So says Randy Brooks' Holdaway to Tim Roth's Freddy Newendyke in *Reservoir Dogs*, instructing him in the art of telling his drug courier anecdote.

There are other nods to these acting classes: 'My motivation is to stay out of jail,' says Elliot Blitzer as he psyches himself up in *True Romance*; 'Let's get in character,' as Jules tells Vincent in *Pulp Fiction*; 'Give me the principals' names,' demands The Wolf – though a scene from *True Romance* where Michael Rapaport's Dick Ritchie auditions for a part in *The Return of T.J. Hooker* is probably the best reflection of the kind of factory mentality that exists in the lower echelons of Hollywood, the world that Tarantino inhabited at that time . . .

RAVENCROFT (the casting director)
In this scene you're both in a car and Bill Shatner's hanging on the

hood. And what you wanna do is get him off. (*She picks up a copy of the script.*) Whenever you're ready. Okay?

DICK (*reading and pantomiming he's driving*)
I'm Marty . . . I'm driving . . . Okay . . . Where the fuck did he come from?

RAVENCROFT (*reading from the script lifelessly*)
I don't know, he just appeared like magic.

DICK (*reading from the script*)
Well, don't just sit there. Shoot him . . . get him.

(*She puts down her script and smiles at him.*)

RAVENCROFT
Thank you, Mr Ritchie. I'm very impressed. You're a very fine actor.

The acting, however, was not going anywhere and a look at his standard publicity shot as an eighteen-year-old – a gawky gang member with bandanna, leather jacket and earring, certainly did nothing to single him out in a town full of wannabes. As a bold attempt to get himself noticed, he even claimed on his CV that he had appeared as a supporting actor in Jean-Luc Godard's *King Lear* (which starred Woody Allen and Molly Ringwald), not only because it would look impressive but also because no casting director would have had a chance to verify the fact. Even though several notable film guides list him in the credits, Tarantino was most certainly not in that picture, but despite such an audacious move, the parts didn't come his way.

'Oddly enough I did a bit more theatre work than I did anything else,' he explains. 'I could never get hired. To tell you the truth, the only legitimate job I got as an actor was on *The Golden Girls*. That was the only work I ever got. I played an Elvis impersonator. It was kind of a high point but it's a glorified extra part. I'm one of eight or nine guys, but we got to sing a song. It wasn't even an Elvis song, it was the Hawaiian Wedding Chant by Don Ho. All the other Elvis impersonators wore Vegas-style jump-suits. But I wore my own clothes because I was like

Courtesy of Connie Zastoupil

'I can't remember a time when I *didn't* want to be an actor.'

the Sun Records Elvis. I was the hill-billy cat Elvis. I was the real Elvis –
everyone else was Elvis after he sold out.'

Screenwriter Craig Hamann was a friend and associate of Tarantino
in the early days. They met in January 1981 at the James Best Theatre
Centre. Neither had made much headway when it came to acting,
Hamann's experience being confined to 'unspeakable low budget horror
movies.'

25

'We hit it off very quickly because we had both seen a lot of movies and° also I just thought really he was a great actor, the best, and I couldn't help but respect his talent.'

Hamann is actually very genuine with his praise for Tarantino as an actor.

'I'd left the school earlier than he did,' he continues. 'They kicked me out. That wasn't unusual for me, I got kicked out of a lot of acting schools . . . I developed a problem, and I know Quentin developed a problem, too. It's just that with acting instructors, after a while you start doing your scenes for *them*, like they're some guru and I don't think Quentin likes gurus. We had a real problem and he left the school shortly after I was kicked out. While we were at the school I don't know how seriously Quentin was taken, but *I* took him seriously and, anyway, we became good friends. We saw a lot of movies together. He introduced me to Chinese cinema, Italian horror films and we decided one day that we wanted to make a movie and we came up with this idea and we talked it over, and we wrote a short script, a 33-pager and it ended up being a film called *My Best Friend's Birthday*. We added scenes to it as we went along and we shot it for about $5000 and almost got it done.'

'It was a comedy, a Martin and Lewis type of thing,' says Tarantino. 'It was never finished.'

The 1986 film, starring Hamann and Tarantino, was designed to be a means to showcase themselves as actors and was made using every available cent that came their way.

'Any way we could, beg borrow or steal,' says Hamann. 'From my credit card and from Quentin working at Video Archives. We used to shoot on weekends. The historical importance [he laughs] of the film is that Quentin directed it, Quentin and I co-wrote it, Rand Vossler, who was one of the producers of *Natural Born Killers*, was the cinematographer and Roger Avary was working on crew, in a crew of about three people. Quentin and I were working on crew, too.'

Part of the film was made in a Westchester bar owned by a friend of Connie's, 'but the majority of it was filmed in my house', she remembers. 'It was like, "Oh Mom. Can I film a movie in the house, it won't be any problem at all?" Three months later I finally got to move back in.'

A monologue from that film, where Tarantino confesses his woes to a radio DJ, gives an indication of the style of writing that was soon to come . . .

TARANTINO

Out of the blue I felt depressed for no reason whatsoever. There was like this dark cloud hanging over my head. I was gonna commit suicide. I was actually gonna commit suicide. I was gonna go up into the bathroom, I was gonna fill a tub with hot water and I was gonna slice open my veins. I was actually . . . I mean I was *actually* gonna do it. Now for a three-year-old to be thinking like that, that's really depressing. You know what saved me? . . . Was *The Partridge Family*, because *The Partridge Family* was coming on and I really wanted to see it, so I thought, 'Okay, I'll watch *The Partridge Family*, *then* I'll kill myself,' and so I watched it and it was a really funny episode. It was the one where Danny got in trouble. It was a really funny one and I didn't feel like killing myself afterwards. It all kind of worked out . . . What were we talking about . . . ?

With Tarantino and Hamann frequently substituting for other actors who hadn't bothered to turn up, the exercise became a labour of love. Unfortunately, it was never finished, 'because we had a lab accident and we didn't have insurance and we lost a couple of cans of film,' says Hamann. 'Looking back at it now, and Quentin said this himself, basically this was his film school, because Quentin and I never went to film school but we learned an awful lot and he had been plugging away trying to make silent Super 8 films and stuff before then.'

'I thought that we were making something really special,' Tarantino reflects, 'but it was kind of embarrassing when I started really looking at it again. But I thought, "I didn't know what I was doing at the beginning and I know what I'm doing now." '

It was back in 1984 that Hamann introduced Tarantino to Cathryn Jaymes, who was to become Tarantino's manager right up through the filming of *Pulp Fiction*.

'Quentin had nothing. He didn't have *My Best Friend's Birthday* done, he didn't have a script,' Hamann laughs. 'He was just a very close friend of mine. That first meeting they had, I'll never forget. Cathryn said to

Quentin, and this is no joke, quote, "You will be a major force in the film industry." And she was *serious* and basically took him on as a client. For a while she was just pushing him as an actor.'

'I met him when he was 21,' says Jaymes. 'Craig just kept talking about this Quentin character in his acting class who was so interesting and so unusual and so kind of off centre. Craig had invested his money and several other people had invested their money in trying to get off the ground *My Best Friend's Birthday*. Craig had made a *mighty* investment in that and Connie, Quentin's mother, had opened up her home and they were in the process of trying to film at weekends. Craig brought Quentin through the door and even at that point Quentin was really determined to be an actor. At the time it was very serious. Everything he engages in, he does with a passion. When the boys were making *My Best Friend's Birthday* they were determined to make a really good short film and one that would generate some attention and some credibility for them and go off and launch their careers across the board. They ran in a pack then – Quentin, Roger Avary, Craig Hamann and Rand [Vossler], he was part of that too.'

In fact, after they had gone their separate ways and Tarantino had gone on to bigger things, Hamann and Avary came in and did some overdubbing on *Reservoir Dogs*, specifically for a background radio play ('We were laughing our butts off the whole time') and with Hamann providing one the voices of the two cops in the car who sit and wait outside Freddy Newendyke's apartment.

Though his claims to be a great actor were not borne out by *Pulp Fiction* where, it has to be said, he does not give a great performance, Jaymes still thinks that Tarantino had what it takes and *could* have made it irrespective of his writing/directing. (His real test will come in his first lead role – in *From Dusk Till Dawn*.)

'I rose to his defence recently with somebody who said he's not a very good actor. I said, "You know that's absolutely wrong. I think he was wearing so many hats in *Pulp Fiction* he was just distracted." You know he's got such an unusual look, he's got such a great kind of frenetic energy. Even when Craig brought him to my door so many years ago, his focus was on acting and it was, "If people aren't gonna hire me as an actor then I'm gonna do my own films", and he started thinking about writing his next script, which was *True Romance*. Craig and Quentin were like brothers. Craig was the one who read all the screenplays and handed them back to Quentin and he'd act out all these scenes for us and take them back to the office, all these napkins with hand scratchings on, and revamp them and put everything into context.'

One such script was a comedy called *Captain Peachfuzz and the Anchovy Bandit*.

'That was the title of the very first script I tried to write. I just wrote twenty pages of it,' Tarantino laughs. 'What you do when you try to write, it's like when you first start off, you start writing and you think it's the greatest thing in the world and then twenty or thirty pages into it, you come up with another idea and it's, "Oh, I can't pay any attention to that, this is so obviously better," and you keep doing that.'

Unfortunately Tarantino's tendency to be easily distracted was a bit of a problem.

'There was no clue really as to how to begin with him because he just had so much energy and was so over the place,' continues Jaymes. 'Back in those days, too, it was questionable, one week to the next as to whether he was gonna have a car and how he was gonna get across the city, you know, so he wasn't always present to comment on what his week consisted of.'

Most of that week, when he wasn't working, would inevitably be devoted to watching movies.

'His mother would offer to take him to Europe every summer because he always had the benefit of a very upper middle class household, his mother has a very substantial income,' says Jaymes. 'That's what's made him the kind of filmmaker he is. He didn't want to go to Europe, he wanted to watch movies instead.'

It is because of Tarantino's single-mindedness that Jaymes is not surprised at his position in the film world today.

'Well, that was the whole thing, that he kind of wanted to be a star. To be an actor, he would write and direct his own stuff so that he could be in it. That really goes back to him wanting to be the centre of attention.

'He was always full of himself. You know he really took risks and took chances even in his formative years. He was bold and very aggressive. At one point he was writing a book. He *wasn't*, of course, because he can't write, but he would call well-known directors and say that he wanted to spend the afternoon with them and talk about their films because he was writing a book about them. But there *was* no book and he really just wanted to sit down and talk to them and *that* was his education. Plus he'd get a free lunch.'

John Milius and Joe Dante were just two of the Tarantino meal benefactors, as have been others through the ensuing years.

'I've read a couple of articles by people where it's like it's cute that he's got all this money but he's barely had a chance to spend it,' chuckles Jaymes. 'It's not that he's never had a chance, it's just that he won't. He's like Scrooge.'

It is probably for this reason that Tarantino has not been quick to move to swanky new living quarters. Even today, he's still living like he was then. Well, almost.

'When he lived down in Los Angeles and you would open the door, really you would have to put on a gas mask,' Jaymes laughs. 'I mean it was *unreal*. I'd never seen anything like it in my life, just unreal. I don't know how anybody could live like that. It's one of his quirks. Everybody's different . . .'

While all this was going on, Tarantino had found gainful employment, having been gifted a heaven-sent vocation for a movie geek, working in the aforementioned video store – Video Archives on LA's bohemian Manhattan Beach.

'Until I became a director it was the best job I ever had,' says Tarantino, who began working there when he was twenty-two.

The original Video Archives has since become Riviera Tuxedo, with the new expanded store having moved a couple of miles to Hermosa Beach. It's an institution that remembers well its former employee – a huge painting of *Reservoir Dogs* hanging in the front window, with *Dogs* Cannes posters and other memorabilia available inside. Its owner, as it was in the old days, is the genial Lance Lawson.

Lawson remembers the first time the twenty-year-old high school dropout walked into the store in 1983, just itching to talk about movies.

'He came by as a film buff one day,' he begins, 'and we started talking about movies and got into a discussion about Brian De Palma. Four hours later we were still talking.'

Tarantino came back to the store the next day and talked about Sergio Leone. Eventually, Lawson offered him a job, working for only $4 an

Courtesy Connie Zastoupil

'If people aren't going to hire me as an actor, then I'm gonna do my own films.'

hour and with permission to sign out as many videos as he liked free of charge.

According to Lawson, Tarantino, dressed mostly in black, drove a silver Honda Civic, stuffed his face with burgers from Denny's and Jack In

The Box, was a voracious reader of crime novels and comic books, nay, pulp fiction, loved Elvis and The Three Stooges and, as legend has it, was so disorganized in his personal life that he amassed $7000 worth of traffic tickets.

'I went to jail about three different times just for warrants on me for moving violations,' confesses Tarantino. 'You'd get stopped and you'd get a ticket and then some other ticket and some other ticket and I just never paid 'em. They had warrants on me for three years and eventually I got stopped and they sent me to jail. They stopped me and it's like three thousand dollars and I was making like two hundred dollars a week. You know what, most people in that class that are making ten thousand a year probably have gone to jail 'cause they can't afford to pay when they get a ticket . . . not women, 'cause women'll get the highest insurance possible, even if they're only making one hundred dollars a week, but guys don't.'

'During that time in jail he overheard all of the inmates talking and on one sheet of a paper in the tiniest writing you can imagine he copied everything down,' says Avary, 'and so a lot of that stuff that Drexl says in *True Romance* came from real life.'

The whole jail experience even gets a mention in *Reservoir Dogs* . . .

MR ORANGE
    . . . Her brother usually goes with her, but he's in county unexpectedly.

MR WHITE
    What for?

MR ORANGE
    Traffic tickets gone to warrant. They stopped him for something, found the warrants on 'im, took 'im to county . . .

'He'd talk so enthusiastically about some movie that a customer couldn't say no,' remembers Lawson fondly of his old employee. 'He could sell you a date in the electric chair.'

In fact, according to his old boss, there was a always a film argument of some sort going on in the store.

'If you had an opinion about something, then, boy, you'd better be able to back it up on your feet,' he chuckles. 'People would thrive on it.'

Roger Avary remembers his first encounter with Tarantino.

'I actually really didn't like Quentin that much when we first met,' he says. 'There was a rivalry. It was about who knew more about films, that videostore geek kind of thing. I was forced to work the same shift as him and after a while I thought, "My God, this is a guy who knows all the same movies and likes a lot of the same films as me that no one else seems to like," like the Jim McBride version of *Breathless*, which at the time *nobody* liked. Then I found out he was trying to write and direct as well and, after a while, we hit it off.'

Tarantino's database memory was too much even for Lawson, who had been to film school himself (as had Avary, who had dropped out).

'I always prided myself on my cinema knowledge – who directed what, who starred in it,' says Lawson, 'but Quentin knew all of that plus *all* of the details – the supporting cast, who wrote the screenplay . . .'

In fact the staff, all cineliterate, completely eschewed the more usual practice of showing Disney and Schwarzenegger on the shop's video monitors for the likes of Jean-Luc Godard and the French New Wave and, later to prove very inspirational, John Woo, turning Video Archives into an earthly paradise for local film junkies.

'This was before *Blockbuster*, when videostores were first starting out,' chuckles Avary. 'The videostore geeks had passion. It was like a club-house. We'd have eight-hour conversations of film criticism, plus you'd have ten thousand films at your fingertips at any moment to prove a point. Each customer who walked through the door was a potential debate. The customer is always right? We didn't have that. The customer was most likely wrong. We'd say, "You know, we don't have *Top Gun* but we have this really cool Eric Rohmer film." That was the real charm of working there.'

And so against this backdrop, with films dissected mercilessly and with Tarantino proving himself to be the king of trivia, he discovered that beyond acting it was actually the *writing* of movies that was beginning to interest him.

John Langley, the film and TV producer who created the ultra-successful LA reality TV series, *Cops*, explains.

'Both Quentin and Roger had this purist appreciation for the medium. Sometimes you would have to wait to get service while they quizzed you about a movie you had done a rewrite on, but these guys knew the whole canon.'

Sometimes too, Langley and the other customers would be treated to Tarantino and Avary's *Top Gun* routine, in which the dynamic duo debated the homoerotic content of that film – a sketch later to be played out by Tarantino in his acting cameo in Rory Kelly's *Sleep With Me*.

Actually, it was Langley, so impressed with Tarantino, who gave him his first production job on a Dolph Lundgren work-out video, where, as a lowly assistant, Tarantino ended up spending most of his time (literally) clearing up dog crap from the studio parking lot so that Dolph wouldn't get his trainers dirty.

Video Archives was indeed tantamount to a film school in its own right. In fact, the video shop film training experience is quite a phenomenon. There are a whole new slew of directors who are products of the video era – Kevin Smith, director of *Clerks* and *Mall Rats*, is another videostore progeny – who have side-stepped film school altogether. 'Rebels with a pause', as *Variety* dubbed the alumni of such establishments.

It's logical when you think about it. When the original movie brats – Coppola, Scorsese, Spielberg *et al.* did *their* training – film school was the only place that you could get any reference material to all things past. Nowadays, just about every film is available at the touch of a button.

'There's this dangerous extreme with some film school kids,' has said Trea Troving of Miramax Films, the company which produced *Reservoir Dogs*. 'They are so pumped up with craft and camera technique that they forget the basics of good storytelling.'

And thus the likes of Tarantino, Avary and Smith come from the cinephile rather than cineaste tradition.

Smith recalled in *Variety*, 'I can't stand hearing some professor interpret another guy's film. The only person I want to hear lecture about a film is the guy who made it. All the great film school directors spawned a generation of people who think all you have to do is to go to film school to be a director.'

'Guys who worked in video stores have seen a lot more films than us, especially Quentin with that Hong Kong stuff,' explains Rory Kelly who worked in the film archive at USC. 'But there is a big difference between watching a clean print on a big screen and watching a video.'

Lance Lawson confirms that since Tarantino's success, interest in working at Video Archives has never been keener, aspiring filmmakers hoping that some of that store's magic might rub off on them.

'Sure we get a lot more attention,' he elaborates. 'For instance, the day after Quentin's David Letterman appearance, the phone was ringing all day long from all around the country. It's crazy, we used to get one applicant per job a month back in the old days and now we must get about ten a week. I actually had a guy come in this last week looking for a job and with his *résumé* he put in a video. He was the director of this feature called *Underground*. We've had people come here who want to become directors, but we've never had anyone apply here who's already directed a film. That was kind of bizarre.'

And so, as Tarantino's interest in writing developed, when he wasn't behind the counter, he was beavering away on scripts of his own. One mustn't underestimate how much time he devoted to this – 'every waking hour', according to one of his associates and by 1987 he had finished two in their entirety – *True Romance* and *Natural Born Killers*. He would shove early drafts under the nose of Lawson, whose counsel was sought on the basis of his film school background.

'It sounds kinda silly but I didn't really enjoy reading his scripts,' confesses Lawson, finding this all rather amusing in retrospect. 'There's a such a difference between seeing a play or a film and reading it on the page.'

Some of the early references were obvious – Elvis and Sonny Chiba have their moments in *True Romance*, and Clarence Worley's birthday treat in that film, a visit to a Sonny Chiba triple bill, is something that Quentin used to reserve for himself.

'That time is captured perfectly in *True Romance*,' recalls Tarantino. 'The things that Clarence says are the things that I and the rest of us said. The things that *he* says are the things that *we* said.'

'Quentin has a mind for dialogue,' says Avary. 'He can repeat a conversation you've had ten or fifteen years ago verbatim.'

Thus *Heroes For Sale*, the comic-book store where Clarence Worley works in that film, is but a thin disguise for Video Archives . . .

ALABAMA
Wow, what a swell place to work.

CLARENCE

Yeah, it's pretty cool. I got the key, so I just come in, you know, read comics, play music.

ALABAMA

You worked here a long time?

CLARENCE

Almost four years.

ALABAMA

That's a long time.

CLARENCE

Yeah, I know, but it's not so bad. I'm pretty friendly with most of the customers. So I just hang out, bullshit, read comic books.

ALABAMA

Do you get paid a lot?

CLARENCE

No, that's where the trouble comes into paradise. But the boss, he's a pretty nice guy, lets you borrow money from time to time if you need it. You wanna see what Spiderman number one looks like . . . ?

A lot of the dialogue also had a familiar ring to it.

'You'd recognize so many things,' muses Lawson, breaking off from serving a customer to whom he'd been giving the hard sell on the French-Canadian film *Léolo*, a particular favourite of his.

'You'd recognize where this came from, where that came from. Much of it was *very* personal. For instance, it got to be such an annoyance that I almost stopped going out to eat with Quentin, because Quentin *was* the Steve Buscemi character in *Dogs*. He wouldn't tip and he had *such* a problem with it. I used to say, "Quentin, these ladies are probably single mothers. They probably live off tips," but he just did not understand the concept. He had no *interest* in understanding the concept, but these things would pop up, and you *knew* where they came from. And he'd say things like, "I'm going for a Jimmy Riddle now," and I'd say, "Quentin, that's a little bit more information than I needed right now." '

This phrase, of course, ended up being uttered by Uma Thurman to John Travolta in *Pulp Fiction*. Lawson, still a close friend of Quentin's and someone who, obviously, still regards him with great affection, digs up some more nuggets.

'You know back then, Quentin was a bit of a homophobe,' he continues. 'He was really a kid who'd never been out of LA county. Being able to travel the world was such a broadening experience and so good for him and that's what I'm happiest about – it's really made him a better person. But you know, I'd kid him back in the old days, you know, "Would you sleep with Elvis?" And the thought just kind of terrified him, and he'd go, "No no no no. I'd have to think about that," and I'd go, "Come on, this is Elvis . . . The King," and he'd go, "Would *you*?" and I'd go, "Not necessarily *Elvis*, but with Bowie maybe," because I was really into David Bowie at the time. And he'd go, "You *would*?" So all those little discussions like that, they end up in the movie.'

In this case, the opening scene from *True Romance*. Indeed, Tarantino pays a touching tribute to Lawson in that picture by having Clarence Worley refer to his kindly gaffer, the comic-store proprietor, as Lance. You don't get much more autobiographical than that.

'And then he named the Eric Stoltz character after me in *Pulp Fiction*,' he points out, rather proudly. 'I said to Quentin after *Pulp Fiction*, if I'd have known you were going to pay so much attention to what I said, I would have tried to have been much wittier.'

Roger Avary, however, remembers someone who wasn't always so cerebral.

'One time Quentin was managing the store,' he says. 'He told this guy to leave and the guy challenged him. All of a sudden Quentin grabbed this guy by the back of the head and – bam! – slammed his head into the corner of the counter. It was like a Quentin movie device. The blood just kind of dripped out of the guy's head into a pool in his eye socket . . . Quentin's funny.'

And that's not all.

'One time a customer came into Video Archives with a tape and it was three months late or something,' continues Avary, reminding us that before each scrap, Quentin would ask his adversary to wait a few seconds while he performed an almost surreal ritual, removing his dangly earring, lest it get ripped off in the heat of the action, a scene that could almost come from one of his own films.

'He had these big hoop earrings, but that's his common logic. You're about to have a fight and it's "Hold on, back up." Quentin told the guy how much it was going to cost in late fees and the guy said, "Oh, that's a lot of money. I'm just going to keep the tape." He started to walk out.

'Well, Quentin went after the guy,' he laughs. 'I don't think the guy expected it. But Quentin, with all his weight, went – boom! – into the guy's chest. He pushes him outside and he's pushing him and pushing him. And this guy was big. The thing about Quentin is, he's not afraid of stuff like that.'

It was probably a case of 'when the cat's away, the mice will play' for, defending the 'mild-mannered' Tarantino to the last, Lawson insists that this couldn't possibly be true.

'The most animated I've seen him is if we went to the movies and there was someone in front of us who wouldn't shut up. Quentin wouldn't be shy about telling them to shut up. I mean, verbally, he'd insult someone . . . insult their intelligence.'

So we'll pose that one to Tarantino. *Did* you get a bit physical?

'Yeah, that happened a couple of times over the five years,' he snickers. 'I mean that stuff *is* true.'

However, in early 1989, after what was, whichever way you look at it, an eventful time, Quentin decided to call it a day at Video Archives.

'At that stage he didn't know what he was going to do – start writing film articles, to be a film journalist. It was a matter of wanting to move on and he was starting to feel a little isolated in the South Bay and, like a lot of people, he thought, if you're gonna get into the business you'd have to come up to the Hollywood area. It had been coming for a while. It was like, "I'll try my fortune there." '

Craig Hamann, however, thinks that the importance of Video Archives has been overblown to suit a better popular mythology.

'Much of what he's doing and the image he's projecting is not being honest, but it's being *smart* because if he didn't do that it just wouldn't work. He *has* to do that. I mean Video Archives is a cool place and I like the guys who work down there, but I don't think that was a big part of his life. Quentin, before he ever got to Video Archives was already a film nut, he already was who he was. It didn't matter, he'd still be where he is. It's almost like it takes away from him. It's not what Video Archives brought to him, it's what he brought to them. But it makes an interesting story . . .'

Tarantino's first job after Video Archives, ironically, was working for Imperial Entertainment, peddling videos to stores like the one he had just left. Tarantino employed a particular scam where he'd phone up a particular store pretending to be a customer and put in several requests for certain videos (all Imperial titles, of course), ones he knew that the store didn't stock. Then he'd phone again some time later as a *bona fide* Imperial salesman and offer to supply the store with the videos that were obviously in such hot demand. Not even Video Archives were exempt from that one. However, he was soon able to quit this and support himself as a writer though only just, and for a year and a half he moved back in with Connie who had remarried and was living in Glendale.

'I'd already written *True Romance*, then *Natural Born Killers* and then I wrote *Dogs*,' explains Tarantino rather glibly. 'I then wrote one script from a treatment that someone else did and then I did a script polish and I had been supporting myself as a writer for about a good year and a half before I got *Dogs* off the ground, which was a big deal – being able to quit my day job, you know, and actually support myself as a writer. That's a bigger leap – working behind a counter, working a day job then doing rewrite work, than it is from doing rewrite work to directing your own film. I mean, just being able to quit, walk away from a day job is *such* a big deal, I can't tell you.'

It is already clear, then, that although the video clerk-turned-auteur theory is true in spirit, the timescale has been somewhat condensed to suit a more tidy anecdote. Tarantino, in actuality, had been trying to make films for nearly ten years. He is no overnight success.

Tarantino was driven by a desperate desire to write and direct his own movie. *True Romance* and *Natural Born Killers* were both written as a means to this end and will, of course, be discussed at length further on. The first, which had gained the most attention – not all positive – seemed the most likely option and Tarantino approached various independent film companies and private parties to invest money in it.

However, tired of empty promises as to its viability, after three years Tarantino decided to sell it in order to provide the budget for a film he could make himself, a third project he was toying with. *Natural Born Killers*, meanwhile, had been written as a means of raising money to direct *True Romance*. It too seemed to be going nowhere, and the rights were naively passed on to his friend Rand Vossler, who had convinced him that he could get a production deal.

Thus, after his script for *True Romance* had been touted round the film companies by Cathryn Jaymes, Tarantino reluctantly agreed to let his baby go and, in 1989, he sold it for the Writer's Guild minimum of $30,000, still a substantial amount of money for Tarantino at that time. He never looked back and thus, with a script credit to his name, a spec script at that, he was actually able to move on to the next step, which was making a living as a full-time writer.

'I thought it was very hard to break in as a writer,' he has said, 'but actually it's really not that hard. It's hard when you don't know anybody and you're out of the blue. But when you actually get to Hollywood and if you're good, if you have something to offer and if you can get inside the industry, you can do it. If you get the script to the people that *should* get it.'

This does not include the readers, the people hired by the film companies to sift through the tons of scripts that they get sent ever year.

'They're almost impossible to get around, I've never had any luck there,' Tarantino continues. 'If these people like what they read, they pass it on to the studio who might take a second look at it for themselves. Should your readers give your script the thumbs down, well then you're out in the cold. You have to do it little by little. By starting to make a name for yourself. For instance, try to become friends with the the writers, sometimes they get offered a job that they can't take because they're already committed to something else. But they like you and perhaps suggest you. The next thing you know, you could be sending out scripts, not to readers but to independent producers, to the people who actually make the decisions. If you're good, you'll make it. I mean, the producers spend years reading crappy script after crappy script. So if your stuff is any good whatsoever, they'll notice it. Readers are just paid to shoot scripts down. But even if a producer doesn't want to touch your script with a ten-foot pole, even if he says, "We don't want to do this," he might just want to hire you to rewrite another piece of junk the studio's got lying around. The thing is, you're in. You get a job, you can make a living.'

And so it was that while he was still at Imperial, Tarantino was finally hired to write a script for $1500 by the special effects people KNB EFX, the deal being that if he wrote a script for them, they would do the effects on his first film for nothing. The result was the horror film *From Dusk Till Dawn*, 'a sort of Desperate Hours with Vampires.' Though Robert Englund, of Freddy Krueger fame, was at one point supposedly attached to it, this had, as with the rest of Tarantino's earlier work, languished on a shelf somewhere, interest only rekindled when Tarantino hit the big time with *Reservoir Dogs*.

From Dusk Till Dawn was filmed and wrapped in August 1995, directed by Robert Rodriguez of *El Mariachi* and *Desperado* fame, who directed one of the segments of *Four Rooms*.

It was the sale of this script that enabled Tarantino to take the next big step.

'I took the $1500, I quit the job and I never had to get another day job again,' he states. 'Then I got another job for $7000 dollars to do a dialogue polish and I just kept getting little increments of money.'

The dialogue polish, his second professional commission, was for a script by Frank Norwood called *Past Midnight*, the 1992 romantic thriller starring Rutger Hauer and Natasha Richardson and directed by Jan Eliasberg, the story of an Oregon social worker (Richardson) who becomes obsessed with her killer client (Hauer). Though shot theatrically, it premièred on cable TV in the States instead.

'They also gave me a credit as associate producer. It was the first credit I ever received in a movie,' he gushes. 'They hired me to do a dialogue polish and it became like a page one rewrite. And then by the time they made the movie it became half of my rewrite and half of the original script. Basically, Natasha Richardson did all my stuff and Rutger Hauer did all the other guy's stuff.'

So the rags-to-riches bit isn't exactly true.

'It wasn't like I went from the video store to the first day of shooting *Dogs*,' explains Tarantino, modestly trying to play it all down a bit. 'It wasn't *that* different from that, but during that entire time I was trying to put together movies. You know, maybe I had spent a little more than

41

six years trying to direct *True Romance* and *Natural Born Killers* that I had tried to raise the money for independently, like the Coen brothers did with *Blood Simple* and Sam Raimi did with the *Evil Dead*, and it just didn't work. I spent six years to no avail, I had nothing to show for it. Out of frustration I wrote *Reservoir Dogs*. I was gonna take the script money and a 16mm camera and that was how I was gonna go about it. Then we got Harvey Keitel and it just started picking up steam and it *happened*. Part of the reason it started happening, though, was because I had started making a living in the industry and I had a script sale to my name, so like, when they hired me to do the movie, yeah, I had never directed anything before, but I *was* a professional writer, there *was* some credit to me. The Cinderella story? It's not *that* different from that, but there's a little bit more in reality.'

There was also the small matter of that *Golden Girls* episode, which had also started to swell the coffers.

'I made a lot of money from that one,' he enthuses. 'It was only one small little thing, but the *Golden Girls* is played very heavily in America and repeated constantly and they took my segment and put it on a best of the *Golden Girls* episode so I was getting residual cheques from both ways.'

And so Tarantino, still intent on making a movie of his very own, and now with the money to do it, began to hatch a big idea.

'Something literally as simple as the fact that I get a kick out of heist films and I hadn't seen one in a long time,' he muses. 'So I thought I'd write one . . .'

Chapter 3

Reservoir Dogs

'I'd had the idea in my head for a while actually, for years and years and years – a movie about a robbery that doesn't take place *during* the robbery but takes place in the rendezvous *after* the robbery, and just the guys showing up one by one,' begins Tarantino. 'That was an idea I had a long time ago. I never investigated it more than that, it was *just* an idea.'

The days behind the counter at Video Archives, particularly the ones where he was left to mind the shop, had served Tarantino well.

'I selected a lot of the films that we bought and whatever and I had like this one shelf, this one section, that was like a revolving film festival. Every week I would like change it to something else – Sam Fuller week or David Carradine week or Nicholas Ray week or swashbuckler movies or motorcycle movies or whatever. And one time I had heist films, like *Rififi* and *Topkapi* and *The Asphalt Jungle* and *The Thomas Crown Affair*. I thought that was a really cool genre.'

One of the perks of working at Video Archives was that the staff could take home whatever videos they liked. Tarantino always made full use of this facility and when mounting his 'mini-festivals' at the store would make a point of taking those particular videos home and watching them all – manna from heaven for a film buff. The self-confessed film geek had seen most of them before, 'but it was in the context of seeing a heist movie every night that I put my head round what a neat genre that would be to re-do because there hadn't been one done in a long long time.

'The thing about heist films actually is they have this built-in suspense mechanism. Even with something like *Treasure of the Four Crowns*, you know, that crazy 3-D *Raiders of the Lost Ark* kind of movie. Even when you look at a movie like that, you're still up there and it's like, "Oh my God, they're getting too close to the beam," and you get real nervous, so I thought, okay, I'm gonna *do* one of these. And I always

43

thought that when I wrote a heist film, I'd write one where they all got away, 'cause I hated it, I *hated* it where they'd do the robbery and they're gonna get away and just by some little quirk, fate steps in and fucks 'em over.'

This, of course, was the origin of what was to become *Reservoir Dogs*, though it has to be said that when it comes to the protagonists in that picture, 'fuck 'em over' fate most certainly *does*.

'Well it didn't work out like that, that's not how my movie ends, but it doesn't have that built-in safety net that a heist film has . . . the actual heist.'

Tarantino, as explained, always had several script ideas on the go at any one time and, after he had completed *Natural Born Killers*, began tinkering with the idea of a script that encompassed three *noir*-ish crime stories that interlocked. This, of course, was to become *Pulp Fiction*, though at that time only two stories existed.

'I didn't *write Reservoir Dogs* to be a *Pulp Fiction* kind of story,' he clarifies. 'I had the idea for *Pulp Fiction* a while ago and started writing the first story, which became Vincent Vega and Marsellus Wallace's wife, knowing that the third story would be about a bunch of guys showing up at a warehouse. I just never did it and then when I came up with the idea to do *Reservoir Dogs*, it's like, "Okay, do that as a whole feature." It wasn't like I started writing it as an episodic thing, I just never got around to it.'

Tarantino has a tendency to put every reference in the context of some film or other – every movie stripped down to its constituent elements and then reassembled before you, as if he were an over-zealous squaddie on bren gun inspection. You may not have ever seen *The Treasure of the Four Crowns*. Watch it today and you'll realize why you never bothered to catch it first time round. He, though, whether they're good, bad or ugly, seems to have seen them *all*.

'When I studied as an actor, I felt totally out of step with lot of the actors in my class because I was really into film, the big picture and the history of it. And *they* didn't give a shit. I mean they didn't care. That's one of the things that made me realise that I was out of step with these people. Just appearing in movies ain't enough, I've gotta make the movies *mine*, because all my heroes were directors and *they* didn't know any of them. They knew who Martin Scorsese was and they knew who

Francis Ford Coppola was, but that was it. They just knew who could give them a job and that's what they cared about. The history of film? They couldn't care less.

'It just seemed to me very sloppy on *actors '* parts. This is their profession. This is what they're trying to do and they're forsaking everything else to do it. It's one of the hardest professions in the world to crack. I was not successful as an actor, I could not make a living, I could not even get close to that.'

Time would prove otherwise, though at the time of penning *Reservoir Dogs*, Tarantino still seemed genuinely in awe of those who managed to earn a living from thespianism.

'All I saw were failures,' he continues. 'Success seemed so elusive and the thing about it was they were trying to make it and they were *sloppy*. Either they didn't take classes, or they took classes and all the work they put in was on that Wednesday when they had *go* to the class. The rest of the time they're fucking around, messing around, not doing a damn thing and they don't know and they don't care, whereas lawyers on the other hand or doctors or whatever, they go to school, they work hard. It's not just that they have to know how to be a lawyer in the courtroom, they have to know the history of law because that perfects them, the knowledge is important to them. Actors don't have that kind of schooling.'

Tarantino, though self-educated in the ways of film, had proven himself no great shakes when it came to the three Rs. Thus his technique for writing scripts is pretty much off the cuff.

'Well, you see, I don't know how to type. I hand write. In fact I don't even hand write, I print,' he explains. 'I got my method and it works very well with me and I'm very happy with it, of just writing in notebooks and whatever. What I do is when I start it off – and I always say, you can't write poetry on a computer – I go to a store and I buy a notebook and I say, "Okay, this is the notebook I'm gonna write *Reservoir Dogs* with," and then I buy my felt-tip pens, usually two red ones and two black ones, and it's like, "These are the pens I'm gonna write *Reservoir Dogs* with," and then during the course of the time that I'm writing the notebook's always with me and the pens are always with me.'

And so, in October 1990, armed with his felt-tipped pens (two red, two black) and a trusty notebook, he sat down to write the script of *Reservoir Dogs*. He managed to bash it out in about three weeks.

'I wrote it real quick, but that's slightly deceptive,' says Tarantino, 'simply because I had done some homework on it before, but dialogue's real easy for me to write and since this movie is nearly *all* dialogue it's just getting guys talking to each other and then jotting it down.'

It was while he was still in the process of writing *Reservoir Dogs* that Tarantino met Lawrence Bender, now his producing partner. A former dancer and pupil of 'Fame' choreographer Louis Falco, Bender had toured New England with a ballet company until he picked up an injury which forced him to turn his hand to acting. He'd managed to land himself a few parts on the New York stage, including a production of *A Midsummer Night's Dream* with Ellen Burstyn and Christopher Walken. Intent on film acting, though, he had moved to Los Angeles in 1985 only to end up branching into film production. By the time he met Tarantino, his credits had included the low budget cult horror tale *The Intruder* for director Scott Spiegel (also the co-writer of *Evil Dead 2*) who, as it turned

Lawrence Bender (second from left) with Tarantino, Maria De Medeiros and Samuel L. Jackson in Cannes, May 1994: 'I had some experience, but not *that* much experience.'

out, was also a friend of Tarantino's. Bender had briefly met Tarantino while in line for a movie, but they didn't really get talking until their second encounter at a party Spiegel had thrown.

'When I ran into Quentin I said, "Tarantino, that name seems so familiar. I read a script but I think it was another Tarantino – *True Romance*, or something like that," and he goes, "That's *my* script," and I go, "Oh really, that was a really cool script, that was really cool." I was nobody and he was nobody and to have read his script, it was kind of a coincidence.'

Bender and Tarantino did not begin their collaboration right away, that process happened over several months. At that time, Bender was still trying to produce movies with Spiegel. Spiegel suggested that Bender get in touch with Tarantino because he knew he needed some help in getting his ideas off the ground.

'At that point he had *True Romance*, but this other guy had the option on it and he had the script for *Natural Born Killers*. I read *Natural Born Killers* and I thought it was a pretty cool script but personally I wasn't sure about that particular project for myself. He said he was gonna do a rewrite on it. He didn't rewrite it the way I thought he should rewrite it but he took the script in a whole other direction and made it pretty interesting. The thing was, he had spent the past five years trying to raise money on *True Romance* and then a couple of years trying to raise money on *Natural Born Killers*. Basically, he had reached his shelf life on these two projects. At that point he said, "I have this other idea, *Reservoir Dogs*, about a bunch of guys who pull a heist, but you never see the heist. The whole movie takes place in one garage where they all come back – someone's been shot, someone's been wounded, someone's been killed, someone's an undercover cop, but you never see the heist because it's a low budget movie." It was one of a few short films that he had.'

Bender suggested that they make a fresh start and use this as a brand new project to tout around, meaning, effectively, that they forget *Natural Born Killers* altogether, which Tarantino's friend Rand Vossler had been trying to produce.

'When he said, "Look, let's make *Reservoir Dogs*," he felt kind of bad because he had been working with Rand for so long and didn't want to leave him out in the cold. So he said, "Rand, look, I'm gonna give you the script and you can take care of it." That's what happened.'

It was this decision to pass on *Natural Born Killers* in this manner that was to blow up in Tarantino's face later on, though at the time it didn't seem a problem. Tarantino simply got on with licking *Dogs* into shape. When he was done, Bender went over to Tarantino's house and read the finished version.

'I thought it was extraordinary,' he says.

It was now November and Tarantino was desperate to get filming. Bender asked for a year to come up with the financing. Tarantino, however, insisted that if they didn't have any funding by January 1991, they would film it in 16mm, black and white, using the money from the script sales.

'I was gonna be Mr Pink and he was gonna be Nice Guy Eddie and we were gonna get some friends to play the other parts,' Tarantino chuckles. 'That's how we were gonna do it.'

'What happened was, I told Lawrence, "Look I'm gonna be writing this film. I'm gonna start with it next month and I'm gonna be finished with it in a few days," and so I write it and I finish it and I show it to him and he goes, "This is pretty good, why don't we try to get this going as a *real* movie," and I go, "No, I've heard that all before. Forget it, I don't trust that" . . . I'd spent six years trying to get deals on films. No one was gonna give me a job to make a new movie. No one was gonna take a chance and go, "Here's a million dollars," and so I took my destiny out of their hands. I had a budget of $30,000 (from the *True Romance* script sale). I could spend it, that was *my* money. I can't tell you how liberating it was. It was so exciting. I had written two other scripts before that I thought I was going to make, but this one, as I'm writing it, I *knew* I was gonna shoot a film on it. I *knew* it. *This* was the one. This was *achievable*.'

Says Bender, 'I started out saying give me like a year option and he said no way, so he finally bargained me down and we wrote on a piece of paper a little deal between us and we both signed it.'

Bender thus had only two months to raise some cash if they were going to do it properly, a ridiculously short period of time to get the wheels in motion. However, events were soon to take a momentous turn.

Bender had still continued his acting classes and, quite by chance, mentioned to his coach Peter Floor that he was trying to produce a script. As they walked down the street to Bender's car after class one afternoon, Floor asked Bender, half-jokingly, who he saw as the lead.

'He just said, "Out of anyone in the world, if you could have the choice, who would you want in this move?" ' laughs Bender. 'I said if we could have anyone in the world, Harvey Keitel would be this one guy. I had *no* connection with Harvey. He goes, "Well my wife Lily (Parker) knows Harvey from the Actor's Studio. Let me give it to her and if she likes it, maybe she can give it to him." '

Lily Parker loved it and swore blind that Keitel would too.

Harvey Keitel *did* love the script and a few days later Bender came to find none other than the Brooklyn strains of Keitel on his answering machine.

'He left a message like, "Hello, Lawrence. Hello, I'm calling for Lawrence Bender. This is Harvey Keitel speaking. I read the script for *Reservoir Dogs* and I'd like to talk to you about it." He'd read it late Saturday night and he rang me first thing Sunday morning.'

Bender, positively sweating with anticipation, rang back and was overwhelmed to hear Keitel stating that not only was it one of the best scripts he'd read in years, but that he'd love to be involved and offering to help get the film made in any way he could.

'That was wild because Harvey was mine and Lawrence's like dream guy for the movie and Harvey is like my favourite actor,' Tarantino enthuses. 'I've worked with him and, boy, I can see what he can do and he's been my favourite actor since I was sixteen years old. I'd seen him in *Mean Streets* and *Taxi Driver* and *The Duellists* and stuff. I didn't write the part for Harvey because I thought it'd probably be, you know, my Uncle Pete!'

'He's one of the reasons I became an actor,' says Tim Roth, who would eventually play opposite him in the movie.

With Keitel on board, *Reservoir Dogs* thus became a whole new ball game.

'At the end of the two months we got a deal that we could have done the movie for $200,000 which begat the deal that we could do it for half a million and then Live Entertainment offered us the situation to do it the way we did it, with $1.5 million,' gushes Tarantino, who was at this stage like a kid let loose in a toy shop. 'You know everything just kept escalating.'

It *wasn't* quite as simple as Tarantino implies. As he has admitted, who on earth was going to give a million dollars to an unknown first-timer? Bender began trying to find ways and means of securing the financing.

'I had produced two movies,' he confesses. 'I had produced my 100,000-dollar movie and a 50,000-dollar movie which was really kind of terrible. I had some experience, but not that much experience. I knew people who would give you 50,000 dollars but I didn't know anyone who would give you a million. There's a big difference.'

In the process of hawking the script around, Bender got in touch with veteran director Monte Hellman – director of two of Quentin's favourite-ever Westerns, *Ride In the Whirlwind* and *The Shooting*. Hellman was so enthusiastic that he offered to mortgage his house and sell a plot of land that he had in Texas in order to finance it. Together with a bank deal that Bender had arranged, this would have given them $200,000.

Hellman was very keen on directing *Reservoir Dogs* himself at this point, 'but after meeting Quentin, he realized that *he* was the guy,' says Bender.

Other people, too, were approached. As Bender explains.

'Quentin and I had several meetings with different people and one guy offered us $1.6 million to make the movie. Now you'll get people offer you a lot of money, but they don't quite see it the same way. At first he said, "Oh, I see it as a comedy," and we said, "Oh, we see it as a comedy, too." But he said, "I see it more as the *Raising Arizona* style kind of comedy where they all get up [at the end]. It's like a sting and they're not really dead." So we got up and left.

'He was someone who was making movies and he had money to give us but we always knew that we had 50,000 bucks we could make this movie for. In the worse case scenario we could turn down what we thought at that point were big bucks. We had one guy in Canada who was offering us $500,000 if his girlfriend could play Mr Blonde. It was such an off the wall idea that we actually went back and talked about it for an hour. I'd heard about it [putting your girlfriend in the picture], but I never thought that people actually did it. I thought it was just an old Hollywood cliché.'

By this time, Hellman had joined Tarantino and Bender as equal partners. He brought the script to the attention of producer Richard

Gladstein at Live Entertainment. The two had worked together previously on a slasher film called *Silent Night Deadly Night 3*. Gladstein, like everybody else, was impressed with Tarantino.

'I have never yet seen a first-time director with so much control over his material and such a clear vision of how he wants to shoot the film,' said Gladstein.

In January 1991 Gladstein agreed to finance and executive produce the picture with Tarantino on board as director according to the actors they got. Harvey Keitel, meanwhile, had shown the script to Christopher Walken and Dennis Hopper. Hopper was keen but had prior commitments. Walken at that stage seemed likely but, ultimately, could not commit either.

On 11 January 1991 the British film trade paper *Screen International* ran the following announcement:

> Filmmaker Monte Hellman switches hats as executive producer of the independent *Reservoir Dogs*. Quentin Tarantino directs his original script about a jewellery store heist that has comic and tragic consequences. Christopher Walken and Harvey Keitel are in the gang for producer Lawrence Binder [sic].

On 4 February, Live submitted an official deal memo and Tarantino and Bender submitted a tentative cast list. Live's Ronna B. Wallace, who had worked on *Bad Lieutenant* and *Bob Roberts*, came on board with Hellman and Gladstein as a third executive producer.

By the end of April, Keitel had officially signed, though Walken did not. Live were actually going to offer more money than Tarantino and Bender ended up with. Without Walken, Live agreed to produce the picture at a reduced budget. It was still $1.5 million, the magic figure that they had been looking for . . .

Should you ever meet him, Harvey Keitel, be warned, is intense – very intense. The dark eyes pierce and a near permanent scowl (his ordinary, relaxed expression – God knows what it's like when he's pissed off) sets you immediately off-balance. He does not engage easily in conversation. Whether it's all part of that deep Method thing or if, indeed, it's just part of some game he likes to play, it's unclear. He may well go home, rip the tab off a beer and regale all and sundry with hilarious tales of his youth,

Harvey Keitel as Mr White: 'Intense – *very* intense.'

but that's not the public persona. Harvey doesn't like talking about the past, Harvey doesn't like talking about the future, Harvey won't talk about anything the director can say better. Harvey will only talk about his character, and even then he doesn't give much away. Instead, he fixes you with that rapier stare, brow furrowed, as if words alone cannot convey the depth of feeling he has for his craft, tossing out a series of aphorisms — 'The analysis of the text is the education of the actor'; 'Rehearsal is a journey, let the possibilities happen' – from the armoury of the Method thespian.

Beneath the bluff exterior, however, beats a heart of gold.

Part of his philosophy has always been to take risks with material and he seems, largely, to have had something of a Midas touch with first-time directors.

'It seems to have occurred that way,' he dismisses modestly. 'It is a bit unusual to me now that I think about it, but yes, there was Scorsese and Alan Rudolph, Ridley Scott, Paul Schrader and then Quentin Tarantino . . . it just seems to have gone down that way.'

Taking risks with material was probably the cause of the hiatus in his career, a career which had never fulfilled the potential first shown in the dynamite early performances of the 1970s, most notably with Martin

Scorsese and Robert De Niro in *Mean Streets* and *Taxi Driver*. Kicked off the set of *Apocalypse Now* in 1976 and replaced with Martin Sheen, Keitel's career proceeded to go downhill and reached its nadir in 1980 with the tragic sci-fi flick *Saturn Three* in which his voice was completely over-dubbed. This film, cruelly and ironically, coincided with *Raging Bull*, which saw his former cohorts at the height of their powers. After a decade in the wilderness, he had started to claw his way back into the frame, with *Thelma & Louise*, *Bugsy* (for which he got an Oscar nomination) and had recently completed *Bad Lieutenant*, also for Live, which despite its weaknesses, showcased a quite stunning performance. Even *Sister Act* had turned into something quite entertaining due to a menacing turn on his part. *The Piano* was about to follow, and though he is now very much back in the major league, collaborating with Tarantino again on *Pulp Fiction* and *From Dusk Till Dawn*, he has still stuck to his philosophy, taking time out to give support to people like British director Danny Cannon, for whom he starred in his début picture, *The Young Americans*.

'You know what, Harvey is a bit of a teacher in a sense and he likes to give his knowledge to people,' says Bender. 'We learned a lot from him working on *Reservoir Dogs*. I think there's something natural about him that's very giving if you give him an opportunity to promote what he feels filmmaking is all about and, I think, especially with directors who are really into actors. He really gave Quentin and I some weight behind us. He was such a wonderful source of inspiration. He would talk to us about acting and he would come to us when we were shooting scenes and he would say, "Lawrence, this is a very important scene and Quentin's under a lot of pressure. If Quentin doesn't have enough time, maybe we can find time another day and cut something else out." '

'I'm always searching for an experience and Quentin came along and provided it – this provocative piece of material,' says Keitel. 'I thought it was a brilliant piece of writing, it dealt with themes that hold interest for me. Universal themes regarding the quest for camaraderie – what it is to be a hero to someone, redemption. It appealed to me in the way Quentin wrote it to me. It was very fascinating and immediate. To me there is a common denominator between Quentin and Marty [Scorsese] . . . there's a certain intensity these people have, a certain vulnerability, a certain insight.'

Tarantino is rather more succinct about his hero – 'He comes in, kicks ass and leaves' – which, in effect is what Keitel did, jump-starting *Reservoir Dogs* with his own cash while the budget was still being sorted out.

'The thing was, we weren't fully financed when we started casting,' explains Tarantino. 'We said, "Look, if we just wait around, nothing's gonna happen." We were based in LA, but Harvey said, "You know we really owe it to ourselves to get a shot at the New York actors," and he bought mine and Lawrence's plane tickets, put us up in a hotel and set aside the weekend for a casting director friend of his (Ronnie Yeskel) to see actors in New York.'

There was the question to begin with of which part Keitel himself would play. Throughout the deliberation Tarantino, as legend has it, proceeded to eat his way through the contents of Keitel's kitchen.

'We read the entire script with Harvey as Mr White and then we'd read it again and he'd be Mr Pink and it was a mutual decision for Harvey to be Mr White,' says Tarantino.

It was the trip to the East Coast that resulted in the recruitment of Steve Buscemi.

Says Bender, 'We had known about Steve Buscemi, but we would never have hired him if we hadn't met him in person. He actually did give us the best audition for that role but there was something about Steve that just made sense for the part.'

'I knew that I was working on something really good,' Buscemi explains. 'It was one of the tightest scripts I have ever read. It even has the descriptions of the camera angles in it – who the camera stays on, whether Mr White or Mr Pink is offscreen – and that's how Quentin Tarantino shot it. It was really faithful to the way he wrote it. When we were making it, it felt really good, but when I saw the film it was even better. But I was just happy that *I* liked it, even though I didn't know if it would reach an audience.'

Buscemi, however, had been singled out by Tarantino even before it came to audition time.

'He saw a videotape of me auditioning for a Neil Simon comedy, *The Marrying Man* [*Too Hot To Handle* in the UK], which I wasn't cast in,' recalls Buscemi. 'He told me that I looked like a criminal. My hair was slicked back and I was wearing this tight 50s-style shirt and I said, "Quentin, that's how I dress." '

Steve Buscemi as Mr Pink and Harvey Keitel as Mr White:
'Just the right combination of fellas.'

'When I first got the script,' he continues, 'I was told to look at Mr Orange and Nice Guy Eddie. Mr Pink was cast – Quentin was at that time serious about playing the part – but when I read the script, Mr Pink was the character that I really responded to. And then I found out just a couple of days before my audition that he *was* available. I don't think I would have played another part.'

Buscemi, of course, would also go on to collaborate with Tarantino on *Pulp Fiction* in a rather ingenious cameo as the Buddy Holly waiter at Jack Rabbit Slim's (what better comeuppance for a man who wouldn't tip than to be reincarnated as a waiter?), though he didn't make the cut of *True Romance* – not feeling comfortable with his casting as either the Chris Penn or Bronson Pinchot character. And, like the rest of the *Dogs*, through loyalty to Tarantino, he was reluctant to get involved in Oliver Stone's adaptation of *Natural Born Killers*, which we'll come to later.

After landing Buscemi, Keitel took Tarantino and Bender out to New York's rather expensive Russian Tea Room.

'Now I'm from New York but I'd never been in the Russian Tea Room because I was always a broke out-of-work actor doing plays for 50 dollars a week or something,' laughs Bender. 'I said to Harvey, "Look, at this point, you've been so much help, we'd like to make you a co-producer on the movie," and he said, "Lawrence, it's about time. What took you so long? I've been *waiting* to hear this from you!" '

As the buzz got out about the casting, the interest of several other New York based actors was aroused.

'A lot of actors came in and tried to read for the parts (including Samuel L. Jackson, who read for the part of Holdaway, the undercover cop played by Randy Brooks).'

Tarantino places great emphasis on the casting which, clearly, is one of his major strengths.

'The thing is, it's not like, "Wow, they didn't make it. It's just that in a lot of situations, in a *different* cast, they could very *well* have made it. With the actors that I saw I could have put this cast together fifteen different ways. I think I found the perfect cast. Rob Reiner was talking about *A Few Good Men* and how when casting is great you look at a movie and you can't imagine anybody else in the movie aside from *those* actors. I think that's totally the case with *Reservoir Dogs*, you can't imagine anybody else in that movie aside from those guys and that's like a total compliment. You know, if Mrs Roth never met Mr Roth and had Tim, alright, that could have affected three other guys in this cast not being in the movie, you know what I mean, because it was just the right combination of fellas.'

One interesting addition was ex-bank robber Eddie Bunker. Though now a writer/actor and advisor on some films, he had in his day had been America's most notorious criminal, at one time the youngest ever 'guest' at San Quentin prison. Turning to writing while still behind bars, his riveting semi-autobiography *No Beast So Fierce*, was turned into the 1978 film, *Straight Time*, starring Dustin Hoffman.

'Quentin Tarantino was at the Sundance Institute and the film he studied was *Straight Time*,' says Bunker. 'Chris Penn and I are very good friends, so when Tarantino was trying to cast the parts, he took me right away. I was just hired as an actor, totally as an actor. In fact, I didn't think it was gonna be that good a movie when I read the script.'

And so the dream team was duly assembled: Harvey Keitel, Michael Madsen, Chris Penn, Steve Buscemi, septuagenarian Lawrence Tierney (veteran of 1946's *Dillinger*), Eddie Bunker and Tim Roth . . . The Reservoir Dogs.

'It's a term I came up with myself and it's just a perfect title for those guys,' chuckles Tarantino. 'They *are* Reservoir Dogs, whatever the hell that means . . .'

In June 1991, Hellman, Tarantino and Buscemi went to the Sundance Institute for two weeks to fine-tune Tarantino's directing ideas. The Institute, in the mountains of Utah and owned by Robert Redford, hosts a series of workshops for young filmmakers with established directors sitting in to impart advice. Tarantino ran through and test-filmed several of the warehouse scenes with Buscemi playing Mr Pink and standing in himself as Mr White.

The first group of directors were not too impressed with Tarantino's preference for long takes, which made the scenes seem very 'stagy'. They did not like, either, the way that the camera, especially for the protracted row in the warehouse between White and Pink, before Blonde shows up, was simply put on the floor, making the shots seem big, wide and very spacious.

Reservoir Dogs: 'It's just a perfect title for those guys.'

In the context of the whole picture, of course, such scenes contrast impressively with the action.

('There's the really long scene with Steve Buscemi talking about what happened and then it just cuts to the chase,' says Tarantino's regular film editor, Sally Menke. 'It just has such great impact.')

A second group, however, including Terry Gilliam and Volker Schlondorff, were enthusiastic and assured Tarantino that he should stick with his vision. Tarantino subsequently thanked Gilliam for his words of advice in the credits to the film ('because directing's kind of weird'). Gilliam likened the claustrophobic atmosphere to that Oliver Stone's 1988 film *Talk Radio*, the story of a shock DJ which is confined to a radio studio. Tarantino didn't particularly go overboard about that film, but liked the way Stone had filmed it. Gilliam, who had used elements of *Talk Radio* in his own *The Fisher King*, a contrast to his otherwise legendary extravagance (*Brazil, The Adventures of Baron Munchausen*), told Tarantino that when you put a film in one room, it's the nearest thing you get to 'pure cinema'.

Tony Scott, too (later to direct *True Romance*, of course), gets the 'special thanks' treatment for some handy hints ('I like Tony better than Ridley,' says Tarantino. 'It's not fashionable to say that, but I do. I love *Days of Thunder*. I think *Days of Thunder* is a great fucking film. it's like a Sergio Leone race car movie').

Despite their words of encouragement, Tarantino was still not totally confident. Tarantino and Bender's friend Scott Spiegel had recently been fired as the director of a movie (*The Nutty Nut*), which made Tarantino a little nervous.

'He was very, very scared, actually, of being fired,' admits Bender. 'I really feel that if Scott had had a good producer behind him, not only would he not have gotten fired but he would have made a really great movie, but they didn't understand what he was doing. He was doing all these crazy, wacky shots first day of shooting, and they were like, well, "What are you doing and how is this gonna cut?" No one understood. He'd storyboarded the entire movie, but nobody bothered to look.'

Bender drew on the experience and thus arranged for Tarantino to put the more conventional shots, ones with lots of coverage, up front in the shooting schedule and the more complicated stuff in the final third, 'so that you're not going to trick anybody. Basically, if you're doing a decent job and you do a shot that's really awful, you can say, "Here's why I'm doing it," and they've already seen some stuff. I came up with all sorts of ways to protect Quentin.'

He needn't have worried. Gladstein later said that unless Tarantino had been a complete jerk, he would have made the movie anyway . . .

Three weeks before shooting began, Tarantino, together with his production designer David Wasco and location manager Billy Fox, began scouting for locations. Tarantino wanted to make his hometown Los Angeles very much part of the fabric of his movie.

'Quentin didn't want to film glistening high rises, so the two storey structures around East LA were a perfect setting to give the feel of old Los Angeles,' says Wasco. 'It's almost like a play and they wanted the city to be almost like a character, as they did with *Pulp Fiction*. We used Highland Park because it was this unchanged older-looking area of one- and two-storey streets, which is where we did the Steve Buscemi running scene. You had this older-looking city backdrop as opposed to that of Wilshire Boulevard, the high tech or the gentrified areas. It allowed us to do this ambiguous time period look, which will allow the movie to age gracefully.'

The buildings found included the Park Plaza Hotel in the downtown area. The hotel had been used many times on film, though never purely for it's bathroom – scene of the segment where Tim Roth's Orange tells his rehearsed anecdote about the dope courier going into the men's room. The coffee shop, Uncle Bob's Pancake House (in reality Pat and Lorraine's on Eagle Rock Boulevard), and the red-brick wall of a bowling alley, against which the Dogs are shot for the opening credit sequence, are again in Highland Park. The fictitious strip club, Boots and Socks, where the gang meet at one point, is a dressed up bar in North Hollywood. The only location to have been overtly used before (in the films *Miracle Mile* and *Short Cuts*) is the diner Johnie's (sic), on the junction of Wilshire and Fairfax. This is used for the meeting between Roth and Brooks, this pair then honing Roth's undercover skills in front of highly graffitied walls downtown at Beverly and 2nd. This location was originally a subway exit to LA's now defunct underground system.

'It's under a freeway, a flyover thing,' remembers Tim Roth. 'It's an incredible place, a big outdoor auditorium and there's a stage. At the side of the stage there's two doors and behind the doors live two tramps. All weekend they'd come and stick their heads out while we were filming. They've been living there for years and neither of them like each other, but they're neighbours and they live this far apart (he holds his hands a couple of feet away from each other) and they really don't like each other, but it's amazing.'

Typically, Tarantino insisted on customizing it somewhat, employing a graffiti artist to come in and spray the word 'Bootsie' (as in the 1970s funkster) in a prime position.

The most important location, though, was to be found at Figueroa and 59th, again in Highland Park – a disused mortuary, since flattened by an earthquake, which served as the warehouse, the post-heist rendezvous where the bulk of the action takes place. Watch the film again and you'll see the coffins lined up against the wall and that the vehicle Michael Madsen's Mr Blonde sits on while slurping his coke is, in fact, a hearse.

'It was scripted to be the back of a funeral parlour so that was our key to that,' says Sandy Reynolds-Wasco, the set decorator, emphasizing that Tarantino had pretty much invented the look of the film in his head already. 'You don't really get a full sense of that because you see coffins and you see a hearse and you think that maybe it's kind of besides the point.'

The mortuary's embalming room was also used (where White and Pink walk off to discuss the fate of Orange) and a room at the back of the building was also utilized – converted into Freddy Newendyke's apartment.

'What didn't come out was that Quentin wanted the Tim Roth character to be infatuated by The Thing (the Marvel comic-book character),' explains Wasco. 'He actually did a scene with Tim Roth walking back and forth in the apartment with this little model in his hand. The producers, and this is before Quentin became the big popular director that he is, they were saying, "Here we have this policeman. Oh my goodness, what are the audience gonna think with him holding a doll," so they cut that out.'

The colour scheme of The Thing, light blue and grey/brown was thus used in the decoration of the apartment, a subtlety that is probably lost, and a reference to The Thing was included instead in an additional line of dialogue when Freddy Newendyke is describing Joe Cabot's appearance.

'It was a subliminal background thing,' says Wasco. 'He wanted the character to be infatuated by the Marvel comic-book character as was the Richard Gere character in *Breathless*.'

One shouldn't underestimate the importance of Jim McBride's 1983 film *Breathless* in influencing Tarantino. A remake of Jean-Luc Godard's 1959 classic, it was not hailed as a critical success. Nonetheless, there are certain themes in it that Tarantino has drawn on – it uses phoney backdrops for the driving sequences (as were used in the Bruce Willis taxi sequence in *Pulp Fiction*), has a rockabilly soundtrack (*Pulp Fiction* does a similar thing with surfing music) and, as with all of Tarantino's scripts so far, the lead character, while being a thoroughly unlikeable person, still evokes our sympathy. The lead character, played by Gere, is also heavily into the comic book character Silver Surfer, as Tarantino was at that time. It is the obsessive traits of such characters which seems to be built into the framework of Tarantino's work (the Silver Surfer also crops up in Tarantino's script polish of *Crimson Tide*).

To give Roth's home a bit more identity, Tarantino also enlisted the help of artists Manuel and David Villalovos to put up posters and other comic book memorabilia.

'They created a new character – Kamikaze Cowboy – for both a poster and a comic book. The character makes its début in the film.'

'You had a hard line to keep it from getting *too* kitschy,' says Sandy Reynolds-Wasco, who ensured that these details didn't become overbearing. 'It's still in the background, otherwise it would be too boring.'

The Wascos also created a scaled down model of Karina's the jewellery store (named after Anna Karina) for a scene in which the robbery is planned. This scene, though filmed, never made the final cut.

Polish-born cinematographer Andrzej Sekula's expertise in lighting enabled him to create the sharp focus and maintain a big depth of field for the interior shots, which is exactly what Tarantino wanted. Sekula, who had trained with Academy Award winning cinematographer Oswald Morris in the UK, uses fast film stock, which requires an awful lot of interior lighting.

'Andrzej brought a quality to the images exactly as I had imagined,' says Tarantino. 'One has to be very skilful to handle the intensity of the lighting so the audience isn't aware of how the scene is lit. It's a time-consuming process, but with Andrzej's sense of lighting and experience

61

with the film it didn't cause us additional production time.'

Costume designer Betsy Heimann created the now-famous black suit and tie look (though each is subtly different) and, thus, from the moment the Dogs swagger forth, Wild Bunch style, to the strains of the George Baker Selection's 'Little Green Bag' while the opening credits roll ('We wanted to go for a more poetic movement. We wanted to give these gangsters a sort of unnatural slowness,' says Sekula), swishing back the curtain on this high testosterone tale of macho bravura, the style and feel have been firmly established.

'Even if our budget were doubled, we couldn't have found a better and more professional team,' says Lawrence Bender.

'I had my vision,' concurs Tarantino, getting philosophical about the art of getting the best out of his troops. 'All I had to do was articulate my desires on a basic level and this team took the ball and ran with it, often-times producing more than I had ever envisioned. I was guided by a quote of Patton's, "If you tell people what to do as opposed to how to do it, they will surprise you with their ingenuity." And that's exactly what everyone did.'

Tarantino's vision lasts as long as it takes Roth's Mr Orange to haemorrhage all over the warehouse ramp and in amongst all the other sets, props, make-up and effects was employed a huge pool of fake blood.

'That was very sticky,' laughs Roth. 'It's a syrup and it dries under the lights, so you're actually stuck to the floor at some points.'

'It was 105 degrees and he lay in that for weeks,' says Sandy Reynolds-Wasco.

'We thought we were going to have to rent a dummy because we thought how can we have this actor lay down for days and days and days,' explains Wasco. 'But Tim Roth just lay on the floor. We had to recreate this pool of blood everyday because we couldn't leave it in this rat infested warehouse.'

And so, with everything ready to roll, the actors went into a week of rehearsal.

'We sat around a table in a room and sort of chatted about the charac-ters and stuff and because it was six or seven actors who like to work in different ways, we had to accommodate each other,' recalls Roth. 'I don't like to rehearse ('Tim Roth didn't want to rehearse the scene in the car,' adds Keitel, 'so we had to adjust to that.') I had to accommodate the other actors, so I would lie there with the script. Harvey always likes to rehearse but he just reads from the script. I don't know quite what goes on in his head, but there's lots of thinking. It's very quiet the whole time he's reading it and nothing really changes until when he's filming and then it all comes together. And when the camera turns, that's it. It was very weird, but it all came together. Mike Madsen, who plays Mr Blonde, doesn't like to rehearse but really enjoyed it.'

Part of that enjoyment came from the rapport that Madsen had struck up with Kirk Baltz, who plays Marvin Nash, the mono-aural man from the LAPD, with Madsen kindly obliging Baltz's foolhardy request to get into the boot of Madsen's car to help Baltz 'find his character'.

'Well actually he only wanted me to drive him around for about ten minutes, but once I got him in the trunk and started to go, I drove around for about 45,' smirks the Elvis lookalike (Vegas period). 'Once I got in the car I thought, "Well this is good for me, too." He was banging and kicking and shouting, so I turned on the radio. I went to Taco Bell and I got a coke. I drove up and down, I did U-turns. I had a lot of junk in the trunk bouncing around and when I opened it up he was all sweaty and real angry. He looked pretty bad, hurhurhur.'

Principal photography on *Reservoir Dogs* duly began on 29 July 1991. It took five weeks to shoot . . .

Chapter 4

Black Tie, White Noise

Sam Fuller to Jean-Luc Godard:
    'You're a goddamned thief, a plagiarist.'
Jean-Luc Godard to Sam Fuller:
    'In America, plagiarism. In France, *hommage*.'

On 18 January 1992 *Reservoir Dogs* made its début at the Sundance Festival, Park City, Utah ('It was completely wild,' says Tim Roth, who was there. 'They were selling tickets on the buses for $100 dollars apiece.') The official festival programme described the film as 'Jim Thompson meets Samuel Beckett'. Although it was a big hit among the paying public, *Dogs*, however, was up against some stiff competition from the likes of Allison Anders' *Gas Food Lodging* and Neal Jimenez and Michael Steinberg's *The Waterdance*, all first-rate fare. *Dogs* didn't win, Alexandre Rockwell's *In the Soup* (also starring Steve Buscemi) running off with the Grand Jury Prize. Interestingly, all of these filmmakers mentioned, the Sundance Kids, have since collaborated at various points with Tarantino – Rockwell and Anders co-directing *Four Rooms* with him, Jimenez and Steinberg on *Sleep With Me*.

There was, though, enough good word of mouth on *Reservoir Dogs* to sustain the momentum over the coming months – through Cannes, where it was shown out of competition and critically lauded, and the various other festivals it played *en route* to its general release in the US in October (including Toronto, where it won Best First Feature). Its release in the States was limited – a mere 26 screens showed it initially (compared with 2000, which is the norm for a big studio picture), but within ten weeks it had made its money back and, more importantly, the rave critical reviews began hailing Tarantino as a major new talent.

By the time *Dogs* reached Europe, it was one of the most hotly anticipated films of the new year, largely due to Tarantino having embarked on an extensive publicity tour on behalf of his baby.

'He was signing autographs for a year,' says Cathryn Jaymes.

Unable to break off his affair with the media for one minute, in April, he even held a press reception at Video Archives, as a sort of thank you to those who had supported him all along.

Opening in the UK on 8 January 1993, *Dogs* cracked six London house records on its first weekend, taking £101,344 from just ten screens, making it an instant number one in the London chart and ninth nationally.

But why did it do so well?

Speaking in November 1992, on the eve of its European release, Tarantino seemed quite *blasé* about it all.

'The standard response is, "Oh no, I'm totally shocked," ' he said. 'I *am* a little surprised, but I'm not *wholly* surprised, because the way it works out every year, there are four or five independent movies that were made on the cheap that come out and get attention and break out from the pack and get a lot of laurels. I always figured *Reservoir Dogs* could be one of those films.'

True. Steven Sodebergh's low budget *Sex Lies and Videotape*, for example, which went on to great critical and commercial success three years before, was almost a blueprint for the events unfolding around *Reservoir Dogs*. A critically acclaimed film with a pedigree – it won the Palme d'Or in 1989 – *sex lies and videotape* notched up enough column inches with a crucial talking point (voyeurism as opposed to violence) that gave it a greater audience than could normally be expected for an arthouse movie.

'I didn't know it was gonna be as *big* as it became,' Tarantino continues of *Dogs*, 'and I'm still surprised by it. I've seen it happen to a lot of other filmmakers, but I always felt that if the film could get a theatrical release as opposed to video, where it would just disappear and no one know anything about it. If it could just get a theatrical release . . .'

The netherworld of video. Visit your local video emporium on a Friday night and you're hard pushed to sort out the good, the bad from the Kickboxer. If you look hard enough, you'll find a film like, say, 1992's *Guncrazy*, which, had it had the backing, would most certainly have made it at the cinema. As it happens, it went straight onto tape in the UK. Tarantino's début, one supposes, *could* have gone that way if the circumstances had not been right, but he knew there was enough of a spark of originality and enough talking points to bring it to the public's attention.

'It's a really incendiary movie,' he exhorts. 'You can't show it to an audience without getting a reaction. I *knew* the movie was like that, all the entire time while I was editing it and getting it ready and everything it was like, "Hey, we've got a powder keg here, I can't wait for audiences to see this." Some aren't gonna like it, but that's okay, but the thing is I *knew* what I had and I'm not saying that everyone liked it because it's not that kind of movie at all. You can't show it to an audience and not expect a reaction. I'm not saying that it's the greatest thing in the world or that's so cool, I'm just saying that I'm not surprised by the response . . .'

One thing that seems to have been unanimously praised is Tarantino's manner of storytelling.

'Part of the thing about the movie is that we're taking the movie off a movie clock and putting it on a real time clock at a rendezvous where they've all showed up,' explains Tarantino. 'Part of the excitement of the movie comes from the fact you don't quite know exactly what happened, it's just everyone's interpretation.'

Thus, by not actually showing the robbery, the viewer's only take on reality is through having each character recount his own separate version of events. Our perspective is their perspective. And each perspective is a little different.

'If a bunch of guys were in combat and were in the middle of a firefight and you asked them what happened, they'd say they all saw the same thing but, you know, the order of the way things went down would probably be different,' he continues. 'You know, "I saw the flash first and I saw this and I saw that," whereas another would say, "I heard their firing first." So that's what I'm interested in. It's not the fact that it's completely different stories from everyone, but a slightly different perspective and you're trying to work it out. Each time they're coming through the door, you're getting a different one and I actually think a little suspense builds because you keep waiting for the robbery, but then about midway through it's become a different kind of movie.'

Roth, whose sudden revelation as an undercover cop jolts the film

Tim Roth as Mr Orange: 'Just like being a little kid.'

toward its *dénouement*, explains just why it was he thinks that *Reservoir Dogs* provoked such a reaction.

'I read his script and it was extraordinary,' he begins. 'You get a stack of scripts sent to you, not necessarily as offers, but you always read them. This was the first refreshing thing I'd read that had real energy and something quite new about it and so I really wanted to do it and it was down to them whether they wanted me to do it.

'It reminded me of playing, just like being a little kid. It's like, if I'm gonna be in this film, it'd be like all the things I imagined I was gonna do as a kid with a gun in the backyard. Jim Thompson is one of my favourite writers and I think if he saw this film he'd be thrilled, he'd love it. Quentin never described the characters and I liked that. He never said 30-year-old, bald, whatever. We just sat around the table.

'Most scripts seem to be the same story told in different ways, generally with a moral, which is very boring. I'd already finished a film up in New York and when I decided to come to LA to see if I could get a job, this was the first one that appealed to me. My agent had put a little note on the front saying, "Look at Orange." I didn't even know what that meant. So I saw it and I thought, "This is wonderful," and then Orange vanishes and, suddenly, it's all revealed. But that was it. Then I went to the office to meet these guys and they said, "So what do you think, Pink or Blonde?" and I was, "No, I want to do Orange," and there was this deathly silence and Quentin went, "Yes, that's a good idea." Then we started talking.

'We had this conversation that it was about *Star Trek* when we were doing it,' Roth continues. 'There are always those guys that go down to the planet (the ones in the red shirts, who you've never seen before) and you *know* they're spares and that was what Quentin said about Orange – he's the spare. We tried to rig the billing up as a cameo, you know, "and Tim Roth", and then it all emerges.'

Thus it was the structure which fascinated Tarantino, this particular quirk being something that was to be repeated in *Pulp Fiction*, the film not being shown in its logical order, events revealed out of sequence.

'I see that as what is particularly refreshing and Quentin's fascinated by it,' Roth explains. 'It's not just beginning, middle and end stuff.'

The main scene in the warehouse is thus inter-chopped with a novelistic method of storytelling, 'chapters' of information being thrown at the audience with no real regard for chronology, shuffling the viewer's traditional sense of perspective. Each chapter flagged with a title card (in this case the character's name), much in the same way as was to be repeated with the three main stories of *Pulp Fiction* and had been scripted in the original version of *True Romance*.

'I actually think that if movies were to follow closer the rules of novels, movies would benefit from that,' elaborates Tarantino. 'I always felt that if you were to adapt a novelistic structure to cinema, the result would be extremely cinematic. I mean, I've always felt that. In the transition from novels to movies, one of the first things that goes is the structure, alright. It's not that I had anything *against* chronological order. If a film would be best served telling the story that way dramatically, well then you tell it that way. I didn't do it just to be a wiseguy, but this is a situation where the actual way of paying out the information actually gives the movie a reason to be.

'You know, this could just be the same old stuff if it was told beginning, middle and end. What I'm going against is that chronological order isn't the only way you can tell a story. You know, I don't see why it should be such a big deal. I always felt that those juxtapositions – if you do it right – jumping around back and forth, would be very cinematic.'

In this sense then, the movie is not told in flashbacks at all, but merely revealed out of sequence.

'It's *not* a flashback. Novels go back and forth all the time. You read a story about a guy who's doing something or in some situation and, all of a sudden, chapter five comes and it takes Henry, one of the guys, and it shows you seven years ago, where he was seven years ago and how he came to be and then like, *boom*, the next chapter, *boom*, you're back in the flow of the action. Is that a flashback? No, I don't think about it when I'm reading it that way.'

Tarantino rams the point home.

'Storytelling is cinematic. Storytelling is seductive, sexy, you know. I don't like the term flashback because normally I don't like dealing with the *term* flashback. It's like they apply terms to movies that they don't to novels. It helps puts handcuffs on movies . . . if it looks like a monkey

Tarantino as Mr Brown: 'A bunch of guys talking a lot of shit.'

and it sounds like a monkey then it's a monkey. Flashbacks, as far as I'm concerned, come from a personal perspective. These aren't, they're coming from a narrative perspective. They're going back and forth like chapters. I like the revealing of information and deciding what I'm gonna reveal and when I'm gonna reveal it. I think a certain suspense comes from that.

'An audience wants to be clear, an audience doesn't want to be confused. I don't know if you're confused in *Reservoir Dogs*, but you're curious about what the fuck's going on. You're probably a little confused right at the beginning, but there's enough immediate dramatic stuff right in your face to deal with.'

And so the actual robbery becomes redundant, although, as Lawrence Bender has suggested, this was initially done as a means of keeping the costs down on a low budget first-time effort.

'It's a joke that if I did a hunchback story, the guy would be cured in the first few minutes and the story would wind up about this guy who used to be a hunchback,' quips Tarantino. 'With *Reservoir Dogs*, I just liked the idea of devoting a whole movie to something that, in a normal movie, would only take up maybe ten minutes of screen time.'

Says Bender, 'Where most movies cut is where Quentin's scenes start getting interesting.'

Of course, in such an intricately plotted film as *Reservoir Dogs*, where the audience is treated to series of surprise plot points, there was concern that the film's key twist was not revealed, the same problem that beset *The Crying Game* shortly before it.

'I am worried about that,' admitted Tarantino at the time of the film's opening. 'Only a few reviewers have spoilt it. I've read a shitload of reviews and I was really worried about stuff like that. A lot of things are spoilt. This movie is so entertaining if you don't know anything about it. It's completely dependent on surprise, after surprise, after surprise and, for me, to ruin it, would be to explain a lot of things. Everyone talks about how Mr Blonde did this, did this and did that, and part of the fun of the script and for people who've never seen that move before, you don't *know* that Mr Blonde's a psycho. Okay, they're *saying* he's a psycho, but when he shows up, he's not doing anything to indicate that he is. Maybe they're wrong, these guys are just fucking like freaking out and then, you know, you find out he *is*. People talk about, "Oh, Michael

Madsen plays a psychopath." That element is impure if you've read those reviews. The film is full of stuff like that and I'm worried about it and I have to be very conscious of not spoiling it myself, which is actually tough because you want to get analytical in some interviews and talk about it. It's really tough for Tim because he can't talk about where his character's coming from in interviews without spoiling it. Actually, I have to say that the press, generally, has been really really cool about it and they understand that this movie's built on surprises and they're being very pure about it . . .'

Not only did most critics keep mum, but reviews of *Reservoir Dogs* were largely ecstatic (more so in Europe than in the US). *Empire* gave it five stars. *Village Voice* called it '*Glengarry Glen Ross* with guns, *Diner* with gore, *GoodFellas* minus girls' – Tarantino praised for his clever use of narrative and plot structure.

Owen Gleiberman, lead critic of *Entertainment Weekly* and one of Tarantino's chief advocates, believes this is the key.

'I think he rediscovered the magic of film narrative,' he explains. 'The scene in *Reservoir Dogs* which got all the attention was the torture scene, but the key scene in the movie which really reveals his talent is the Tim Roth character memorizing his script to become an undercover cop. He's learning to do this convincingly as we are watching the process of dramatizing this story. And that's what Tarantino does, he allows us to watch him present a story and part of what thrills us is the joy he takes in presenting a fiction.'

There was also the sheer attitude of the whole venture. Analogies were drawn between *Reservoir Dogs* and Stanley Kubrick's *The Killing*, a non-sequential film about a racetrack robbery and John Huston's *The Asphalt Jungle*, about the plotting of a crime and the gathering of a gang to pull it off. Tarantino was suddenly finding himself referred to in the same breath as the likes of Dennis Hopper, James Toback, John Cassavetes, Jean-Pierre Melville and, perhaps inevitably, Martin Scorsese – *Dogs* being touted as a new *Mean Streets*, Scorsese's breakthrough movie of 1973, Keitel's Mr White, like Keitel's Charlie in Scorsese's film, acting as a minder to a doomed colleague.

'I think people make this analogy because of the talent that Quentin and Marty have in common,' says Keitel. 'Charlie could never do the things that Mr White does, he'd be scared to death, he's a whole different person.'

Of course, there are many themes to *Reservoir Dogs* – honour amongst thieves, betrayal, redemption, etc. – but the only real relationship that develops in the film is that between Keitel's White and Roth's Orange, almost like a father/son story, with Orange blubbing to White, right at the end, that he is, in fact, a cop.

'I think that's up to the audience to work out why I confess to Harvey at the end,' says Roth. 'I mean *I* know why, Harvey knows why.'

As Tarantino will readily admit, he is a big Brian De Palma fan, De Palma's *Casualties of War* being one of his favourite war movies and a source of inspiration for one line of dialogue in *Reservoir Dogs*. In *Casualties of War*, there's a scene where Sean Penn is taking care of his best friend, who's just been shot and is being carted off on a stretcher.

'Look into my eyes, I'm gonna fuckin' hypnotize you, you're fine,' he tells him.

Not a million miles away from what the squealing Mr Orange begs of Mr White as he demands to be taken to a hospital.

'Just look into my eyes Larry, look in my eyes. Just tell them anything, you'll be safe man.'

Keitel may shoot cops ('not real people') and may happily instruct his *protégé* on the art of cutting off a bank teller's finger before merrily going for a taco, but despite his brutal behaviour, has taken it upon himself to acts as Orange's guardian

('I've never played a violent character,' insists Keitel. 'I've played people who are in conflict and had a need sometimes to commit violence as a result of this conflict.')

In telling his name to Orange, White is the only one to reveal his true identity to another. White also takes it as his personal responsibility that Orange has been shot. ('The bullet in his belly is my fault,' he yells to Pink and Blonde at one point. 'Now that might mean jack shit to you, but it means a hell of a lot to me.')

The dialogue was indeed drenched with macho utterances, particularly of the white American male variety. But as for racism (something that would cause a more serious reaction in *True Romance*) – references to, 'black semen pumping up white asses', 'a Jew who wouldn't have the balls to say that', and unprofessional hoods 'acting like a bunch of niggers'?

'That's just the way these guys talk,' he states. 'The thing is, do I think these guys are true racists? No. I just think they're a bunch of guys getting together and talking a lot of shit. There's a difference there. Do I think, you know, when Mr White says a couple of things in the movie, do I think Mr White thinks that blacks are like lesser human beings than him? No, I don't. The main thing these guys are coming from is that they don't look at blacks as professionals in their job, alright. They rob liquor stores. Now if there was like a black guy, say, a gunman that they trusted, they'd be different . . . you know, "Marvin's different, he's a good guy, you can trust Marvin, he's a goodfella." But I don't think they walk round thinking about it. They're just walking around talking a lot of crap. But that is also how those guys talk, and that was an important part to me to bring it in. They could have very easily took it out. Oddly enough, the violence in the movie at the script stage wasn't really brought up so much but that (the language) *was* because it was inflammatory. But to me, inflammatory stuff *should* be brought up, *should* be dealt with in some way and also I think it's very indicative of those characters.

'Again, it falls into the situation of where I wanted you to get behind these guys. I wanted you to hook in to them dramatically and care about what happens to them, but I wanted to make it real hard. I wanted to go the exact opposite way of how Hollywood normally works. I wanted to show you them warts and all. I wanted you to hear them say very ugly things. I also wanted you to hear them say profound things. I wanted them to come across like fucking idiots in one moment and then, in another, come across as brilliant geniuses. I wanted you to see wonderful humanity and incredible brutality. One after another, after another, after another, just piled on top of each other.'

In its 30 October 1992 edition, *Entertainment Weekly* carried the following as part of its top-mark Grade 'A' review.

'Michael Medved (chief exponent of "family values" films) probably won't agree, but some of the most enthralling movies of our time have come down to the spectacle of raging macho blowhards hurling profanities and hell-raising wisecracks at each other,' wrote Owen Gleiberman. 'That's true of Martin Scorsese's *Mean Streets* and *Raging Bull*, films that forge a gutter poetry out of the 'F' word, that makes those characters seem so tantalizingly alive and true. Perhaps it's simply this. In a civilized world where people have to watch their tongues on the job, in the classroom, even perhaps when speaking to their loved ones, there's something primal and liberating about characters who can let it all hang out, whose ids come bursting forth in white hot chunks of verbal shrapnel.'

At the University of Southern California Film School library, *Reservoir Dogs* is still the second most checked-out script – after *Taxi Driver* . . .

A few critics ran away with the 'maleness' of the whole thing, some suggesting that Mr Brown's rant in the film's opening 'Madonna' conversation was a conscious retort to the 'all men are bastards' attitude of *Thelma & Louise, Mortal Thoughts* and, perhaps, a finger to the caring, sharing, New Age man philosophies of *Regarding Henry, The Doctor* and *Unforgiven*, films that had all done the rounds in recent months.

It is a fact that women do not feature strongly in *Reservoir Dogs* – Madonna is talked about in fairly disparaging terms, one woman gets shot and another is pulled through the windscreen of her car. Tarantino finds this highly amusing.

'There's a few other ones, too,' Tarantino chuckles. 'Pam Grier is mentioned, this cocktail waitress Elois, who fights against her husband and, even more importantly, there's that scene in the Mr White chapter. Harvey talks about when he used to partner with a woman and when Joe is hiring Mr White, he's expecting her to come along with him, alright. He's surprised that it's not a team. He speaks about her with a great deal of respect. People forget about that, you know.'

The woman referred to is, in fact, Alabama, the lead in *True Romance* (*Pulp Fiction*'s Marsellus is also mentioned as the man who can shift the stones).

'I'm not even saying (affects silly voice), "Well see, I talk nice about women." I think it's funny that in a movie where they don't have any women, they still talk about them all the time.'

As he says, 'It would be like women turning up on the submarine in *Das Boot* . . .'

What *was* apparent was that *Reservoir Dogs* was attracting a cross-over audience, appealing not only to those who enjoyed it as a straight piece of tense macho drama but also to those who preferred it for the dialogue and the knowing humour that went with it: 'The first coffee house action movie,' as *Vanity Fair* dubbed it, suggesting that it was the kind of film that would appeal to those who thought they were way too cool for *Lethal Weapon*.

Certainly the idle banter that goes on between the guys was one of the major talking points . . .

MR PINK

I don't tip because society says I *have* to. Alright, I mean I'll tip if somebody really *deserves* a tip, if they really puts forward the effort I'll give 'em something extra, but I mean, this tipping automatically, it's for the birds. I mean, as far as I'm concerned, they're just doing their job.

MR BLUE

Hey, this girl was *nice*.

MR PINK

She was okay. She wasn't anything special.

MR BLUE

What's special? Take you in the back and suck your dick?

(*They all laugh.*)

NICE GUY EDDIE

I'd go over twelve per cent for *that*.

MR PINK

Look, I ordered coffee, right? Now we've been here a long fuckin' time, she's only filled my cup three times. When I order coffee, I want it filled *six* times.

MR BLONDE

Six times! Well you know, what if she's too fuckin' busy?

MR PINK

The words 'too fuckin' busy' shouldn't be in a waitress's vocabulary.

'That was totally my credo for years, that whole tip speech, from Steve Buscemi's perspective,' Tarantino laughs. 'Yeah, I totally believed that stuff. Not so much any more because I can afford to tip now, but it was more of a situation when *I* was making minimum wage, alright, and they're making minimum wage and no one was tipping me. I didn't have a job that society deemed tip-worthy. Oddly enough, I changed my ways a little bit, but it's really funny. My friends, that is, like, my friends who've known me for years, that is their least favourite scene for two reasons. One is they're bored by it. They've heard me say that shit, you know, a zillion times. Two, they just hate the fact that I got the last word.'

'Usually I have to overcompensate for my tipping to show that that really wasn't me,' chuckles Steve Buscemi. 'Recently I forget to tip a cab driver and I thought, "Oh my God, if he sees the movie he's gonna say, 'That's the guy . . .' " '

Spouting their own unique brand of homespun philosophy, the ultra hip Dogs certainly drip with style as they cruise around in their big sedans.

'It was important to Quentin,' says Wasco. 'I mean, obviously we had some cars which were present day but we wanted to do an ambiguous time period so that if you look at the movie some time from now, it's not really dated. He tried to do that in *Pulp Fiction* too.'

Nonetheless, the cars used certainly have a Seventies feel.

'The stuff that he showed us that he liked was starting to focus into that time period,' explains Sandy Reynolds-Wasco. 'The Seventies stuff just sort of came to me from LA road movies and cop shows like *Chips* and *Police Story*, that kind of thing. So when we were doing the sets that kind of came through a lot, too. We didn't have to say Seventies, but it read that way.'

There was, however, one aspect of the automobiles that was imperative.

'We were very specific about all the different car interiors,' chuckles Reynolds-Wasco. 'We were looking for white interiors because they show the blood.'

The use of certain cultural reference points also adds to the Seventies feel . . .

EDDIE
You know who she looked like? She looked like Christie Love.

'Member that TV show *Get Christie Love*? About the black female cop. She always used to say, 'You're under arrest, sugar.'

MR PINK

What was the name of the chick who played Christie Love?

EDDIE

Pam Grier.

MR ORANGE

No, it wasn't Pam Grier. Pam Grier was the other one. Pam Grier did the film. Christie Love was like a Pam Grier TV show, without Pam Grier.

MR PINK

So who was Christie Love?

MR ORANGE

How the fuck should I know?

MR PINK

Great, now I'm totally fuckin' tortured.

'It's, funny people say that, but at the same time they're making constant cultural references to right here and now,' differs Quentin. 'The first thing in the movie is the Madonna speech. When they talk about Madonna, there's a kind of immediacy there.'

'You know, Madonna liked the movie a lot and wanted to meet me,' he chuckles, keen to get to the bottom of the 'Like a Virgin' hypothesis ('it's a girl who digs a guy with a big dick'). 'So we got together and so I sort of go, "Am I right about the song?" because I really believed that was the subtext. She goes, "Were you serious about? No, it's about love. It's about a girl, you know, who's been messed over and she finally makes love to this one man who loves her." I'd just been in Brazil – and they still make albums in Brazil as opposed to just CDs – so I bought the *Erotica* album and when I showed it to her, she hadn't even seen an album of *Erotica*. She signed it "To Quentin. It's not about Dick, it's about *love*, Madonna."

'I was proven wrong,' Tarantino concedes. 'But I actually did believe that. I wish I could take credit for the theory but I can't, some friends of mine came up with the theory. I'm a strong believer of "you know the truth when you hear it." I said, "That's it man, that's what that song's about . . . that's what it is." I really thought that was actually the subtext of the song and I was positive that I was gonna meet Madonna and she was gonna say, "That's what it is." '

Nevertheless, though discussions such as this most definitely set the film in the 1990s, it certainly has a classic look, due to the use of the black suits, black tie and shades – a throwback to the standard outfit of 1950s *film noir* and also the same kind of gear worn in the Hong Kong bulletfests of John Woo, a director Tarantino's clearly drawn inspiration from. In fact the image of Keitel walking towards the police car, blazing away with an automatic in each hand could be a scene straight out of a Woo movie.

'As far as the look of the movie, I was really conscious about having the film be cinematic, especially when we were trying to get the money to make the movie,' Tarantino elaborates, mindful of the fact that his movie could almost be staged as a theatre piece. 'People would read the script and go, "This isn't a movie, this is a play. Why do you want to do this as a movie?" And I said, "No, no, no, no" – I don't like movies from plays, normally – "It's gonna be a movie, don't worry about that. It's *gonna* be a movie." '

'That's what I like, I like *movies* and I wanted it to work first and fore-most as a movie, so the look was very important – the use of the camera, the moods in it, the colour scheme. You know, it changes. In the ware-house you have a certain set of colours – the black suits, the green walls, the red blood – and that's about it, but then when you go outside of the warehouse, the colour kind of explodes every time someone walks through the door, like they're wearing some kind of technicolour car-toon shirt. I was very conscious about that. And as far as the black suits, it's *always* cool.

'There are a few things in the movie that are like this, when you can achieve two effects with one thing. The suits totally function in that capacity. On the one hand, the guys look cool. You know, you can't put a guy in a black suit without him looking a little cooler than he already looks. It's a stylistic stroke. It looks like I'm doing a genre movie and my genre character's in uniform, like Jean-Pierre Melville's trenchcoats, or Sergio Leone's dusters that he'd have his characters wearing. So it does have that cool jazzy thing.

'It also has a foot in reality. What will happen, not all the time, but sometimes in a robbery, is that the robbers will adopt a uniform – it could be black suits, it could be Raiders jackets, it could be parkas. But the whole idea is that everyone has a uniform look, so when they go and they do a robbery, with the people afterwards, when the cops show up later and they talk to the witnesses, they say, "How do I know? They looked like a bunch of black suits. You know, I think one of them had red hair maybe. I don't know, I can't be sure. One of them, I think, had blonde hair but I'm not for sure, you know, they all blend in." You *know* you're watching a gangster movie when you see those guys walk in on the opening credit and you think, "Oh God, these guys look like they're gonna go out and do something you know," but in real life, if a bunch of guys in black suits walked in here, I'm not gonna necessarily think they're gonna rob the joint.'

A not entirely convincing argument, especially if the experience of Eddie Bunker is anything to go by, who claims the whole heist business in *Reservoir Dogs* has little founding in criminal reality.

'What? Picking a crew up like that?' growls the old lag. 'You know, if you're gonna pull a caper, you really wanna know the people really well. If you have that many people in a gang, you're gonna get caught, because somebody's gonna talk to his wife.'

And as for the black suits.

'I mean it was absurd,' he snarls. 'There were these guys going to pull this big robbery and they're sitting in a coffee shop all dressed alike and the waitress knows them and they're tipping her (or not, as the case may be). If they went and pulled this big million dollar robbery, she'd pick up the newspaper and say, "Hey, I know these guys . . ." '

So it looks like the 1950s, is set in the 1990s but acts like the 1970s, again accentuated by the masterful deployment of an oldies soundtrack in the form of a radio show, K BILLY's 'Super Sounds of the 70s' and the deadpan voice of its DJ, comedian Steven Wright.

'It falls again into that whole thing of doing two effects for the price of one,' says Tarantino, whose hoods, amongst other things, step out to the frenetic dope paranoia of the George Baker Selection's 'Little Green Bag', and joyfully beat up a cop to the 'hit me' refrain of Joe Tex's 'I Gotcha'.

'One. I mean, I love the use of music in movies. I think the right combination of the right scene and the right visual and the right piece of music is as close as you get to pure and simple. And I always like it when you take an existing piece of music and you put it to a scene and it has a cinematic pull and feel and excitement. That's just incredible and from thereon, whenever you hear that song, you think of that movie.

'You know, "The Ride of the Valkyries" has been around for a hundred years but I defy anyone not to think of *Apocalypse Now* and to see helicopters when they hear that piece of music. And when I hear the opening strands of The Ronettes "Be My Baby", I see Harvey Keitel's head hit the pillow in *Mean Streets*. And the same thing, I see Dean Stockwell whenever I hear "In Dreams" from *Blue Velvet*. But the thing is also, because the movie takes place in real time, you're basically in that warehouse for an hour, the same time that the characters are and so there is, like, no soundtrack to that movie, no movie music . . . *everything*'s source.

'I like the idea. In LA you have a lot of oldie stations and what they do is they'll have special weekends – you know, the Motown weekend, the British Invasion weekend, 60s weekend, Beatles weekend, you know, and so I came up with the idea of a Super 70s weekend. And I like the idea of the movie having an invisible character kind of running through it – that's the function Steve Wright's K BILLY DJ has.

'Now when it came to choosing the 70s music, I didn't want to go for the serious 70s stuff. I didn't want to go for Black Sabbath, I didn't want to go for Led Zeppelin or Marvin Gaye or Parliament or Kiss or Elton John or any of those big touchstones . . . Fleetwood Mac . . . not that I could afford any of those guys, anyway. I wanted to go for the super sugary bubblegum sound of the early 70s. One, is because some people are annoyed by it. Two, because I have affection for it. I grew up with it. It's my childhood. But it's also special because it's the last bastion of bubble gum rock in rock and roll. You know, that was the last time you would hear a song and just go to the store and buy a 45. After about '75, everything became album oriented. But the bubblegum songs, it does two things. On one hand, in some scenes, the sugariness of it, lightness of it, the catchiness of it, kind of really lightens up a rude rough movie, makes it a funnier, makes it a little bit more enjoyable, gives it a kick. But in the torture scene the lightness, the sugariness, the catchiness, makes the scene even more disturbing. That scene would not be as disturbing without that song because you hear that guitar strain, you get into it, you go, "Yeah yeah," and you're tapping your toe and you're enjoying Michael Madsen doing his dance and then, *voom*, it's too late, you're a co-conspirator. People have told me that whenever they hear that song from hereon in they're gonna just see Michael Madsen doing his dance. It's the ultimate compliment.'

Tarantino is fond of using Abbott and Costello – as in *Abbott and Costello Meet Frankenstein, Meet the Mummy*, etc. – as an example of getting 'two great flavours' for the price of one, the scary scenes being scary, the comedy routines being funny. As a child this was the first time he became aware of genre distinction in movies and the idea of contrasting humour with brutality is clearly evident in *Reservoir Dogs*.

Not since a rape was juxtaposed with 'Singin' in the Rain' in *Clockwork Orange* has a piece of music been put to such disturbing effect, heightening the tension on a quite harrowing scene, the one, of course, which became the film's main talking point . . .

The *New York Times* of 23 October 1992, at the end of its review of the film, ran the following paragraph.

'*Reservoir Dogs* is rated 'R' (under 17s require accompanying parent or guardian). It has a great deal of obscene language and scenes of explicit brutality, including one in which a policeman who is tied to a chair is attacked by a man with a razor.'

MR BLONDE (to the cop)
   Look, I'm not gonna bullshit you, okay. I don't really give a good fuck
   what you know or don't know. But I'm gonna torture you anyway,
   regardless. Not to get information. It's amusing to me to torture a cop.
   You can say anything you want 'cause I've heard it all before. All you
   can do is pray for a quick death, which you ain't gonna get . . .

Regardless of anything else in the movie, it was the torture scene that became the main talking point of *Reservoir Dogs*. That it became known simply as the movie 'where the guy gets his ear cut off' is still a great deal of concern to Tarantino.

Violent? Certainly. Gratuitous? That is a moot point.

Certainly Michael Madsen, whatever else he does, will forever stick in the mind as malevolent toothpick-chewing Mr Blonde – severing the ear of the LA lawman and drawling into the freshly detached lughole. It's a scene that still haunts Madsen, not for its sheer brutality, but because he can't understand why audiences were not dancing in the aisles as he set about his impromptu brand of reconstructive razor surgery.

'Well I don't know too many people who like policeman,' he muses hoarsely. 'I mean, I didn't find Mr Blonde that bad a guy . . . I couldn't understand why people cheered when he was shot. I would have thought they'd be sorry to see him go, especially as he gets shot by a rat. He didn't bullshit anybody, he just wanted to tell the truth, hurhurhur.'

In fact, when Madsen was first offered a part in *Free Willy*, the nice family film about a boy and his pet killer whale, he naturally assumed it was because they wanted him to blow the orca's brains out. Probably because that image of Mr Blonde is too haunting.

'I think you have to have an understanding of the people you play,' he chuckles, crinkling his brow and intimating that life and art might not be that far apart after all. 'Either way you're slicing.'

Many found Mr Blonde's torturing of Marvin the cop just a little too hard to stomach. In fact, when the film was shown at the Sitges festival in Spain, even horror director Wes Craven headed for the exit. *Today* newspaper called for that scene to be cut from the movie with others jumping in to attack the 'arthouse designer violence', as one magazine put it, most taking umbrage with the fact not that Mr Blonde tortures, but that he tortures so darned gleefully.

Tarantino considers, and disregards, these objections.

'I just don't think it is gratuitous, alright, but I don't even know what the hell gratuitous means,' he retorts. 'To me violence is just one of the many things you can do in movies. Saying you don't like violence in movies is like saying you don't like slapstick comedy in movies or like saying you don't like dance sequences. I think it's gratuitous if it screws up the movie, if its badly done. It's gratuitous, like, if you have a musical that has like six good songs and a seventh really bad one. They were kind of gratuitous with that bad song. They shouldn't have had it in the movie. It would have been better if that bad song was left out. That's how I look at it – completely aesthetically. My mother doesn't like slap-stick comedy. If I was Buster Keaton she would like my stuff because I'm her son, but she wouldn't get it, she wouldn't appreciate it. I love the Three Stooges, alright, and other people don't. To me, literally, it is that black and white.

'I get a kick out of violence in movies. I don't get a kick out of *badly done* violence or action scenes in movies. It's like, "How far is too far?" Well, if they do it well, there shouldn't be, "How far is too far?" I don't agree with the fact that it's gratuitous because the whole movie is kind of building up to that scene, alright. That whole first half of the move, it's like this powder keg that builds and builds and builds and builds and then there's the explosion in the middle. Then, after that explosion, it turns into a different movie. It becomes a different movie with a differ-ent pace and a different rhythm and a different tension. I didn't think it would would be really cool to have a torture scene because it would really freak everybody out. That's what Mr Blonde would *do* when left alone with that guy.'

Some tried to intellectualize about the torture scene, pontificating on the theory of the director standing in for the character and the hostage cop representing the audience. Certainly in the original script, the cam-era's point of view is that of the cop.

'That's for film enthusiasts and journalists and critics to articulate and it's silly of me to say, "Yes that's right," because I was certainly thinking of the story,' ponders Tarantino. 'I do understand the thoughts behind it and I actually kind of agree with it. There wasn't a gigantic conscious decision that I was doing it but I do understand the thought process behind it.'

Regardless of all this, most detractors failed to notice that when it comes to the ultimate moment of terror (i.e. the severing of the ear), the camera pans away to the wall . . . you never actually see it, concurring with the Hitchcockian notion of what you don't see being scarier than you actually do see. Though, having said that, the sight of the big hole on the side of Marvin's head is hardly pleasant.

'He shot once where you see the ear being cut off and then the second he shot it with his hand away, which I think is more gruesome,' says Tim Roth. 'The walkouts were wonderful. It always starts with the razor coming out, you get a couple, and then with the ear, *fwick*, everyone's

83

out. Then when the gas comes, the next stage . . . I find it hard to watch and I was there.'

Some have suggested that Tarantino copped out by turning his camera away at that crucial point. He can't win either way and though he said that, as an eight-year-old, seeing Bambi's mum get killed is probably more frightening than anything in *Dogs* (this writer always had great difficulty with the Child Catcher in *Chitty Chitty Bang Bang*), it'll go down in cinema infamy, not least because it took place to the incongruous strains of Stealer's Wheel's hitherto harmless little ditty, 'Stuck in the Middle with You'.

'It was just the perfect song for that scene,' says Tarantino. 'I can't tell you why, it just works. Let me tell you something, they do *not* play "Stuck in the Middle with You" on oldie stations, at least in LA, it's not on the rotation and when Michael Madsen drove home that night, *pow*, it just came on the radio and it freaked him out.

'Look, I never went to writing school: 'Write A Screenplay In 27 Days', Robert McKee or any of that nonsense. Everything I learned as an actor I completely applied to writing and one of the things you get taught as an actor is, when I'm writing, I just get the characters talking to each other – whatever happens is what happens and what they say is what they say. I didn't write that scene to write this really bitchin' torture scene. I didn't know Mr Blonde had a razor in his boot until he whipped it out – it's like, "Oh, my God." The truth of it is that was what Mr Blonde would do when left alone in a room with this cop. To pull back on that because some people might not like it would be lying.'

Tarantino has had to field questions on violence on numerous occasions. He's got his answers down pat, using such analogies as a car crash being more interesting than seeing it park and saying that he's put violence on the screen because he doesn't like violence in real life. Regardless of rhetoric, it *is* a fact that that scene is disturbing, making *Reservoir Dogs* a film that lives with you for a long time after you leave the cinema. Certainly not a 'parking lot' movie as they call it in the States – one which you've all but forgotten about by the time you've shifted into second.

Tarantino, once again, refers back to literature to conclude his point.

'Even in the way novels deal with characters. You know, in movies everybody has to be so fucking likeable, the audience has got to be

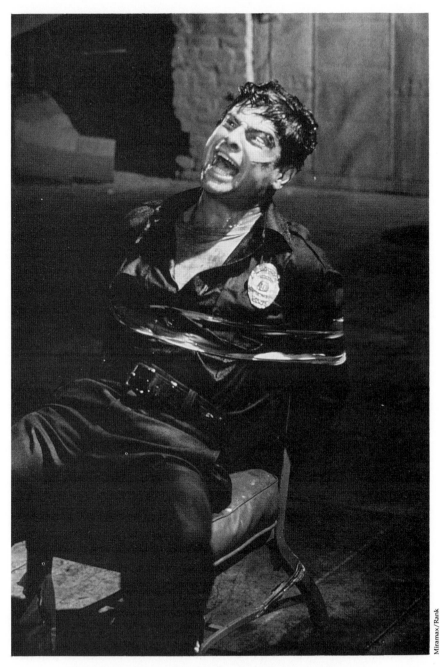

Miramax/Rank

Kirk Baltz as Marvin the Cop in the infamous torture scene:
'I don't even know what the hell gratuitous means.'

behind him, the audience has got to root for him,' he says. 'You can write a novel about a perfect bastard, right. It doesn't mean you don't want to turn the page. You're just reading a story about a bastard and that's okay, it's interesting . . .'

But what of the level of violence in the movie? What is worse, Arnold Schwarzenegger saying 'Consider that a divorce' and putting a bullet through his wife's brain before moving swiftly on to the next scene, or to see a man shot in the gut and watch him squeal through the consequences? People don't die cleanly from that in real life, it's a slow, painful, bloody mess. As Tarantino has pointed out, you tend to get penalized for doing violence well.

It can be argued that in *Reservoir Dogs* and in *Pulp Fiction*, for every cause there is an effect. Those who scoff tend to condone acts of brutality that are done in a 'cartoon' context. Maybe it's the sheer realism of it that we find so upsetting. One thing that can be said in Tarantino's defence is that the violence in *Reservoir Dogs* is *always* integral to the plot. In this sense it is *not* gratuitous.

Under the old Hays Code, baddies could be baddies as long as they got their comeuppance. Do they get their comeuppance in *Reservoir Dogs*? They all get killed, that's for sure.

Unfortunately, mud sticks. Released uncut at the cinema – 18 in the UK, R in the USA – when the time came for UK video certification, *Reservoir Dogs* got lumped in with *Man Bites Dog* and *Bad Lieutenant*, two other strong movies, all three becoming part of the media debate about 'New Brutalism' (a nice, neat media-friendly expression). Thus, at the height of the public debate about the moral responsibility of filmmakers in the wake of Britain's James Bulger case (in which a small child was abducted and brutally murdered by two older boys), where *Child's Play 3* was erroneously blamed for affecting the juvenile murderers, scapegoats were thus sought. The British Board of Film Classification, rightly sensitive to public opinion, misguided though that opinion might have been, were thus pressured into action.

Board Head James Ferman denied that the BBFC had asked video distributors to delay submitting titles but, in the wake of research that had been commissioned in March 1993, he admitted that, 'there *is* a serious problem. If 18 really means 12, as it appears to do, and there have been some court cases recently indicating that it's quite easy for children in some shops to get videos *way* under age, then it makes it very difficult to pass films like these. There's no way we can pass them until there can be some demonstration that 18 actually *means* 18, not just in the shops but in the *home.'*

Reservoir Dogs was thus made unavailable on video in the UK (though, surprisingly, *Man Bites Dog*, a disturbing *cinema verité* style drama about a Belgian serial killer, was treated with more leniency, the argument being that as it was in the French language, it would have only minimal appeal – a nonsensical point). The ban was lifted in June 1995, three and a half years after the film's Sundance première, but its existence explains why *Reservoir Dogs* has enjoyed an extended run at several cinemas in the UK making it, unofficially, the longest general release since *Gone with the Wind* (a statistic officially denied as, according to records, *Reservoir Dogs* was re-released mid-way through its run). The release of the alternative cut has certainly given it 'legs'. Nevertheless, at places like LA's New Beverly Cinema and London's Prince Charles cinema, it still attracts cult followings to midnight screenings, like *The Rocky Horror Picture Show* and *Eraserhead* before it, some customers even dressing up in all the *Dogs* paraphernalia especially for the occasion.

'I think the ban's unfortunate because there are people who only see the big commercial films and then, when they're looking for something on video, they'll be a little bit more adventurous,' commented Steve Buscemi at the time.

'They're such wankers,' says Tim Roth.

'It's like Orson Welles, people telling him, "Oh, you're real big in Europe", or old vaudevillians saying, "Oh, I'm real big in Des Moines",' laughs Tarantino. 'It's weird. It's like *Dogs* is so much in the culture of Britain. Even if people haven't seen it, they know what you're talking about.'

The Last Temptation of Christ and *The Life of Brian* (Christians), *Basic Instinct* (gays), even *Shakes the Clown* (clowns) – there have always been special interest groups who take offence at particular movies. Interestingly, considering that the main victim of violence in *Reservoir Dogs* is a cop, the police have never once complained about the film. Cynics may say this is because the police have long accepted that their lot is never a happy one when it comes to the movies, some that had the torturer been black (the film came out around the time of Ice-T's 'Cop Killer', banned because it 'advocated' rather than 'portrayed' violence), it would have been a different kettle of fish. Nonetheless, there have never been any recorded copycat incidents of violence based on Tarantino's film, although, amusingly, a botched bank robbery in San Francisco soon after the film came out, had the members of *that* gang all using the same colour-coded names as in Tarantino's film.

It has to be said that Tarantino and Roger Avary (whose *Killing Zoe* is also about a bank robbery that backfires) would not go very far in the heist business . . .

As with most films, there are in-jokes: the woman that Tim Roth shoots is, in fact, his dialect coach, Suzanne Celeste ('They drive you crazy, so I got her the job. She shoots me and I shoot her. We were very pleased about that.'); the jewelry store is called Karina's, after *Bande À Part*'s star Anna Karina; Lawrence Tierney, star of the 1946 film *Dillinger*, utters the line 'dead as Dillinger'; and, as Steve Buscemi runs along the street chased by the cops, you just about hear the cry 'Sally, Sally', the name of the film's editor. Some have even pointed to the orange balloon blowing in the wake of Nice Guy Eddie's car as a clue to the rat's identity.

There is an even more obscure code.

'In the warehouse there was a note on the wall that said, "Tony, don't turn this switch on" and, on the outside of the building, "Tony, don't park here" ', explains David Wasco. 'There's a one-frame shot of this in *Pulp Fiction*, where Bruce Willis is running to the pawn shop. He had us recreate, "Tony, don't park here," in spray paint. Nobody saw it. Nobody read it, but he got a kick out of it.'

But, beyond this, it was the fact that the film is very knowing that provoked comment. It draws quite blatantly on its sources – *The Killing*, *The Asphalt Jungle*, John Woo (whose bulletfests feature the same black and white suits and a similar flash gunplay) and even *The Thing* (the stranger in a group – albeit an alien – who is not what he seems). *Reservoir Dogs* also pointed to the films of the French New Wave directors, Truffaut and Godard, taking the old films of Bogart and Cagney and setting them in Paris and Marseilles – Tarantino taking them one step further and showing all the gore that we were never allowed to see first time round . . .

There followed inevitable accusations of plagiarism.

'Quentin doesn't have a single bone of originality in his body,' claims his main detractor, *Natural Born Killers* producer Don Murphy. 'Any that he has have long since died of loneliness.'

The question really is when does *hommage* end and plagiarism begin? Woody Allen, after all, has been drawing on Ingmar Bergman for years without objection and Tarantino again refers to other source material in *Four Rooms* – his section of that film making no bones about being a rehash of a short Alfred Hitchcock feature, a fact that Tarantino freely acknowledges.

As the Irish playwright Denis Johnston commented, there are only seven original plots in storytelling, and all the rest are based upon them. These are Cinderella (unrecognized virtue), Achilles (the fatal flaw), Faust (the debt that must be paid), Tristan (the love triangle), Circe (the spider and the fly), Romeo and Juliet and Orpheus (the gift taken away). Although he was referring to theatre rather than film, he did add an eighth one for cinema, The Indomitable Hero (*à la* Indiana Jones). This theory renders just about every film ever made of similar substance to another.

The key to *hommage* is either when you are making a nod to something obvious or when you acknowledge your source, easy in literature, not so clear-cut on film. However, as *Reservoir Dogs* and *Pulp Fiction* are not esoteric movies, but fall within a certain genre (gangster/*film noir*), Tarantino is more or less doing this.

After all, if you pursue the argument of the purists, there would only ever have been one Western made, all the rest would have been rip-offs.

Says Matt Mueller, editor of *UK Premiere*, 'Nothing's really original in terms of what he's doing but it's *how* he does it, how he puts it together. The way he combines all these elements is what makes it so unique. It's like Elvis or Buddy Holly, when they created rock and roll. They took black music that had been around for years and years and made it accessible for a popular audience. He's doing for movies what they did for music. If it was just about *hommage*, it would be a very select audience, but he's appealing to a multiplex audience. Directors are ripping each other off all the time – they're ripping old films off, they're ripping scenes off. I think there's nothing wrong with what Tarantino's doing. In many ways, he's doing a service to all these old films – you actually want to go and see them. He's almost like a one man revival.'

Plagiarism is a different matter to *hommage* and implies a more under-handed manner, especially if you are plundering a little-known work rather than something that is generally known – using someone else's invention for your own gain.

The style of the Hong Kong action movies is obvious in *Reservoir Dogs*, but in 1993, *Empire* magazine ran an item by this author, pointing out, in jest, similar elements in *Dogs* and Ringo Lan's 1989 Hong Kong flick *City On Fire*. This matter was soon picked up on by various other publications and championed in the American alternative magazine *Film Threat*. There was even a twelve-minute short film made by Michigan film student Mike White which juxtaposed scenes from both films. Entitled *Who Do You Think You're Fooling?*, this was due to play at the New York Underground Film Festival in March 1995. It was pulled at the last minute, allegedly under pressure from Miramax.

City On Fire, starring Chow Yun-Fat, one of Tarantino's favourite actors, is an obscure picture that, until recently, was unavailable in the US or UK on video.

Consider what happens in a portion of that film – a gang of code-named robbers (Brother Joe, Brother Chow, Brother Fu and Brother Nam) leg it after a bungled diamond heist. The heist has been bungled because one of them, a psychopath, started shooting. The cops were lying in wait, tipped off by Brother Chow, an undercover cop. In the get-away, Brother Chow is 'minded' by the older Brother Fu, who sickens Chow by emptying a pair of barettas through the windscreen of a police car. Chow shoots an innocent bystander and gets wounded himself. Fu carries him to the rendezvous, a disused warehouse. Fearing that they were set up, the boss (Big Song) is called. Big Song accuses Chow of being a cop and pulls his gun on him. Fu protests Chow's innocence and draws his gun, too. A four-way stand-off ensues. Sound familiar?

Though we already know which one's the undercover cop and we actually *see* the robbery, the similarities cannot go unnoticed. The basic premise is the same as *Reservoir Dogs*. In mitigation, this section of Lan's film is only one twenty minute part of the whole picture and, given everything else – style, structure, dialogue – when the two films are viewed together they are extremely different. Nonetheless, if one *can* level accusations of plagiarism, it is, perhaps, in this case.

This subject became a press conference favourite and Tarantino answered accusations in Cannes.

'I love *City On Fire* and I have the poster for it framed in my house. It's a great movie. I steal from every movie. I steal from every single movie ever made. I love it. If my work has anything it's that I'm taking this from this and that from that and mixing them together and if people don't like them then tough titty, don't go and see it, alright. I steal from everything. Great artists *steal*, they don't do *hommages*.'

'Some of his little techniques and quirks are nicked wholesale, but regarding the whole thing – *Reservoir Dogs* and *Pulp Fiction* – I don't think you could say they were plagiarized,' says Philip Thomas, managing editor of *Empire* and *UK Premiere*. 'The good thing about Quentin is as soon as people mentioned *City On Fire*, he said, "Yeah, it's a fuckin' great film. I've got the poster on my wall. I accept that. If you think I'm repeating the story, then so be it." '

Through general *bonhomie* he came away from this allegation remarkedly unscathed. The truth is, had Tarantino admitted the similarities up front, no one would have batted an eyelid.

Others claimed that *Reservoir Dogs* was simply too stagy (but so were *Dog Day Afternoon*, *Interiors*, and *Come Back to the Five and Dime Jimmy Dean*). Some that the 'Mexican stand-off' climax was a rip-off of *The Good the Bad and the Ugly* and *For A Few Dollars More* .

It most certainly is and until Tarantino's universe ceases to exist purely of movies, it is unlikely that this flow of references will be abated.

Roger Avary, in a *Vanity Fair* interview, made an interesting point: 'The one problem that people have with Quentin's work is that it speaks of other movies instead of life. The big trick is to live a life and then make movies about that life . . .'

It was the geometric complexities of the film's final shoot-out, the ultimate conclusion to what Alexander Walker described as a latterday version of a 'Jacobean revenge drama', that led to an amusing on-running debate through the letters page of *Empire* as to 'Who Shot Nice Guy Eddie?'

Think about it: Orange is shot by Joe; Joe is shot by White; White is shot by Nice Guy Eddie? So who shoots Eddie?

In the absence of the script or a copy available on video, in April 1993,

Empire posited its own theories under the title 'The Magic Bullet Theory', in response to the sackfuls of mail it had received regarding the confusion.

Officially it is White who shoots both Joe *and* Nice Guy Eddie, though Chris Penn reveals that the confusion among the speculators is not without foundation.

'Ha, that's the most asked question,' he laughs. 'Let me set the record straight, *nobody* shot Nice Guy Eddie . . . it was a mistake. What was supposed to happen – and I don't know if Quentin's gonna like me giving this away, but it's too late now, he never told me not to – was Harvey was supposed to shoot Lawrence, then shoot me, then get squibbed. But what happened was the squib (a small explosive charge resembling a bullet hit) on Harvey went off right after he shot Lawrence, so he went down, but my squib went off anyway, so I went down. So basically *nobody* shot Nice Guy Eddie. It was really a tribute to Quentin's sort of brilliance in a way. We were really pressed for time, pressed for money and had to finish the picture. It was sort of the last thing we did and Quentin started thinking about it – where we were going to get the time – and he said, "You know what? Everybody on God's green earth is going to ask who shot Nice Guy Eddie. It'll be the biggest controversy of the film. We're leaving it." And he was definitely right.'

Some critics, though, couldn't see the lighter side of it all. Australian magazine *Metro* even postulated, in all seriousness, a homosexual bonding between White and Orange.

'Homosocialism', it labelled the imperilled individuality and masculinity of the principal characters, 'phallocentric braggadocio'.

'Even the title is polysemically perverse,' screeched that magazine, suggesting that it was a play on *Straw Dogs*, *Sleeping Dogs*, *White Dog* or even *Dog Day Afternoon*. 'Dogs returning to their vomit, like fools to their follies, perhaps?'

'It did come from somewhere,' says Tarantino of the title. 'But people come up to me and they tell me what they think it means and they're knocking me out with their ingenuity and their creativity. The minute I say, "This is it," it all becomes official and all that creativity just dies and turns to dust.'

Connie Zastoupil has been a little more explicit, revealing that the name came from a joke made when Tarantino's girlfriend had wanted him to go and see a Louis Malle film.

'I actually busted him', laughs Connie. 'He was refusing to tell people how he came up with the name and people interviewed me and I said, "Oh, that's when Grace wanted him to see *Au Revoir Les Enfants* and he said 'I don't want to see no darn *Reservoir Dogs*.' " I didn't realise that was a secret . . .'

Chapter 5

True Romance

13 August 1993. The anally neat 'burb of Westwood, Los Angeles, wedged between the affluent retreats of Beverly Hills and Brentwood, with its designer boutiques and its small cluster of cinemas, art deco and otherwise, in the area's central village, is exactly the kind of place that *Falling Down*'s D-Fens – had he the time – would happily have stopped off at. Just a short walk – though no one does in the City Of Angels – from the manicured campus of UCLA, this is a safe haven, in an age where pre-empting audience reaction has become Hollywood's all-important marketing tool, for filmmakers to test their product away from the hubbub of the studios.

For tonight's unpublicized preview, however, word is out and the invited gaggle of hacks have been supplemented by an orderly yet excitable line of young hopefuls – stretching a full two blocks back from the small cinema complex – here on the off chance of filling up the empty seats. Such is the buzz on *True Romance*, Clarence and Alabama Worley burning rubber to this very city with a suitcase full of nose candy and the mob on their tail and the biggest hail of bullets since Butch and Sundance decided to leg it out of their Bolivian shack.

Those managing to squeeze past the guards on the door are not disappointed, bestowing, as the final credits roll, an enthusiastic standing ovation, the ultimate seal of approval, one would have thought, for director Tony Scott and, of course, Tarantino, whose first script has finally made it to the big screen. But there is something rotten in Denmark . . .

'It's heartbreaking,' grumbles Scott, back at the palatial Westwood Marquis Hotel afterwards. 'Each year the ratings board gets tougher, especially in terms of violence. They don't like movies like this . . .'

True Romance was Tarantino's first script and, as explained, was sold in 1989 after it became apparent that it would never be made with himself at the helm. He originally wrote it to direct himself and, just as he would partner with a buddy producer on *Reservoir Dogs* and *Natural Born Killers*, the partner in crime on his first project was Roger Avary.

'Quentin and I were going to be like the Coen brothers but that never really happened,' says Avary, 'It was just a 100,000 dollar film.'

At one point the script was optioned by producer Stanley Margolis, but Tarantino was adamant on directing himself. After three years of promises, with Margolis and Tarantino constantly being told that a deal would be 'two weeks away', Tarantino decided to sell it, receiving the Writers' Guild minimum of $30,000 for the privilege, the money that would ultimately convince him to make a movie of his own: *Reservoir Dogs*. It was this script sale that was, without question, Tarantino's big leg-up.

It is also his most personal film. The hero Clarence Worley, 'a total movie kid', according to Tarantino, lives and breathes movies, acts according to their prophecies, positively revelling in trash culture along the way – 'That's totally true. I love movies, I love TV shows, I love breakfast cereal. You know, I love all that stuff. I grew up with that. It's like 100 per cent my consciousness.'

In fact, through Clarence, Tarantino is able to indulge his obsessions – Elvis, kung-fu movies, junk food ('I never had a hamburger that tastes so good,' declares Clarence minutes after slaying Drexl). Other pop culture motifs are there – Vegas-Elvis aviator shades, the '75 Cadillac, Alabama's Love Boat locks and blaxploitation leopard prints and the box of Animal Crackers ('Leave the gorillas').

In a few lines cut out from the film, Tarantino hints at his youth . . .

ALABAMA

I didn't know they had stores that just sold comic books.

CLARENCE

Well, we sell other things too. Cool stuff. Man From UNCLE lunch boxes. Green Hornet board games. Shit like that. But comic books are our main business. There's a lot of collectors around here.

(*She holds up a little GI Joe size action figure of a black policeman*)

ALABAMA

What's this?

CLARENCE

That's a Rookies doll. George Sandford Brown. We gotta lotta dolls.
They're real cool. Did you know they came out with dolls for all the
actors in The Black Hole? I always found it funny that somewhere
there's a kid playin' with a little figure of Ernest Borgnine . . .

In Alabama, too, Clarence has found his soul mate – sexy, streetwise
and, essential for the ultimate movie junkie, not averse to sitting through
a Sonny Chiba triple bill ('Six foot six of half breed fury and a man who
keeps his word').

'God yeah, I've *seen* that triple feature,' gabbles Tarantino. 'I went to a
drive-in and saw that triple feature. In fact a good buddy of mine said,
"Oh Quentin, I'm so fucking pissed," and I go, "How come?" and he
goes, "Well, I'm driving round and all of a sudden I see this Marquee –
Streetfighter, Sister Streetfighter and *Return of the Streetfighter* – and I said,
'Oh my God.' I pulled the car over right up to the theatre and then I realized they were making a movie. It's, "Oh, this is fucking Quentin's
movie. Oh *shit*." He freaked out because he thought they were playing
that triple feature. One of my favourite things in *True Romance* is seeing
Sonny Chiba on the big screen from *The Streetfighter* in this beautiful gor-
geous print in 'scope, you know widescreen and everything – just seeing
Sonny Chiba up on the screen again . . .'

So what of *True Romance*? If one is to attempt to pigeonhole it, the story
is effectively a bittersweet romantic action comedy, the bitter aspects
being very bitter indeed. A sort of latterday *Bonnie and Clyde*-cum-
Badlands, Detroit movie nerd Clarence falls in love with rookie hooker
Alabama, killing her pimp, with the pair taking off on the road to
Hollywood with a suitcase full of cocaine (as in *Reservoir Dogs* and *Pulp
Fiction*, the briefcase full of booty functions as a *raison d'être*, though not
a McGuffin in the strict Hitchcockian sense). Then, as they try to peddle
their wares in a caricatured world of film executives, the mob and the
police close in.

So far, so B-movie.

Unfortunately, when the script was first tendered, no one would
touch it with a barge pole, largely because of the controversial nature of
the dialogue – incessant profanities, alleged racist utterings, extreme

violence and the same kind of chronological plot distortion that was employed in *Reservoir Dogs*. The movie was since restructured in a more linear format for shooting (and, crucially, the ending was changed), but the original script structure meant that an unsuspecting innocent reading it for the first time could certainly be hit in the face with some provocative material.

On pages 1 and 2, for example, there was a debate on whether one would or would not have homosexual sex with Elvis ('I don't say it now. I wouldn't cornhole Elvis, man,' jokes Tarantino. 'Way back then, when I was a big Elvis aficionado in my early twenties, I did say that').

Then, on page 3 begins a heavy-duty jive-talking diatribe on cunnilingus (which never made the final cut of the movie, sacrificed in order to maintain other sections of controversial language/violence) . . .

FLOYD (*He takes a hit off a joint*)
> There used to be a time when sisters didn't know shit about getting their pussy licked. Then the 60s came and they started fuckin' around with whiteboys. And whiteboys are freaks for that shit.

DREXL
> Because it's good.

FLOYD
> Then after a while, sisters get used to gettin' their little pussy eat. And because you whiteboys had to make pigs of yourselves, you fucked it up for every nigger in the world everywhere.

BIG DON (*solemnly*)
> Drexl. On behalf of me and all the brothers who aren't here, I'd like to express our gratitude.

FLOYD
> Go on pussy-eaters . . . laugh. You look like you be eatin' pussy. You got pussy-eatin' mugs. Now if a nigger wants to get his dick sucked he's got to do a bunch of fucked-up shit . . .

'There was no way the MPAA was gonna let them sit around and have a fifteen-minute conversation about cunnilingus,' laughs Samuel L. Jackson, whose role as Big Don was virtually made redundant by the paring down of this segment. 'I was annoyed, especially when it's the only performance that you're doing in the film. It's kinda like I just showed up, said something and got killed. I did a little bit more work than that.'

The 'foot massage' conversation that takes place between Jackson and John Travolta in *Pulp Fiction* can almost be said to have been a more censor-friendly version of the same dialogue.

However, consider that by page 6 a shotgun massacre ensues and it is quite easy to see why it all might have been a little too much for an uninitiated script reader, even though we now accept all this as part of the Tarantino canon.

'Cathryn Jaymes took calls around from people in the industry who were just livid at that script,' says Craig Hamann, who was still associated with Tarantino at that time. 'They absolutely didn't like it at all. One person who's very prominent in the film industry sent the script back to Cathryn and said, "I will seriously reconsider reading anything else that you send me again if this is the quality." I mean that kind of hostile thing was going on and I'm not sure even Quentin understands that completely, but then after *Reservoir Dogs* everybody was, "Oh we really like this film." Another prominent producer called Cathryn up after *Reservoir Dogs* and started going, "Oh, I'd really like to read all of Quentin's old stuff," and we're talking a big, *big* company. Cathryn said, "Oh, I thought you didn't like Quentin's writing?" and the guy said, "Oh, I've changed my mind." '

'It had a very different structure in the original script. The French producers who originally bought it put it back together that way,' says Tarantino.

In the original version, for example, Clarence and Alabama become an item and the circumstances of their initial meeting are not revealed until after they reach LA.

'The bottom line is that I would have done it the way I wrote it. I actually think it would have worked. However, it works *this* way. It's not like, "Oh they ruined it." It totally works this way and, to be self-critical, maybe that wasn't my best juggling act. It wasn't the best one I ever did but it works just fine this way.'

It is, however, wrong to suppose that *True Romance* was made purely on the back of *Reservoir Dogs'* success. The script, after all, had been purchased way before *Dogs* was even formalized and began its life as a movie while *Reservoir Dogs* was still in pre-production.

There is much talk in film of the *auteur* theory. This is a phrase that was coined in the 1950s by the French New Wave directors, Godard, Truffaut, *et al.* Essentially, the term is applied to a director who is the creator – the author – of the piece. This is not a widely embraced concept – the likes of screenwriter William Goldman, in particular, tend to be sceptical of such labels that overlook the team nature of filmmaking (in his excellent book *Adventures In The Screen Trade*, Goldman claims that the only true *auteur* at work today is comic-porn king Russ Meyer as he fulfils every function of making his own films including operating the camera and editing).

Nonetheless, Tarantino does fit very much into what the French perceived as the *auteur* definition, i.e. someone who writes, produces, directs (and even acts) in his own films. ('The best work comes out of single visions,' says Tony Scott.) The two full-length features that we *can* call Tarantino films – *Reservoir Dogs* and *Pulp Fiction* – have a particular cinematic style. *True Romance* is *not* a Tarantino film. It is wrong to treat it as such and is a great injustice to Tony Scott, who has not only got the best out of the screenplay but has also imbued Tarantino's story, his most overtly comedic so far (the climactic Mexican stand-off, almost a direct repeat of *Reservoir Dogs*, is this time played for laughs) with a fairy tale, dreamlike innocence – some achievement for a film that contains no small degree of brutality. Look at the final shoot-out, for example. The upholstery feathers falling like snow through the air against the music-box melody seems almost like a pastiche of *It's a Wonderful Life* or *Edward Scissorhands*.

'One of the best mainstream action thrillers for a decade,' said *Empire*. 'Even if Tarantino had directed it himself he wouldn't have come up with anything more entertaining, violent or downright funny.'

It is a fact that the movie was out of Tarantino's hands by the time it came to shooting – he never revised the script or once visited the set. *True Romance* is Tony Scott's vision and unlike *Natural Born Killers*, which Tarantino has effectively disowned, it's something that Tarantino's extremely proud of. When the film was being publicized,

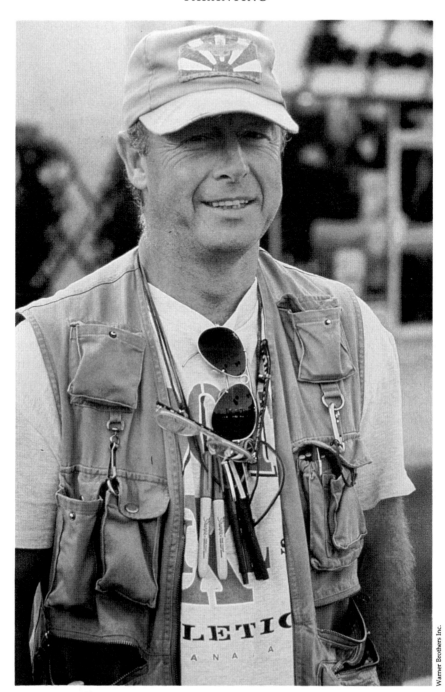

Tony Scott on the set of *True Romance:* 'I read the screenplay and loved it.'

Scott was under no obligation to invite Tarantino to take part in any of the media promotion. He did, however, and generously let Tarantino take centre stage . . .

'I had met Tony through a mutual friend and I was a big fan of Tony – *Revenge* is one of my favourite movies of the 80s. I love *Revenge*. I think along with *Revenge* this is his best movie,' enthuses Tarantino. 'He was like, "Oh, I'd like to read something that you've written." I'd just gotten *Dogs* off the ground and he had heard who my cast was and he said, "Oh, that's a great opportunity for a first film." So I sent him *True Romance* to read.'

The script at the time was owned by August Entertainment's Gregory Cascante and French producer Samuel Hadida.

'Tony said, "Oh, I really like it, I wish there was something we could do about it," and I said, "I want *you* to do it." And so they went about it and it took a long time to work everything out.'

Tarantino's recollection of events differs from the far more messy reality. Originally the script was under option to producer Stanley Margolis, who had then passed it on to Cascante with a director already attached. As August Entertainment didn't put up money, Cascante then called Hadida in Paris to see if Hadida's Metropolitan Filmexport would provide the cash. So enthusiastic was he, he literally read him the script over the phone and Hadida agreed to finance the film on the spot.

Hadida, however, has since said that he had already read the script two years before when he had met Tarantino in LA. Tarantino had had a stab at doing a script rewrite for him on another project. Hadida was not that impressed with what Tarantino had done but had asked if there was anything else he had written. Tarantino gave him *True Romance*. Whether, technically, Tarantino should have done that if it was already under option to someone else is open to conjecture. 'Naivety or just enthusiasm,' say Roger Avary.

Regardless of this contradiction, the end result was that Cascante and Hadida went into partnership to produce it for 6 to 7 million dollars with August handling the overseas distribution and Harvey Weinstein of Miramax signing up the US rights.

Meanwhile, Tarantino, at a party, ran into Scott, Bill Unger (Scott's producing partner) and whiz-kid screenwriter Shane Black, who had just received $1.75 million for the script of *The Last Boy Scout*. Word was out about Tarantino as, by that time, he was in pre-production on *Reservoir Dogs* with Keitel on board. Unger read *True Romance* and liked it, but Scott was still immersed in *The Last Boy Scout* and by the time he agreed to get involved, the Miramax deal had been finalized. As a director of clout who would bring with him a guaranteed big-name cast through the agency that represented him, CAA, the scope for the budget therefore increased considerably, making it too big a picture for Miramax to handle. Miramax were therefore paid off, though they gave Bob and Harvey Weinstein an executive producer credit as they did Stanley Margolis, who had also surrendered his stake. Morgan Creek then picked up the rights for the US and UK with a production deal through Hadida's Davis film and foreign sales done through August. Sound confusing? It is, which is why the budget of $16.5 million probably never reached 20 with all the various settlements. ('They had to pay people off because it was in semi-pre-production when they bought it', says Scott.)

'I read the screenplay and I loved it,' explains Tony Scott. 'But it was already attached to somebody else and I had the weaning process of getting it away from the other guys. I'm not a good reader but I read it in one sitting and I thought it was brilliant. I thought it was very fresh and very different and totally character-based. My love of the piece was based on how much I fell in love with the characters, so therefore it's an actor-based movie and it's the first time I've had one of those. After *Top Gun*, the movies that I was offered were, for better or worse, what you'd call hardware action movies.'

Indeed, after his début, *The Hunger*, and with the exception of 1990's *Revenge*, Tony had proved to be the more bankable of the Scott brothers, notching up a string of glossy action pictures that have all – *Top Gun*, *Beverly Hills Cop II*, *The Last Boy Scout* and even *Days Of Thunder* – put a very great number of bottoms on seats. *Crimson Tide* has since made him one of the most commercially successful directors around.

'You know, it's funny, people seem to think that films land on my lap and I do them, but I always struggle. You see I was being criticized for the way I was dealing with violence in *The Last Boy Scout* and I thought, "Oh, here's another violent movie," but it wasn't. What I fell in love with were the characters, so I chased it.'

102

At this stage, though, Scott was still not sure whether he would direct it or produce.

'The opportunity was somewhat open for me on *True Romance* if I wanted to direct it,' explains Tarantino, who by this stage was working on the script of *Pulp Fiction*. 'Tony and Bill (Unger) said, "How do you feel about this?" 'cause Tony hadn't decided if he wanted to direct it, he thought maybe about possibly just producing it. Tony takes a long time to make up his mind and there was, "Well, Quentin. How do you feel about it?" and I said, "Whoa, I would love Tony to direct it and everything and away we go." I think Tony wanted to do it but it was open for discussion, but you know I didn't want to, so I turned it down. I wrote them all [*Reservoir Dogs*, *True Romance*, *Natural Born Killers*] to be my first film and then I *made* my first film, so I didn't want to do them any more. The next film I directed, I wanted to be my *second* film and your second film is different from your first. And, more importantly, it's like the time had passed as far as what I wanted to do. It's like an old girlfriend, it has a shelf life. But Tony was different, he loved it. Tony's shelf life was going strong. You know what I mean? I think by far he's the better guy to have done this movie and also it was exciting, the idea of seeing my world through Tony's eyes and have it look like that.'

Principal photography began on 15 September 1992 with Samuel Hadida, Bill Unger and Steve Perry producing and Scott assembling a lot of his regular crew for the twelve-week shoot – cinematographer Jeffrey Kimball (*Revenge*, *Beverly Hills Cop II*, *Top Gun*), production designer Benjamin Fernandez (who had worked on *Revenge* and *Days of Thunder*) and costume designer Susan Becker (*Days of Thunder*). Fernandez created the various sets, including Clarence's apartment (with a blue neon Elvis head looming over Clarence's bed), Drexl's dodgy Detroit lair, created in a gutted Victorian home, in a tough neighbourhood bordering LA's South Central area, with its tacky zebrastriped furniture and Cliff's mobile home (the interiors shot on an LA soundstage). Becker put Alabama in the pink and turquoise numbers that jar with the monochrome drab of Detroit, the stark contrast of Detroit and LA being captured effectively by Kimball.

'We did a week in Detroit for that whole title sequence and the exterior of Drexl's,' explains Scott. 'All the establishing shots at the beginning of the movie we did in Detroit. We were lucky because we got snow and

I really wanted Detroit to be one planet and LA to be another, so it worked out perfectly.'

'I love the contrast between Detroit and Los Angeles,' agrees Tarantino, who'd scripted it to take place in these two cities. 'It's such a good contrast and part of the thing that happens to Clarence – I didn't know it when I wrote it and it took me almost four years to figure it out – is that once you actually get into the Hollywood area and you start meeting people, it's a very, very, very small town. One person leads to another person. I didn't know that in real life, I didn't *do* it in real life. Clarence knows Dick and he knows Elliot and Elliot knows Lee Donowitz. It's a *very* small town. Clarence was hip enough to understand that and I wasn't.'

There were a number of locations used, including the Palmdale Desert, the mansions of Pasadena, the shabby streets of downtown LA, the bungalows of Hollywood Hills where Dick and Floyd live, a Malibu beach for the film's finale, a building site adjacent to LAX airport and the ultra-kitsch Safari Motel on Olive Boulevard in Burbank (also used in *Apollo 13*). One notable setting was the Ambassador Hotel, the Beverly Ambassador in the film, where Lee Donowitz's suite was created. Scott chose to have Donowitz run dailies (of his film *Bodybags 2*) on a projector. This was based on a real event, when Scott went to pitch a project to a producer who ran a projector all the way through the meeting. Bear in mind that Lee Donowitz has been created more or less to resemble Joel Silver, legendary producer of the *Die Hard* and *Lethal Weapon* series . . .

The reputation of Tarantino, who was, by this time, hot on the tail of *Reservoir Dogs*, was enough to have Tinseltown's finest falling over themselves to be in it. As is the process with most films, those who end up being in the picture aren't necessarily the names originally bandied about. For various reasons, often due to contractual obligations elsewhere, original choices can't commit. Jennifer Jason Leigh, Matt Dillon and John Turturro were all attached to *True Romance* in the early days. Nonetheless, Scott still ended up with a top notch cast.

Says Scott, 'For me some of the greatest actors alive today are in this movie and I was very pleased that they wanted to do the movie.

Quentin should be flattered that they were beating down the door because of his script.'

Christian Slater as the movie's linchpin Clarence Worley was extremely keen.

'After I did *Untamed Heart* I wanted to do a movie that was *outrageous*,' muses Slater. 'I really wanted to do, you know, a *performance*. I don't want to allow my image to rule the choices that I make. It was a daring movie. For me the challenge was to be, in a way, a sympathetic character in all this madness.'

So what of the madness? As you'd expect from a film that's a whirlwind of bullets, sharp one-liners and a cachet of Colombia's uncut finest, it is never short of incident. What is also apparent that once again Tarantino has made us sympathetic with a character who is, in effect, a killer. We are made to feel comfortable with him, though never to the extent that we can't believe him turning round and doing something irrational. To this end, Tarantino has used quite a neat little plot device – Clarence doesn't kill of his own accord, he does it on instructions imparted by the ghost of Elvis Presley, although for fear of a hefty legal bill from the Presley estate, the character is simply referred to as 'Mentor'.

For the same reason, a line from the film, used as the ultimate measure of female ugliness – 'Elvis wouldn't fuck her with Pat Boone's dick' – is deleted, and Charlie Sexton's 'Graceland', recorded especially for the film, is used as the opening song rather than a genuine Presley number . . .

CLARENCE
Look he's haunting me, you know. And I do want to kill him. But I don't want to spend the rest of my life in jail.

ELVIS
Hey, I don't blame you.

CLARENCE
If I could get away with it . . .

ELVIS
Get away with it? Killin's the hard part. Getting away with it? That's

easy. Do you think a cop gives a fuck about a pimp? Listen, if every pimp in the world gets shot – two in the back of the fuckin' head – cops'll throw a party, man. As long as you're not at the scene of the crime, smokin' gun in your hand, you'll get away with it.

(*Clarence looks at Elvis*)

ELVIS
Clarence, I like ya. Always have, always will . . .

'That's one of the things I should get a big kick out of,' guffaws Tarantino, 'As opposed to *Play It Again Sam* with Bogart telling Woody Allen how to get in with the chicks, Elvis is just saying, "*Kill* that guy . . ." '

'Val (Kilmer) spent eight hours in make-up trying to look like Elvis and he looked brilliant,' continues Scott. 'Originally I showed it so you could see his face, but there's only one person in the world who looks like Elvis and that's Elvis so I redesigned it. But Val is brilliant, he *became* Elvis three months before we did it and he only had two days' work – I'd talk to him on the phone and it's like (affects Elvis voice), "Hey." He only plays dead rock and rollers now.'

Thus, we never really see Elvis full-on.

'It's difficult to say if Clarence is really crazy or not,' Slater continues in his best Jack Nicholson, sucking on one of a long line of Marlboros. 'You know he had to make up a kind of fantasy world for himself and Elvis is sort of the one he chooses to be his guidance counsellor.'

The King, it has to be said, would never get a job with the Samaritans, what with urging an innocent to blow away Gary Oldman's unsavoury pimp, Drexl Spivey.

'He was just confused,' apologizes Slater, rather unconvincingly, 'I thought he was sweet and sensitive. He loved the movies. He always wanted to be a part of them in some way and Alabama opened the door and gave him the opportunity to be the hero. Somebody said to me it sorta picks up where *Taxi Driver* left off.'

Which is exactly the effect Tarantino intended.

'What I like about what Clarence does is that he makes a *choice* to go in there and kill this pimp and it's funny because it's kind of psychotic.

That's very erratic behaviour for the lead in a movie. But he's been movie-fed, he's seen a zillion movies about pimps beating up whores and he remembers the scene in *Taxi Driver* when Harvey Keitel is talking about Jodie Foster, describing it in all these real graphic terms. He can imagine this pimp, who he's never even met, talking about his gal, his *lady love* like that, so he has to go out there and execute him. It's not because he's ever met a pimp in his life, it's just because of what he's, like, seen in the movies.'

In fact, in the original script, there is a whole scene with Clarence imagining a monologue from a pimp talking about Alabama, virtually replicating that between Keitel and Robert De Niro in Scorsese's film.

'I think Clarence is very human. Part of the thing, though, is that he's had as much a brush with this kind a stuff as anybody else. Everything he knows about this, he knows through seeing movies and when he goes to take out Drexl, you know he's like a guy in a movie, he's thinking of himself as coming in there and kicking ass and doing what a movie hero does. He shows up there but he comes somewhat into the real world when he goes down to this pimp's place. It takes a lot of bravado to knock on that door and go into that room.'

Not an orthodox justification for murder, though one we are left to live with, which is precisely what Clarence *didn't* do in Tarantino's original draft, expiring from a bullet to the eye rather than recovering to leave a set of tyre marks all the way to Mexico.

'I think it's very nice and sweet that we do end up together,' rasps Slater. '*And* it's a beautiful sunset . . . but, yeah, in the original script, that's a rap, which made complete sense because they were living such fast and insane and chaotic lives. But this *is* the movies . . . and I'm really proud of it.'

Scott actually brought Roger Avary in to redraught the film's conclusion.

'At that point I'd been rewriting the script for over four years,' claims Avary. 'I'd been trying to produce it and at the time I thought what a producer did was just to try and make movies better. Over that time I had a lot of input in the script.'

'It was very faithful to the *first* script that I read,' says Scott. 'That was the script that I executed. That was the script that I shot and I changed very little. It's much more linear now than the *original* draught that I

Tarantino on Scott: 'He just cut loose on this movie and I really loved what he did.'

read, and also the ending is different. I think Quentin originally thought that I was trying to make a commercial ending because Christian lives, but I began my life as a painter and I function from my gut. I was saying by the time it got near the end of the movie I wanted to see Christian live. It wasn't a political choice, it was a creative choice . . .'

Though Clarence may be quasi-autobiographical, it is actually the enigmatic Alabama who is the film's central character and, as Scott has filmed it, the narrator of the piece, her monologue bookending the film.

This monologue is a direct reference to a similar speech given by Sissy Spacek at the beginning of *Badlands*. In fact, the title music, by Hans Zimmer, is a reworking of the *Badlands* theme. At the time of promoting the film, Scott was happily clomping around in a pair of hand-painted cowboy boots similar to the ones worn by Martin Sheen in Terrence Malick's film.

'If people say this is similar to *Badlands*, I'd be flattered,' he adds. 'It's one of my favourite movies and it's timeless.'

Interestingly, while *Badlands*, based on the Starkweather killings, was the result of youths murdering simply because there was nothing else to do, Clarence kills because he's seen it in the movies.

According to Scott, Tarantino confessed ('during a moment of weakness') that Alabama was written as sort of an ideal girlfriend at a time when Tarantino wasn't having that much luck with women.

'It's like 'Bama isn't a *dream* girl for me,' counters Tarantino. 'I wish I could be a fly on the wall when Tony says this stuff. Basically, I had never had a girlfriend before I wrote this, just a bunch of first or second dates. What happened was that she wasn't like my ideal but she was sweet and fell in love with Clarence, not because he was the coolest looking guy in the world, but because he was *good* to her. He was romantic. She responded to his ideas of romance, she responded to his tenderness. That's how she fell in love with him. I thought it was equally romantic in *Yentl* when Amy Irving falls in love with Barbra Streisand. She falls in love with her because Yentl treats her with respect and is nice to her. I thought that was very moving. It was that aspect with 'Bama . . .'

Alabama, though, has an undisclosed past ('I might be from Tallahassee, but I'm not sure yet,' she tells Clarence at one point).

'You're supposed to believe anything you want, but she's not always telling the truth,' waxes Patricia Arquette. 'For starters, as far as I'm concerned, she doesn't really have that Southern accent, that's an affectation. She decided that was sexy and she was gonna be that Southern Belle.'

In one scene, cut from the final version, Alabama even gets a chance to explain her unusual name . . .

ALABAMA

When my mom went into labour, my dad panicked.

He never had a kid before and crashed the car. Now, picture this: their car's demolished, a crowd is starting to gather, my mom is yelling, going into contractions, and my dad, who was losing it before, is now completely screaming yellow zonkers. Then, out of nowhere, as if from thin air, this big giant bus appears, and the bus driver said, 'Get her in here.' He forgot all about his route and just drove straight to the hospital. So, because he was such a nice guy, they wanted to name the baby after him as a sign of gratitude. Well, his name was Waldo and, no matter how grateful they were, even if I'd been a boy, they wouldn't call me Waldo. So, they asked Waldo where he was from. And, so there you go . . .

Unfortunately, it was the plight of Alabama that was the main stumbling block for the ratings board of the Motion Picture Association of America (MPAA), who insisted that cuts be made in the finished version of the film (the American, European and British versions all differ slightly) in order that it qualify for an R (restricted) rating, rather than the box office poison of NC-17.

'To be honest, I think it's two and a half minutes cut,' explains Scott. 'In most instances it's blood hits and bullet hits that have been cut, but in two cases it's what I call "the story". The major one for me is Patricia originally got to shoot Chris Penn (Officer Dimes) at the end of the movie, which enabled her to open the door and be instrumental in terms of their release and getting the money. That, for me, was the fulfilment of that character at that particular point in the piece. Now an incidental character, the Italian lying on the floor, gets to shoot Chris, so it wasn't fulfilling story-wise or character-wise.

'When we presented the movie to the MPAA there was a big public outcry against police being shot by civilians and therefore they didn't want the star of the movie to be seen to shoot a cop and also, what made it even worse, was that it was a woman. That's what they said, "a woman shooting a policeman", and that makes it even worse. The guy's called Hefner, not Hugh Hefner, Richard Hefner. If it was Hugh Hefner on the ratings board it'd be a lot easier. You have to be very civilized, otherwise they cut your head off. You've just got to say yes.'

The other scene to be affected was the one in the motel room in which Alabama, about to be murdered by Virgil the hitman manages to kill him. In the original version, after Alabama had shot him, using up her shells, she continues to batter him with the butt of the gun, incanting a religious verse.

'I think that scene was a very well crafted scene in terms of what was on the page and the dynamic arc of the scene,' explains Scott. 'Basically, it's about taking the underdog to the lowest common denominator and it's, "My God, this woman is gonna die even though she's the star of the movie," and then she comes back and wins through and winning through means that she exhausts her physical energy and all the power that she's got. It was a tough scene to watch but that's what I thought was the truth of the moment and the truth of the character. It was a shame it went but, you know, when we had test screenings with that in, it was frightening the way that they were actually cheering.'

Tarantino agrees.

'*True Romance* got hit big. It got hit *real* big. I saw Tony's original cut of it and it kicked my ass. I thought it was wonderful. It's what I wrote. It was great. But, what's funny though about the ratings board, it's a weird situation. It's so easy to bang them on the head with a hammer but at the same time with me on *Dogs* they were very reasonable. I'd been hearing all these horror stories about them, but I found them to be okay. What's very interesting is the thing they objected to wasn't Alabama getting beaten up. They freaked out about when she fought back so violently – they literally said the words, "She's like an animal." There was a thought, "Well maybe someone from the ratings board should see it with an audience to see how it reacts when that scene plays," but you know, it was, "Nonononononono. That would make it worse." If the audience is like, "yeah", that would freak them out even more. The number one thing the ratings board is doing that's freaking me out is like going through old movies like the *Wild Bunch* and slapping an X on it. You start thinking about all the films that came out in the 70s. *Deliverance* would get an X now, that's really freaky. Whoa, whoa, whoa. Things are supposed to get better in the course of ten years as far as progressiveness is concerned. You're not supposed to go backwards. What's going on here?'

Tarantino's views on violence have already been documented. His execution of it onscreen, too, is different to Scott's.

'The violence in *Reservoir Dogs* is different to the violence in *True Romance*,' says Scott. 'Quentin's is a much more dark and unforgiving piece. I find it difficult at times to watch and that's rare for me. The violence is in the anticipation, so you have this long build up to this guy getting his ear cut off, whereas the violence in *True Romance* is on you and it's over. It's much more flowing.'

Nonetheless, in the context of storytelling it serves to have dramatic impact, a technique that is referred to as a 'left turn'. That is, logic dictating that events will take a normal cinematic turn, only for the audience to be thrown. Tarantino is fond of this plot device. He uses it again in *Pulp Fiction* when John Travolta's Vincent Vega takes Uma Thurman's Mia Wallace out for the evening. When they return to Mia's house after visiting Jack Rabbit Slim's, Vincent goes to the bathroom, trying to compose himself. The audience expect the next step to be whether he can avoid making a pass at the boss' wife. What we *actually* get is Mia OD-ing on heroin. Likewise in *Four Rooms*, Tarantino plays with the normal process of cinematic tension with the 'finger-chopping' scene.

The Alabama motel room scene fits into that category.

'I was thinking particularly about the effect this would have on the audience,' explains Tarantino. 'Not to be a wiseguy, it's just fun. I like movies and everything and I'm not about calculation, but part of the thing of being a storyteller is a problem with movies recently is that you pretty much know what's gonna happen before it happens. The average moviegoer, even if it's just subconsciously, they know when a movie's gonna turn left, they know when it's gonna turn right. Pretty much in the first ten minutes of any movie you see, it pretty much says, "This is the kind of movie we are. This is what we're gonna do." You know when to kind of lean up towards the screen, you know when to sit back.

What I like to do is use that against you psychologically – you turn left and then *I* turn right, not just for gamesmanship but because I'm trying to be an interesting storyteller.'

'Quentin writes brilliant characters,' says Scott. 'The real twist is that all the characters have a sense of humour. You get the guy who beats the shit out of Patricia and in the middle of all that he gives this monologue about the first guy he killed. Quentin's got such a bizarre mind, you can never anticipate what people are gonna do or what they're gonna say.'

Tarantino continues.

'One of the things I discovered in the process of watching movies, I saw this movie *Silver Bullet*. It was this Stephen King thing, Gary Busey and two kids, and I realized something when I saw that movie about character construction. The final thing happens where there are two kids and Gary Busey fights this werewolf. There's this young girl who's narrating the movie and the other one was this kid who was in a wheelchair. Well you don't think *he's* gonna die. Gary Busey could die. Dramatically, they could kill Gary Busey at the end of the movie and that wouldn't have broken anything. I was really *scared* for Gary Busey when I watched that scene and one of the things that I think makes the scene with Alabama work dramatically is that she could die. She *could* die. You know she's up for grabs. You put her in danger in the first ten minutes of the movie, she might be a heroine but you know she's not gonna die. She could be offed and the film could still go on for the next twenty minutes. That's one of the things that I think is so powerful about that scene . . .'

Definitely up for grabs was Gary Oldman who, as Alabama's pimp Drexl Spivey, turns in one of the most unpleasant screen villains in recent years.

Tony Scott remembers their first meeting.

'I'd never met him before and he said, "Come on down to the hotel for a drink" – and he shouldn't have been drinking. So we had a drink and he said, "Tell me the story of the movie." But it's very difficult to say. I said, "You've got to read it," and he said, "I don't fucking read, I don't read scripts, so tell me the story." So I started to tell him the story and I could see him going (imitates snoring) and he said, "Tell me about my fucking character, what's my character?" and I said, "He's a white guy who thinks he's black and he's a pimp." He said, "*I'll do it.*" He's mad.

'He'd just been working on *Romeo is Bleeding* and there's this guy who he'd been hanging out with on the set who was like the security guy and was a drug dealer. This guy had spent ten years of his life in Jamaica and he had a sort of half Rasta, half Queens accent. It was the weirdest accent that he came up with, but he was great in the piece. It was difficult for him because it was such an outrageous role to play. He likes time to put his head in the right place but he didn't have it. He's not particularly articulate in terms of the intellectual sense, he can't tell you why he's doing things, but he's got the best instincts. He's almost Dickensian, he's got this strange laughter. There's certainly something very dark and very dangerous.'

It is the creation of interesting minor characters that seems to be one of the strengths of Tarantino's scripting generally.

'Each of the minor characters is treated as guest star,' said the *New York Times*, including on this occasion the stoned waster Floyd, played by Brad Pitt.

'You know Brad has a mystery and a darkness. I think it comes from the chequered life he had before,' smirks Scott, motioning his thumb and forefinger to his lips, puffing on an imaginary joint. 'That's a character that he knew and hung out with at his house. This guy came for a week and stayed for two years – a pothead who never got off the sofa.

'But the bong was my invention,' he adds triumphantly, referring to the sweet jar Floyd uses to inhale his weed. 'There's a guy I go rock climbing with who has this bong, a honey bear that you can buy across the counter – he calls his Russ. That was a homage to Russ.'

Saul Rubinek's fictitious action producer, the aforementioned Lee Donowitz, is another brilliant addition.

'It was Tony who turned him into Joel Silver,' adds Tarantino, who at the time of writing didn't move in such esteemed circles. Tarantino actually based Donowitz on his acting coach, Allen Garfield.

However, it was the interaction between two other supporting characters, Dennis Hopper and Christopher Walken, which gave the film its biggest talking point, supplanting the allegations of gratuitous violence in *Reservoir Dogs* with racism for *True Romance*.

Hopper, who plays Cliff, Clarence's father, is at the mercy of Sicilian

Gary Oldman as Drexl Spivey: 'I don't read scripts, so tell me the story.'

Mafioso Vincenzo Coccotti (a part that was originally going to played by Michael Madsen. Interestingly, one of the minor Italian hoods is called Toothpick Vic, a nickname that Madsen's Vic Vega has in *Reservoir Dogs*).

Coccotti has been boasting about his ancestry – his father being 'the heavyweight champion of Sicilian liars'. Cliff, knowing that he will be tortured, putting his son's life at risk, therefore taunts Coccotti into killing him . . .

CLIFF

You know, I read a lot. Especially things about history. I find
that shit fascinating. In fact, here's a fact I don't know whether you
know or not, Sicilians were spawned by niggers.

COCCOTTI

Come again?

CLIFF

It's a fact. You see Sicilians have black blood pumping through their
hearts. And if you don't believe me, you can look it up. Hundreds and
hundreds of years ago, you see, the Moors conquered Sicily. And the
Moors are niggers. You see way back then, Sicilians were like the
wops from Northern Italy. They all had blond hair and blue eyes. But
then the Moors moved in there, they changed the whole country.
They did so much fuckin' with Sicilian women that they changed
the whole bloodline forever. That's why blond hair and blue eyes
became black hair and dark skin. You know, it's absolutely amazing
to me to think that, to this day, hundreds of years later, Sicilians still
carry that nigger gene. I'm quotin' history. It's a fact. It's written. Your
ancestors are niggers. Your great, great, great, great grandmother
fucked a nigger and she had a half nigger kid. Now, if that's a
fact, tell me, am I lyin' . . . ?

'I actually think it may be the most taboo word in the English language,' says Tarantino of his liberal use of the word 'nigger'. 'It's almost volatile. Words should not have that much power and anytime you have a word that has that much power, you should strip the power away. What's being said is obvious, he's trying to insult these guys, insult them in a way that they, in particular, would be insulted. But I love that speech. I think that speech is really funny. It was actually a black guy who told me that whole story.'

Says Scott, 'Quentin wrote two scenes – that scene and he also wrote the scene with Sam Jackson, which unfortunately got cut, about pussy-eating and I don't find them offensive. I don't think the black population of the country will find it offensive either. It seems it was said in good heart, in good spirit. It's not like it's said that it's damning. I've seen it with a black audience and they loved the scene and it was basically a dating audience, kids eighteen to twenty-five with their dates, black kids, and they loved it. They felt that they were being pulled into the spirit of the thing as opposed to being singled out and criticized. It's funny, a black audience responds even stronger than both Latin or white audiences. They go with it. That's what Quentin writes. He writes street vernacular and it's poetry. You can say the word nigger and the word pussy without it being offensive as long as you have the right guys to then deliver those words on screen.'

There is no better person to pass judgement on this matter than Samuel Jackson.

'As Quentin said, he's trying to de-sensitize the word,' he comments. 'I think that as an actor you try and be true to the director's vision, to the truth that you as an actor want to tell. You say the things that are written, that are as true as you can say them. Now, I look at what he writes and I say he's taken the word nigger and he's used it every possible way it could be used. He's used it as a descriptive, he's used it as a term of endearment, he's used it as a derogatory, he's used it as a generality. It's just a word that's used and it happens. That's one of the best speeches I've ever heard and if you are a *true* racist you will sit there and go, "Yeah, that's right." If you are a liberal, you will sit there and go, "Oh my God, that's awful." But that's what actors are supposed to do. I am supposed to solicit a reaction that will generate conversation that will hopefully generate change, so in that respect he's totally successful at doing what he's trying to do.'

'Yeah, I was more worried about the Sicilians,' grins Dennis Hopper

117

menacingly. 'I figured that it would probably rub a few people the wrong way, but that's okay and, anyway, as a screen actor, you don't have speeches in movies anymore. *This* is a speech. I'm a great admirer of Tarantino's writing.'

Christopher Walken, whose character 'hasn't killed anybody since 1984', is equally unconcerned.

'That amount of dialogue is unusual in movies. You don't usually talk too much, but there's three pages of dialogue and it's unusual and in this case I think it's very good. I don't ever confuse movies with real life and I don't think other people do. With that scene there's a surreal aspect to it and I think that what he was saying was so outrageous that how can you respond to somebody saying that to you? So there was an element of that in it, of just being absolutely flabbergasted. I think that's a quality of the scene and it's one of the things that's amusing about it. He really, in a sense, gets shot for offending me.'

'Think of Mark Twain,' adds Hopper. 'He was dealing with the same things. There's a couple of guys running away on a riverboat going down a river. I mean that's a strange juxtaposition, but we're in the 90s now. How can you write about it and not make some reflection on your culture? Quentin Tarantino, he's the Mark Twain of the 90s . . .'

True Romance was generally well-received critically – 'Dynamite. A full throttle blast of action and fireworks, a savagely funny thrill ride,' said *Rolling Stone*. 'There is an undeniable allure to this film. That is what will make it one of the top films of 1993 – perhaps the decade,' proclaimed *Dramalogue*, though the question of violence never strayed far from the qualifications in reviews. (And indeed surfaced again in June 1995 when Republican Senator Bob Dole, a presidential hopeful, castigated Hollywood for producing films which crossed a line 'not just of taste but of human dignity and decency'. *True Romance* and *Natural Born Killers* were cited as twin harbingers of evil which 'revel in mindless violence and loveless excess', though his admission that he hadn't seen either film left him easy prey for Tarantino and Oliver Stone who deftly picked him off in the press.)

'There may be something darkly disturbing about the appeal of crime films themselves,' sang the *New York Times*, positively shovelling on the praise. 'For they speak to some deep need to release violence. By exploit-

On the set of *Reservoir Dogs*, August 1991: 'I had the idea in my head for a while – a movie that doesn't take place *during* the robbery but *after* the robbery.'

Quentin Tarantino and the cast of *Reservoir Dogs*, August 1991: 'Her casting is great. You can't imagine anyone else in the movie aside from those actors.'

Quentin Tarantino directs *Reservoir Dogs*, August 1991: 'The entire time it was like, "Hey, we've got a powder keg here. I can't wait for audiences to see this." '

Pulp Fiction's Jack Rabbit Slim's: 'The one set extravagance that Tarantino allowed himself.'

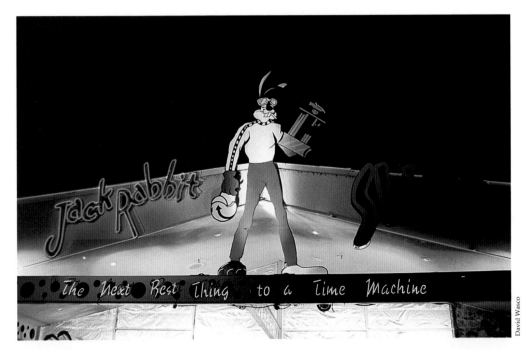

David Wasco

Jack Rabbit Slim's: 'The big mama of the '50s diners. Either the best or the worst, depending on your point of view.'

David Wasco

Filming *Pulp Fiction*'s Twist sequence, November 1993: 'Something so camp it was not to be missed.'

The Hawthorne Grill, Los Angeles, a location for *Pulp Fiction*: 'In Los Angeles, life and loneliness revolve around restaurants.'

Pulp Fiction's quirky adornments: 'Little customized props which give the film its own distinct style.'

Uma Thurman in a *Pulp Fiction* publicity pose: 'The idea, originally, was gonna be like three short stories, like the old *Black Mask* magazine.'

ing the genre so cleverly, Mr Tarantino reveals the virtues of being a video kid.'

American *Humane Movie Review* even added its own footnote – 'Animal action is minimal. In one scene where Clarence confronts Drexl, Clarence punches him, sending Drexl flying backwards into a row of fish aquariums he has in his home. He crashes into the aquariums, breaking two of them, sending glass and water flying. The two aquariums that the actor fell into were made of candy glass and contained no fish.'

True Romance – or 'Reservoir Snogs' as *Time Out* called it – duly premièred amid scenes of typical hullabaloo before a hip young crowd at Mann's Chinese Theatre, a place where Tarantino had applied for a job eight years before and been rejected ('Apparently there were other people more qualified,' he jokes).

There were, though, some detractors, *True Romance* having the misfortune to coincide with the quite nasty and far more sinister road movie, *Kalifornia* (which starred Juliet Lewis in a sort of mirror opposite role to that of Mallory in *Natural Born Killers*).

'At the moment, killing someone seems to be the only addiction Americans can have on the road,' said *New York Magazine*. 'Two movies about young lovers on the run advances the curious proposition that in America you have to knock off someone in order to become a human being.'

'*True Romance* is anything but truthful and not even remotely romantic,' said Kenneth Turan of the *LA Times*. 'Nothing is more irritating than a dumb film that thinks it's hip – and *True Romance* is this year's model.'

'One of the endless variations on the couple on the run subgenre, it provides some amazing encounters, bravura acting and gruesome carnage,' commented *Variety*. 'But it doesn't add up to enough as preposterous plotting and graphic violence ultimately prove an audience turn-off and will limit the film's prospects.'

The prediction of *Variety* turned out to be true. *True Romance* opened officially in the USA on 10 September 1993 and in the UK on 15 October. It took $12.2 million in the States, an underachiever as far as Warner Brothers were concerned. In June 1993 in the UK it had the dubious distinction of following *Reservoir Dogs* into being put 'on hold' by the

British Board of Film Classification when it came to video classification, though by December 1994 it gained a release, unaltered from the cinema form, with an 18 certificate.

Scott is still unhappy at the way the film was promoted, coming over, as it did in the main promotional poster, almost like a teen movie, with Slater and Arquette in a passionate embrace.

'I think they mismarketed it, the selling of this movie. For me, I'm from advertising, there's a perfect vehicle in the title, really contradicting the overall tone of the movie. My belief is that the broad stroke of it should have been the title *True Romance* and behind it Christian Slater pulling the gun on Gary Oldman because, with the advertising now, people think this is another Christian Slater movie, which is a gentle, softer kind of movie. The concept of the advertising should be the contradiction of the title versus what the movie is really about and I don't think they used that in the way they should. They take the trailer to shopping malls and do marketing research and with this sort of movie it's very difficult. You really have to follow your instincts, it's not a normal sort of movie.'

That is not to say that he's disappointed with the end result. Despite the constraints placed by the MPAA, Scott still considers it his 'best work to date' and the critics are overwhelmingly in his corner.

'I'm a bit close to it, but where *Reservoir Dogs* is a much more psychological movie than *True Romance* in the anticipation of the violence, *True Romance* is much more a rollercoaster ride and an adrenaline rush. *Reservoir Dogs* is much more of a head trip. I found *Dogs* very disturbing. What I get from an audience of *True Romance* is that it's like doing speed for two hours, it's a sort of exhausting experience.'

Box Office magazine perhaps bestowed the highest praise of all: 'From the giddily poisonous pen of Quentin Tarantino, it plays like a bigger-budgeted sequel to *Reservoir Dogs* . . . As it stands, *True Romance* is, in its way, even more impressive: that Tarantino's writing is trenchant enough not only to survive an all-stops-out, big screen treatment by a far more seasoned director, but that his corrosive stamp is capable of eating right through even a far more seasoned directorial signature . . . Between *Reservoir Dogs* and *True Romance* we could have the makings of a new genre, "Brute Farce". '

'I love what Tony did with it,' concludes Tarantino. 'I'm a big Tony

120

Scott fan. As a filmmaker, when I do my own stuff, it couldn't be more different. You know, the look is different. I like long takes, for Tony a long take is twenty seconds. You know, the whole aesthetic about how the film looks and how it plays. I like that, I like it, it's just not my way. This gave me the opportunity to see my world through Tony's eyes. He just cut loose on this movie and I really *loved* what he did . . .'

Chapter 6

Natural Born Killers

Though Tarantino went out of his way to endorse *True Romance*, it is a different story with *Natural Born Killers*.

'My name'll get brought up from time to time but I think I've done a pretty good job of distancing myself from the film,' he states. 'Basically, if you like it, it's all Oliver. Good, bad or indifferent, it has very little to do with me.'

Tarantino has still not seen the film and is unwilling to talk about it at any length. All parties involved in the making of this film feel they have been wronged and there is still a great deal of acrimony.

'I'll see it in a hotel room someday,' is Tarantino's standard put-down to discussions on the subject which, though it may sound churlish, at least prevents him from having to get drawn into talking about it.

'I *was* getting curious but then I ended up being in Japan and Korea for the actual opening and so I missed it. Then I came back into its third weekend or something like that and I had like one day to see it before I went to Europe and it was just like, "I'll pass on it." If I was here on its opening weekend, the excitement of it might have made me go see it, but I didn't go and I haven't gone since . . .'

The original *Natural Born Killers* was written by Tarantino after he had completed *True Romance*. It is a far more brutal piece than *True Romance* and went through several drafts before emerging as anything near the final film that Oliver Stone made. Mickey and Mallory Knox are husband and wife serial killers, who, by perverse logic, become media darlings. Eventually captured, they become the star attraction on a TV show called *American Maniacs*, which is broadcast live from their prison. A mass breakout and riot ensue and the TV show host, Wayne Gale, and his crew then become implicit in proceedings.

'It's definitely *not* my screenplay,' declares Tarantino categorically.

Indeed, substantially rewritten by the Stone team, new scenes have been added, others deleted and the whole thrust of the story slanted to suit Stone's purpose.

That is not to say that it has been bastardized. Large chunks of the original script remain intact and if you watch it a number of times, the rhythms of the dialogue still seem in places like Tarantino, especially with the lines spoken by Robert Downey Jr and the odd snap of Woody Harrelson.

Though it lacks the humour of *Reservoir Dogs*, *True Romance* and *Pulp Fiction*, what Stone *has* made is an incredibly powerful film. Released on 26 August 1994, it came as a violent slap in the face after the wistful summer of *Forrest Gump*. A savage indictment of the media, it has become a comment on recent *causes célèbres* such as the Menendez case, the Lorena Bobbit case and the Geraldo Rivera TV interview with Charles Manson. Quite by an outstanding stroke of coincidence, that June OJ Simpson went on his chase down LA's 405 freeway. With the route lined with people cheering him on and waving banners, Stone's message achieved a new poignancy – that the media must take their share of responsibility for the decline of modern America.

A 35-million-dollar picture, it is a big showy film and as an audio-visual experience it is awesome, using a relentless barrage of trickery – different film stocks (as in *JFK*), back projections and a thrash metal soundtrack – all tightly edited into a parody of the MTV attention-span style that has become the hallmark of modern American television. Graphically violent, the overall result is an overwhelming assault on the senses that certainly leaves a bitter taste in the mouth, which is what Stone intended. Though, unlike *True Romance*, which offset its bitter moments with comic sweetness, such moments do not appear in *Natural Born Killers*.

Commercially, it was a big success, taking over $50 million in the States and upward of £2.6 million in the UK. Critically, it again delivered the goods though it was often unclear as to whether critics were praising it as a piece of stylish filmmaking or for the message that it brought which, due to the paradoxical nature of the film, may have been lost on that great section of the USA's public known as Middle America. It also resurrected, yet again, the whole question of copycat violence with several brutal incidents on both sides of the Atlantic pinned on the movie. It was subsequently banned in Ireland and then put on hold in the UK, released three months after its intended November opening. As noted previously, it was later one of the films singled out by Senator Bob Dole in his June 1995 attack on Hollywood, and mentioned again in a Senate debate on 27 June. 'Senator Dole's renewed attack on my film is a shameless act of political grandstanding and hypocrisy coming from the man who is leading the campaign to repeal the assault weapons ban,' reacted Stone in an angry statement. 'It doesn't make much sense to condemn make-believe guns but promote real ones.'

A popular misconception is that Tarantino is credited with the screenplay. As he has already stated, he is not. The screenplay is, officially, by David Veloz, Richard Rutowski and Oliver Stone. Tarantino takes a lesser 'story by' credit, at his own request, the obvious sign that there is a certain lack of harmony between the parties.

Though the final version is markedly different from Tarantino's original draft, the lovers on the run aspect certainly is loosely similar to that of *True Romance*, in concept rather than detail. In fact, when both simply existed as scripts, and were referred to in one-line synopses, the two would often be confused, though, as both films went into development, confusion ended there.

This is not without reason.

'When Quentin started writing *Natural Born Killers*, it was actually part of *True Romance*. It was originally called *The Open Road*. He was even thinking about calling it *Be-Bop-A-Luah*,' explains Craig Hamann.

'What happened was there was a script that I wrote,' explains Avary. 'It was more like *After Hours*. Quentin loved it and said, "Oh, you've got to rewrite this," but I just wasn't into it. He went off and rewrote it and what it became was parts of *True Romance* and parts of *Natural Born Killers*. *The Open Road* literally vanished,'

Hamann at that time used to type up a lot of Tarantino's scrawlings.

'What happened was Clarence, the lead character in *True Romance*, was writing a screenplay as all this was going on. What he was writing was *Natural Born Killers* with Mickey and Mallory.'

With Mickey and Mallory as tantamount egos for Clarence and Alabama, Tarantino was soon confronted with the obvious problem.

'It was getting *really* long,' remembers Hamann. 'Quentin got to the point where he said, "This is crazy," and he took Mickey and Mallory out, which is the right thing to do. What he had was *True Romance*.'

What happened with *True Romance* is now history but, as already recorded, Tarantino had passed on the rights to his colleague Rand Vossler, almost as an apology for switching his interest to *Reservoir Dogs* and Lawrence Bender. In a similar process as had been employed on *True Romance* and *Reservoir Dogs*, Vossler had tried to raise enough money so that he and Tarantino could make the film independently, Vossler touting Tarantino as the next Scorsese and Tarantino camping up the image, turning up to meetings in leather jacket and shades.

It is from then on that history is open to conjecture. Two things are for sure. One: Oliver Stone, perfectly legitimately, purchased the script and made his own movie. Two: Tarantino has kicked up an almighty stink over the manner in which the script passed from A to B.

The fact is that the script came to Stone through two up and coming producers, Don Murphy and Jane Hamsher and their company JD Productions. Murphy and Hamsher, both friends of Tarantino when they picked up the option on the script in the summer of 1991, have now fallen out with him spectacularly and publicly, the dirty laundry being done through the pages of *Premiere* magazine in November 1994 and January 1995.

In an interview with executive editor Peter Biskind, Tarantino alleged that with his script a 'skulduggerous theft happened.'

'That was really a mean article. It really distorted the facts and was unkind,' says Jaymes. 'I feel so ashamed of him for saying things like that.'

'I'm not saying he's the Antichrist, I'm saying he's the egomaniac from hell, there's a difference,' says Murphy, still stinging from that tirade. He promptly replied to Tarantino, quite savagely, through the letters page of that magazine . . .

So what really happened? The answer is pretty much open to conjecture, largely due to the fact that Tarantino now considers *Natural Born Killers* a dead issue, but seems to revolve around the part played by Rand Vossler to whom Tarantino had passed the rights, someone who has since disappeared off the scene.

Tarantino claims that when he had passed the option to Vossler, he had made it conditional on the fact that he shoot it guerrilla style, 16mm, as had been the original plan with *Reservoir Dogs*.

'But he didn't do it that way,' Tarantino told *Premiere*. 'He met some people, Don Murphy and Jane Hamsher, who said, "No, no. Fuck that. We'll get a budget of $3 million for you." He goes, "Really?" He made a deal with them. Three days later they fired him. That's why I never, under any circumstances, would have given these people the rights for the script.'

This is quite an accusation, probably prompted by an earlier dig Murphy had made through the pages of *Details* magazine in which he queried why anybody would take a chance on a director whose movie (*Reservoir Dogs*) 'had grossed less than *Leprechaun*'.

'We rewrote [*Natural Born Killers*] because it's like all of Quentin's scripts, a good idea built around a lot of swearwords and no plotting,' continued the acerbic comment.

Irrespective of such vitriol, when Murphy and Hamsher met Vossler, then working at an MGM Cable company, Vossler was in possession of the script which was, at that time, a loose *Badlands* analogy with a David Koresh-style guru in the story. Murphy and Hamsher were breaking into production and had just made 'this piece of shit *Double Dragon*' (by Murphy's own admission) for Imperial, ironically the same company where Tarantino ended up working after he left Video Archives. Thus, the three got to know each other well. At this stage Tarantino, still unknown, was attached as the director to *Natural Born Killers* and it languished on a pile somewhere in Murphy's office. However, Tarantino furiously reworked it over the coming months. At a party, a friend of Murphy's told him about a hot script that he'd just read called *Natural Born Killers*, a substantially revised version to the one that Murphy had read before. He told Murphy to definitely get a look at it as it would appeal to him, given that Murphy had a particular interest in the Manson killings. Murphy and Hamsher thus gave it a second crack. The script now had the Wayne Gale character inserted in the story.

'Jane reads the script and goes, "Fuck, this is one of the best things I've read in five years," ' says Murphy.

Tarantino, however, had since gone off to do begin pre-production *Reservoir Dogs*, then only perceived as small million-dollar movie. Thus Rand was left holding the baby.

And here's where the trouble comes into paradise.

While the Tarantino camp claim that Vossler was fully in charge of proceeding with a deal, Murphy says that Tarantino never really for one minute expected Vossler ('who's not Mr Follow-Through', according to Murphy) to get the wheels in motion.

Conditional to Vossler's acquisition of the option on the script, Murphy claims Tarantino had provided Vossler with a bizarre caveat. Vossler, in six months, had to come back with twenty minutes of the movie (the *American Maniacs* interview section) already filmed to prove his worth.

'You can direct it, you can produce it with another director, your mom can direct it,' Murphy claims Tarantino said. 'But you must have shot that as a 16mm film because that's what it's supposed to be.'

At this point the two realities become blurred. If the above scenario *did* exist, was this the letter of intention or did Tarantino imply that the whole rest of the film be subsequently shot in this manner, i.e. guerrilla style? Nobody really knows because at this point it was all done on a gentlemanly basis. No one really knew, either, when the six-month period actually started and couldn't really confirm anything while Tarantino was incommunicado, shooting *Dogs*.

Vossler was confident at this stage that he would be the director of the film and, despite Murphy's reservations, $10,000 was raised to shoot this segment, Murphy and Hamsher knowing that if that sequence worked then they would have a fifth of the film in the bag, and if it didn't, then they would get a new director and retain Vossler as co-producer and allow him to keep his rights.

Murphy's take on all this is that Tarantino had cynically insisted on this precondition because he never wanted to get the film made but wished to retain *Natural Born Killers* and rework some of the scenes into later material, panicking when it looked like the movie actually might get made after all. Tarantino's implication is that he trusted Vossler and that Vossler was cheated by Murphy and Hamsher. In any case, the time came to put the deal down in writing.

'And that's when Rand pulls out his ace in the hole,' says Murphy, this ace being an old, previously undisclosed contract between Vossler and Tarantino, which, according to Cathryn Jaymes, gave Vossler the rights 'in perpetuity'.

Lawyers were summoned to look at that agreement, one which tended to contradict the point of an option, options, by their very nature, having a termination date – a year, two years. This was an option for ever. There was a further complication. Who was to determine that what Vossler filmed was any good?

According to Murphy, a new deal was drawn up by Tarantino's lawyer, by which a fresh two-year option on the script was sold to Murphy and Hamsher's JD Productions for $10,000, this figure being brought up because Tarantino, Murphy claims, had wanted to buy a new car. This was deemed preferable by Tarantino's lawyer to a one-year renewable option. Tarantino, allegedly, asked permission to keep back pages 24 and 25 for himself, which was granted.

Desperate to raise cash, a novel idea was hit upon. Vossler ran into a pair of hulking Scandinavian body-building twins, who were trying to make a name for themselves as actors. They pledged $270,000, firstly on the condition that they could be in it – a bit like the producer who wanted his girlfriend to lay Mr Blonde in *Reservoir Dogs* – and secondly that JD Productions could match it.

Roger Avary was enlisted to write a scene for them – Mickey and Mallory take a hacksaw to their legs and the twins end up giving enthusiastic interviews on *American Maniacs*, praising Mickey and Mallory from their wheelchairs.

This agreement didn't work out . . .

The next stage is, again, blurred. Vossler was removed as director. Tarantino claims that Murphy and Hamsher fired him, Murphy says that as the ball got rolling it appeared Vossler wasn't up to the job and that he thus was moved sideways, 'retaining his full status as co-producer and keeping his full directorial fee.'

'I say it now, without fear of contradiction that we never would have done it had not Quentin embraced the idea (to oust Vossler). I'm not gonna say that Quentin came up with the idea, I'm not gonna say that. He said, "Go ahead and do it." '

Other up and coming directors were approached, including Marc Rocco (*Murder in the First*) and various companies touched for money, including CB 2000, who tried to come up with a package with Sean Penn as director. Penn didn't seem the right choice but a budget of $5 to 10 million seemed likely and Brian De Palma, David Fincher and Barbet Schroeder were all interested, though Murphy has since alleged that, despite Tarantino having directorial approval, Tarantino actively got in contact with the likes of De Palma and Fincher and asked them not to be involved.

Tarantino, by his own admission, declined the opportunity to direct it himself. Meanwhile, Vossler launched a lawsuit against JD Productions, claiming he was erroneously fired. This came to nought.

While all this was going on, Sean Penn gave the script to the producer of *The Indian Runner*, Thom Mount.

'Mount had gone to this testosterone party with Oliver Stone and John Milius,' says Murphy. 'The script got passed to him, Oliver reads it on a plane and then I get the phone call, "Oliver would like to direct the movie," and I'm (sarcastically), "Yeah, *right*." '

Says Oliver Stone, 'Jane and Don said, "This guy's very good." I read it and said, "This is terrific, I'd like to buy it," and then Thom brought Don and Jane in and they made a very difficult deal. They were very ballsy for young producers. They insisted that I make the movie right after *Heaven and Earth*. Usually you buy a script and you have a little freedom with it, an option to develop it, but they insisted that it be made right away.'

There was a reason for this. Murphy and Hamsher, who had already had a year lapse on their two-year option, needed to move fast.

At this point it must be made clear that *Reservoir Dogs* had not been released yet and Stone refutes allegations that the script was purchased simply because Tarantino was hot. Stone had been toying with the idea of making a crime film for a while and was very keen on the script, though not in its existing form.

'Having written *Scarface* and *Year of the Dragon*, I wanted to return to the gangster genre and do a story about American criminality,' he explains. 'I did it in '82 and '85. A long time had gone by and I wanted to direct that kind of a movie, so in a sense, this was a channel. Quentin's original script was a combination of the road movie and the prison movie, the two energies could be combined under the aegis of a gangster film and at the same time put the spin on to it of the 90s media, which never existed in a gangster picture to my knowledge to date. It was a new twist.'

129

Mount and Vossler subsequently sat down and came to an agreement and thus Vossler remained as co-producer. Stone took on the project but insisted that the script be substantially rewritten . . .

Oliver Stone believed that any differences that Tarantino may have had with Murphy and Hamsher he could circumvent. Thus he tried to win Tarantino on to his side.

'He meets with the guy and it is his worst nightmare,' accuses Murphy. 'He thinks he's Mr Movie Encyclopaedia and he goes, "You know that scene where Mickey Rourke talks to John Lone in the *Year of the Dragon*? What the hell were you thinking of when you fuckin' wrote that? What *was* that?" Oliver considers himself first and foremost a writer. There's some kid pissing on a script he wrote.'

Stone denies that it was confrontational.

'He came into the office twice and we had fairly genial conversations and he told me about his pain and about being rewritten and hating Don and Jane. I told him the story of how I wrote a film called *Eight Million Ways to Die*, which I loved. I found the book, I bought the book. It was all set in New York and Hal Ashby took it over. I went to Mexico to shoot *Salvador*. It was somewhat a similar case and when I came back I was stunned out of my mind to find that the script had been entirely rewritten. Robert Towne had come in and rewritten it and they had reset it in Los Angeles and it was another story. Towne did call me and said, "I'm sorry". Hal never bothered to tell me. It was a terrible movie but it had nothing to do with my writing, but I never went public with it.'

Stone does agree that there then began a process of non-co-operation on behalf of some of Tarantino's *Reservoir Dogs* actors who were subsequently approached to be in *Natural Born Killers*.

Michael Madsen was one of them.

'Oliver Stone called me up to offer me a part,' he says. 'We started to have a conversation on a day to day basis and then had meetings about it but he'd started to change some things in the script. Quentin advised me not to do the film – he told me that he was trying to get his name taken off it.'

Madsen was actually the first choice to play the Mickey.

'Then Oliver Stone told me about the choice of Woody Harrelson and Robert Downey Jr – Oliver likes to work with a lot of these people. It

Oliver Stone on the set: 'I wanted to expand the script for more of a social political commentary about the 90s.'

didn't turn out to be the film that I wanted to do. Every other Dog was offered a part – Steve Buscemi, Chris Penn, Harvey – and they all did the same, which made Oliver very angry.'

'Yeah I believe that,' says Stone of the so-called conspiracy theory. 'Tim Roth came up. I liked him but, you know, he promptly pulled out, but it was no big thing because there are so many good actors. I was simply responding to good actors and trying to be fair. Whatsisname Madsen. I offered him the role, I admitted as such, but the picture, when it was rewritten, budgeted out at considerably more because we wanted to try a lot of different effects and Warners said, "We will not partner with you on this film with Madsen." I strung him out for what I ultimately don't think was that long. He was very bitter.'

Murphy even alleges that Tarantino's agents, the William Morris Agency, began a stalling tactic to let the option lapse and revert to them.

Nonetheless, Stone did try and recruit people who were associated with *Reservoir Dogs* and *True Romance*. Tom Sizemore, from *True Romance*, appeared, though he was, as Stone points out, in *Born on the Fourth of July*. Stone didn't, either, feel the need to change the name Jack

131

Scagnetti, so obviously a reference to another Scagnetti, Seymour, the probation officer in *Reservoir Dogs*.

'I like the name,' declares Stone.

Even Kirk Baltz, Marvin The Cop, crops up.

'There was *no hommage* aspect . . .'

So why did Oliver Stone rewrite the script?

At the suggestion of Hamsher and Murphy, David Veloz was brought to collaborate with Richard Rutowski, an old partner of Stone's, on reworking it. Together with Stone they share the credit for screenplay. Tarantino, wanting to distance himself from it, settled instead for a story credit, though he *did* retain his screenwriting fee.

Oliver Stone explains.

'Listen, I've written many scripts myself and I have five or six writing nominations from the Academy. I'm not the type of person who feels that I *have* to rewrite something. I'm not driven by ego. I have many collaborators. If you check all my writing credits, I've been very generous with my collaborators. I've tried to use the best of a lot of people. I don't have much of an ego. I wrote most of *Year of the Dragon* and Michael Cimino participated and his name came on it. I'm not hogging the credit.'

Stone, at that time shooting *Heaven and Earth*, gave instructions to Veloz and Rutowski as to how he wanted it changed.

'I said, "Here's the areas I want to redo. I want to expand the script for more of a social political commentary about the 90s, more about Mickey and Mallory and more about violence and aggression and the implications of violence in this century." I had read a couple of David's earlier scripts. I brought him to work alongside Richard and they did it over a period of several months. Then I essentially pounded together the whole thing the way I wanted to shoot it.'

According to Stone, by Tarantino's own admission it was a first draft screenplay which Tarantino wanted to do himself and no longer had any need for after he got *Reservoir Dogs* off the ground

'He said he didn't want to direct it, so he went on to do his second movie and I agree with him, I think it (*Reservoir Dogs*) is a wonderful first movie. I thought *Natural Born Killers* was good, but for me as a director making my tenth or eleventh movie, it isn't what I had in mind as a movie in its overall attack on where society is. What is aggression, what is violence, what is TV, what is our relationship to TV, what are the implications for the twentieth century? – the apocalyptic feeling that we get from society. That was not in that screenplay. Mickey and Mallory were stick figures, to be honest, they were supporting characters. It was mostly about Wayne Gale and jokes about Wayne Gale and his crew. All his crew had an identity. You know, it was cute stuff, I'm not putting it down, but I said, "I don't really care about Wayne Gale. He's good in parts, but I don't really want to make the movie about Wayne Gale." '

'It *was* a satire about the media and celebrityhood, that it *was*. That was the outstanding idea in the screenplay. We added layers of socio-political commentary with imagery. We added the Mickey and Mallory story, pretty much, the bit with Rodney Dangerfield. We added the Indian, the pharmacy and the concept of remorse was introduced. The concept of the interview was expanded, based on the Charles Manson–Geraldo Rivera interview. The concept of the riot taking place, which was a metaphor for the world coming to an end, we expanded into enormous proportions. The concept of the style of the movie itself. The style was done to reflect present-day television, to make a kaleidoscopic refraction and making it highly subjective – by the time we've finished 'A' we're in the killers' driver's seat. They have fun killing, we have fun killing. That starts to make the audience re-examine its own attitudes and we change styles with Mr Downey, with the magazine format, and we changed style with Mr Sizemore, with Tommy Lee Jones as the warden. Each character brings with him a different subjective style into the picture.'

Thus changes were made accordingly and various little touches that are characteristic Tarantino – a lengthy diatribe by a judge detailing the rights and wrongs of the electric chair; a two-page donut shop discussion between Wayne Gale's TV crew, debating which was the best of Steven Spielberg's films – were chopped out. One scene, a film within a film of Mickey and Mallory on the road, called *Thrill Killers*, culminating with Mallory having her head blown off, was removed completely and replaced with the TV sitcom episode, written by David Veloz, the intention here being to create sympathy for the anti-heroes.

Tarantino, perfectly legitimately, feels aggrieved that his work was tampered with, though nothing seems to have been done underhand legally. The accusation of 'theft' may be just a careless remark, having far more emotive connotation than is the actuality – you cannot simply steal a screenplay, writers must sign a chain of title document, guaranteeing originality, executed before lawyers. This *was* done . . .

Tarantino and Bender put the release date of *Pulp Fiction* back so as not to coincide with *Natural Born Killers*, fearful that the press would lump the two films together. Unfortunately, for all concerned, Tarantino then proceeded to make some pretty disparaging remarks about Stone in the aforementioned *Premiere* article.

'He and I are pretty much at odds as far as our sensibilities and styles are concerned,' he said of Stone, adding that while Stone makes 'films', he makes 'movies'. 'I don't like to show things, I like things unexplained. He's obviously not into that. I would imagine that if Oliver Stone showed his movie to a thousand people and a thousand people didn't exactly get the point that he was trying to make, he would think he failed. To me the best thing about him is his energy. But his biggest problem is that his obviousness cancels out his energy and his energy pumps up his obviousness. He's Stanley Kramer with style.'

Although he held out an almost touchingly ridiculous olive branch by offering to play the Platoon board game with Stone, this did not prevent Stone's retort that he, as a filmmaker, was making films about a life he'd lived till his forties, Vietnam and all, but Tarantino was still making films about his twenties.

Stone reflects on that brief skirmish.

'I think the nature of the business is one of highly strung egos and hurt feelings, a combination of arrogance and hurt, but it's one thing to feel hurt and it's another thing to go to the press with it. There are newspaper accounts from here to Israel, France, Italy, Spain and now the US where he has attacked me and attacked the film without having seen it.

'The thing that you have to bear in mind is that I am a writer. I wrote five screenplays and each one of those five was, in one way or another, tampered with by directors, producers. I don't always agree, but I never went public. Whatever fights I had with Brian (De Palma) on *Scarface*, I never went public. There were times I was angry, but badmouth the movie? I never did that. The press gives us enough of a hard time as it is. Why then kick in and destroy the reputation of another artist, another filmmaker publicly? He's compared me with Stanley Kramer. Not only is that an insult to Kramer but that's an insult to me because he's assuming he has the knowledge to sum up another filmmaker's films. It's a terribly arrogant action. That's what movie critics do. It's something else when you make films and you respect the people who make them who understand the difficulties. He's done that to others, too. James Ivory, I've read the worst stuff he's said. I respect him very much, he's been through the mill and he's earned his stripes. For this guy to attack Stanley Kramer, to attack James Ivory, to attack me. He's extremely arrogant.'

Stone does not, either, like the accusation of being ambiguous.

'I find that very insulting. Anybody who's seen *Natural Born Killers*, because you can see, it's a highly subtle film that does not have one easily attributable message. It's a highly ambivalent film with many meanings and to say that about me is insulting and he has hurt my feelings because he hasn't experienced the nature of compromise in his life probably.'

No one can really tell if what Tarantino said really damaged *Natural Born Killers* as the film still took over $100 million world-wide, a very healthy performance. It has been suggested that the success of *Natural Born Killers* and the ensuing fracas between Tarantino and Stone even helped the performance of *Pulp Fiction*, though there is no evidence to prove this.

What is clear is that Tarantino not only made a $350,000 fee for the script but will continue to receive 50 per cent of the residuals ('I did okay,' says Tarantino).

'If you're noble about your intention, you should not take residuals,' says Stone. 'He's made a fortune on this film. More than he's probably ever made.'

Tarantino could, actually, have taken a pseudonym, which the Writers' Guild permits, and which might have avoided this mess altogether . . .

Natural Born Killers has since passed and the extraordinary acclaim for *Pulp Fiction* has since engulfed the dispute over Oliver Stone's film, which was a success in its own right.

There is a tendency for those who were once associated with someone who's riding high to bite the hand that once fed them, though this is not to suggest that this happened regarding Tarantino *vs* Murphy/ Hamsher. There is certainly no love lost between the parties, who are both bitter about matters for their own good reasons.

'Don and Jane certainly have a different view (to Tarantino) of the way things came down and it's so different that the grey area between them is vast,' says Craig Hamann.

Now that the dust has settled, though, Tarantino and Stone seem to have put it behind them. Stone, spiritedly, even offering to take up the invitation to play the Platoon board game.

'It's still a sore point, but I don't walk around thinking *Natural Born Killers, Natural Born Killers* until someone brings it up,' says Tarantino, quite indignantly. 'Oliver Stone? We're reconciled. Don Murphy? I don't have any blood between him good bad or otherwise, he doesn't even exist as far as I'm concerned. And as far as the movie is concerned? It's just over. The bottom line is, I don't care about it anymore.'

The popularly misconstrued villain of the piece, Oliver Stone, a veteran filmmaker, has probably been the voice of reason amid all the accusations and it is more than likely that had the same scenario occurred ten, or even five years down the line, level heads would not have let it blow up into such a storm.

While he can seemingly do no wrong, Tarantino has demonstrated ability to charm his way out of such situations and, though possessed of a very sharp mind, his personal lackadaisical approach has been enough to get him of the hook. Fortunately he still has the support of some good people who have stuck by him over the years.

Jaymes, his manager of ten years, was dismissed shortly after *Pulp Fiction*, though she will defend him to the bitter end.

'He was pretty funny about it because he simply said, "You know you've done a fabulous job. You've done such a fabulous job and I'm gonna be so big now, that I don't need you any more." Only Quentin would say something like that. It was really funny actually, he had me fired in the morning and called me in the afternoon to ask me to do him a favour.'

She believes that the *Natural Born Killers* affair was simply born out of too much too soon.

'Well, I think he thought he lost control of that. Quentin had a habit of . . . he has a highly selective memory and, you know, I used to have to deal with that. You know, he'd have one conversation with me and instruct me to stop an option on something and then I'd call the person and say, "I'm not gonna pursue this option," and then they'd say, "Quentin just called me and told me that I *could*." And then Quentin would call me back and say, "Cathryn, I've been thinking," and I'd say, "Oh no, he's been *thinking* again," because he'd change everything. I mean, even with *Reservoir Dogs*, I don't think, up to a certain point, he was cogniscent of the fact that it was really going to open up his career and what happened with *Natural Born Killers* is that he had signed a napkin agreement to give Rand the rights in perpetuity for like a minimal, minimal, minimal amount of money. I think what it really came down to was, just at a certain point, Quentin realized there was a buzz around town about *Reservoir Dogs* and the fact that his career was going to take off and he wanted to pull back in material he considered to be innately his own. Don and Jane were incredibly supportive of his wishes right from the start, I mean, were very respectful and went to great lengths to accommodate him and to check with him every step of the way.'

Of course, criticism will always be equated with jealousy at success, but unfortunately, Tarantino seems to have let this side slip on occasion. Until the Oscars, no one really knew, for example, the full extent of the part that Roger Avary had played in *Pulp Fiction*. Ironically Avary, who officially wrote the middle third of *Pulp Fiction* (and unofficially contributed to *True Romance* and *Natural Born Killers*), relinquished *his* screenplay right and settled for a story credit on that film. Avary, gentleman that he is, will not reveal beyond what is established fact and has remained tight-lipped, subsequently suffering the indignity of seeing his own film, *Killing Zoe* (executive produced by Tarantino), marketed more or less as a 'Tarantino film' (though this is not Tarantino's fault).

In January 1995, when Tarantino won the Golden Globe for Best Screenplay for *Pulp Fiction*, his first major award, he enthusiastically bounded to the stage and made an entertaining, if inebriated, speech to rapturous applause.

'I feel like an aunt or something, but I was ashamed of his behaviour,' says Jaymes, 'because not only did he not acknowledge the calibre of company in which he was nominated, he was oblivious to the *Forrest Gumps* and the *Shawshank Redemptions*. He didn't acknowledge Roger. He didn't acknowledge anybody really.'

Britain's *Mail on Sunday* suggested that there had been a heated altercation at that event between Tarantino and Avary's wife Gretchen, with her screaming at him to 'fuck off' after he had failed to acknowledge Avary in his speech.

'That's probably true,' says Avary, 'but then she kissed him and we all went out and hung out that evening.'

Tarantino has even tried to sell the screenplay publication rights to publishers Faber & Faber (who have printed the other Tarantino screenplays), forgetting that, after all of the above imbroglio, he doesn't actually own them.

It must be stressed that even those in his own camp who have been critical of Tarantino's role in the *Natural Born Killers* affair, with the exception of Don Murphy, speak highly of Tarantino as a filmmaker and indeed as a friend, though being perceived as a lovable shit-for-brains can wear thin after a while.

'You see Quentin's always been able to express himself so unabashedly without concern for the impact,' says Jaymes. 'What he does, he does. I have said to people, "I think he's a wonderful filmmaker but I think he ought to learn some manners." Just to be a little gracious to the people who really have been supportive of him. Sometimes it's just too much, you know.'

Perhaps it is fitting that it is *Natural Born Killers* – a film about the nature of celebrity – that has thrown this into sharp relief . . .

Chapter 7

Pulp Fiction

Pulp *n*.
1. A soft, moist, shapeless mass of matter.
2. A magazine or book containing lurid subject matter and being characteristically printed on rough, unfinished paper.

Soon after *Reservoir Dogs* had débuted at Sundance, Tarantino took off for Amsterdam, where he was to spend the best part of five months, on and off. It was the first time he'd ever been abroad.

As Clarence says to Alabama in the original script of *True Romance*, 'I been in America all my life. I'm due for a change. I wanna see what TV in other countries is like.'

There was no specific reason for choosing that city ('Some friends of mine had just been there and it seemed a cool sort of place') but any doubts were dispelled when he found out that there was a Howard Hawks festival playing there.

'One of those God things,' he says.

Thus in March 1992, two months before he unveiled *Reservoir Dogs* at Cannes, Tarantino flew to Holland, found himself an apartment, deliberately choosing one without a telephone, and cut himself off from all but the chosen few. Throughout the ensuing weeks he did what most people do in Amsterdam, hang out at hash bars and drink into the early hours of the morning. During the day he spent his time holed up in dingy cinemas, watching obscure French gangster films and also began a bout of voracious reading, consuming such books as *No Good from a Corpse* by Leigh Brackett and Anais Nin's diaries (is it a coincidence that in the film *Henry and June*, Anais Nin was played by Maria De Medeiros, opposite Uma Thurman?).

'I hung about and bummed around and everything and, to tell you the truth I, like, enjoyed living in Europe for the first time. It was just a great loaf time. I saw movies all the time and then in morning I'd just get up, take a book and go down by the canals.'

There was a reason for his sojourn, though, for without even having seen *Reservoir Dogs*, Stacey Sher, President of Jersey Films, had offered him nearly a million dollars to write and direct a second movie. This was based on the advice of her producing partner Danny De Vito, who, even before *Reservoir Dogs* had gone before the cameras, had liked that script so much that he urged they move fast and make a deal for Tarantino's next project.

Fuelled on his experiences in Amsterdam, Tarantino duly began writing that next script, *Pulp Fiction*, so-called because of the pulp novellas that were to be its inspiration, although unable to tackle the writing head-on as the *Reservoir Dogs* promotional machine began cranking in to motion in the wake of Cannes. The script wasn't to be finished for another year, with the final third completed while on the festival circuit.

With all this in mind, Vincent Vega and Jules Winnfield's opening exchange seems to make a lot of sense . . .

VINCENT
You know what the funniest thing about Europe is?

JULES
What?

VINCENT
It's the little differences. A lotta the same shit we got here, they got there, but there they're a little different.

JULES
Example?

VINCENT
Well, in Amsterdam, you can buy beer in a movie theatre. And I don't mean in a paper cup either. They give you a glass of beer, like in a bar. In Paris you can buy a beer at McDonald's. Also, you know what they call a Quarterpounder with Cheese in Paris?

JULES
They don't call it a Quarterpounder with Cheese?

VINCENT
No, they got the metric system there, they wouldn't know what the fuck a Quarterpounder is.

JULES
What'd they call it?

VINCENT
Royale with Cheese.

JULES (repeating)
Royale with Cheese. What'd they call a Big Mac?

VINCENT
Big Mac's a Big Mac, but they call it Le Big Mac.

JULES
What do they call a Whopper?

VINCENT
I don't know, I didn't go into Burger King . . .

Tarantino even invented a fantasy past for the character of Vincent – a quasi-autobiographical musing based on his Dutch adventure – in which Marsellus Wallace owned a club in Amsterdam, Vincent having been despatched there to run it for a while.

As mentioned in his construction of *Reservoir Dogs*, Tarantino has long coveted for filmmakers the freedom of expression that novelists have, with the liberty to not only play about with chronology but to allow characters to float in and out of different stories, often citing J.D. Salinger's 'Glass Family' stories as an example. This was the basis for *Pulp Fiction*.

'The idea, originally, was gonna be like three short stories, like the old *Black Mask* magazine,' he said as he finished writing. 'Raymond Chandler, Dashiell Hammett – a lot of their novels appeared first as short stories in magazines. It's not like that at all any more, but that was the jumping off point. It's three stories – they're interlinked, they all share the same characters. the same characters float in and out of the different stories.

'It's funny, because it's a weird situation right now. You know, as much as I love Don Siegel – and I would be very lucky to be as good as him – I just don't want to be the gun guy. I want to do many different types of movies. But I love the genre, I have a lot of respect for the genre and knowledge about it, so I like the idea of introducing myself with it and then I like the idea with my next movie, exploding it into smithereens which is what I intend to do.'

Pulp Fiction in its purest sense needs a little definition. It refers generally to the crime stories from the 1930s and 1940s, the cheap, garishly illustrated news-stand publications of which the aforementioned *Black Mask* was one – a hard-boiled world of footsore private investigators, two-bit hoods, corrupt cops and, of course, black widows. Dashiell Hammett, Cornell Woolrich, James M. Cain, W.R. Burnett and Raymond Chandler were all exponents of the art which, in turn, triggered the *films noirs* of the 1940s like *The Maltese Falcon*, *The Big Sleep* and *Double Indemnity*.

Whole books have been devoted to defining what actually *is* a *noir*, though through all the conjecture and categorizing, the critics can only agree on one thing – that it is a French term, applied to these American films in retrospect.

When the American *noirs* had run their course, the directors of the New Wave – Truffaut and, especially, Godard – reinvented the genre in the late 1950s and early 1960s with the likes of *À Bout de Souffle* and *Shoot the Piano Player*. They had shifted the settings to Paris and Marseilles and their work was the kind of fare Tarantino boned up on while in Amsterdam. Given the cyclic nature of cinema, the French *noirs*, too, had then faded, to be revived again by filmmakers such as Scorsese who had dipped into the *milieu* again in the early 1970s, manifest in 'Little Italy' films like *Mean Streets* and *Taxi Driver*, and also Roman Polanski with *Chinatown*.

The genre was, once again, ripe for revival, but Tarantino wanted to achieve something approximating the short story spirit of the original literature. He thus decided to use three main plot developments as the means to his end.

In fact, way before *Reservoir Dogs* even got off the ground, Roger

Avary remembers Tarantino sitting outside Stanley Margolis's office and talking about a fledgling project called *Black Mask*.

'After three years of trying to get *True Romance* made, the idea was to do three short films, just make them about a common theme,' says Avary.

Roger Avary: 'We kind of rushed everything together.'

'The stories would be the oldest chestnuts in the world. You've seen 'em a zillion times, alright – the guy who's supposed to take out the boss's lady, "but don't touch her"; the boxer who supposed to throw the fight but doesn't; and the third story is kind of like the opening five minutes of every Joel Silver movie – two hitmen go and kill somebody. We hang out with those two hitmen for the whole rest of the morning and we see what else happens. I love the idea that each of these characters could be the star of their own movie and, as far as they're concerned, when they come in, they are.'

However, in the beginning, those stories were yet to be determined. As rookie writer/directors, Tarantino was going to write one story, Avary a second and then someone else would be brought in to complete the trilogy.

'But we never really found the third guy,' says Avary.

Thus Tarantino took on the third story himself. The name of the project became, tentatively, *Pulp Fiction* and, while the first story revolved around a couple of hitmen, the third instalment became a tale of a bungled jewellery heist. This became too big a proposition to be contained within an anthology, so Tarantino went off and turned it into *Reservoir Dogs*.

As a project, *Pulp Fiction* languished, and Avary expanded his contribution, a story about a boxer who refuses to throw a fight, into a full-length script called *Pandemonium Reigns*.

'When Quentin had done *Reservoir Dogs*, he called me up and said, "Roger, they're offering me all these different projects, but the one thing I gotta do is *Pulp Fiction*." And I said, "Great, go to it." So we went back and we got *Pandemonium Reigns* and we squashed it back down and it became *The Gold Watch*. We took a scene that I had written for *True Romance* and that had been written out of the script (about someone's head being blown off inside a car) and things that Quentin had written for other movies and we just kind of rushed everything together.'

'We got together in Amsterdam and mostly the middle story is mine,' explains Avary. 'It was funny because Kit Carson once said that for Quentin he was waiting, he was waiting, he was waiting for the evil to arrive and, I don't know, I guess that meant me. I guess I'm the one that comes up with the really diseased stuff and Quentin comes up with the funny stuff.

'When I sit down and write I just let the movie unfold before me. Sometimes it doesn't unfold very well, sometimes you walk into the darkest recesses of your mind and that's the joy of writing, that's what makes it fun – all of a sudden they're bringing out The Gimp and then they start butt-fucking. Where does that come from? I have no idea. I'm a really normal nice guy. This stuff just spills out of my head. There are two things you can do, you can either censor yourself or you can walk down that path and see where it goes and I prefer to walk down that path.'

However, Avary needed money and fast. 'Marriage was one of the reasons and the other was to go to Cannes and get *Killing Zoe* made.'

He thus sold his interest to Tarantino for the Writers' Guild minimum up front and settled for a 'story' credit. The official billing is therefore as follows: Written and directed by Quentin Tarantino; stories by Quentin Tarantino and Roger Avary.

'There is no defined rule,' says Avary by way of explanation. 'The Writers' Guild may tell you that there is, but there is no defined rule as to what it does or doesn't mean. That's like asking what does an associate producer credit mean. Sometimes, you know, it's Michael Douglas's brother, who hangs around a lot and doesn't really have anything to do, so they give him credit on the film. In this case it was the deal that was offered to me that I took.'

Until Avary, too, received an Oscar for his troubles, there had been some doubt as to the extent of his contribution to the overall picture, with a swell of media opinion suggesting that Avary had almost been duped out of his share of the credit. As with the furore over *Natural Born Killers*, the end result is that everything is legally sound and done by consent. While such stories were circulating, Avary was out of the country for several months and not available to set the record straight.

'Any decision that I made, I made under counsel, with attorneys and with agents,' he explains. 'It was ultimately my decision and made of clear mind and body and I certainly, especially at this point, don't regret anything I've done. Even before I got the Oscar, I didn't regret what happened because the certain sacrifices that I made enabled me to get *Killing Zoe* made. I didn't want to be a writer my whole life, I wanted to be a writer/director and so now I find myself in a very good position and even if I *hadn't* won the Oscar I'd still find myself in a very good position. It just means now I can make a little bit more money doing what I like. There *is* no bad blood. If there was, it was probably inflated by the press or maybe created to make a good story.'

That credit came on the night of 27 March 1995 when the Academy decided to give Oscars for Best Original Screenplay to both Tarantino *and* Avary, though Avary and his attorney still had to fight to get a mention in the Miramax press thank-yous ('He [Tarantino] probably felt I didn't deserve it,' says Avary), a confusion fuelled by the fact that, at some of the awards ceremonies in which *Pulp Fiction* was honoured, both Tarantino *and* Avary received the prize for Best Screenplay jointly, such as at the LA Critics' Awards and the BAFTAs. At others, like the Golden Globes, it had been Tarantino on his own, a decision purely up to the awarding body.

'Roger wrote a script that I wanted to use, so I bought it from him,' Tarantino told the *Los Angeles Times*, rather matter-of-factly. 'Then I came up with all the other ideas and characters and so I adapted his screenplay the way you would adapt a book. But having said that, I don't want Roger getting credit for monologues. *I* write the monologues. There is only one scene that has pure Roger dialogue, that's the scene in the bathroom where Bruce explains everything he's going to do. I love that scene. I suppose Roger has little lines interspersed throughout that story, but that's the only full-on Roger scene.'

'There *were* parts that were used verbatim, there *were* parts that were changed because we had to fit in the other stories,' counters Avary. 'For instance, there was one thing that Quentin changed on me that I was actually mad about. Originally the girl in the hotel room [Fabienne], her name was Christine and she was an American girl. Quentin changed it to a French girl and that was a little too close to home for me, but for the most part it's pretty much the same.'

Nonetheless, with Avary's collaboration, two stories were in the bag, and with various false starts on the final instalment, Tarantino decided to return to Jules and Vincent to see what happens to them *after* they'd executed the yuppies. This is the chapter that became The Bonnie Situation and, thus, *Pulp Fiction* as we know it, was born . . .

Like *Reservoir Dogs* before it, the whole business of mounting *Pulp Fiction* was very much premeditated. Even when *Reservoir Dogs* was playing at Sundance in January 1992, Tarantino and Bender were on the verge of signing a deal for what looked like being their first major studio picture. Stacey Sher, Danny De Vito and Michael Shamberg's Jersey Films had a production deal with Bender and Tarantino's newly formed A Band Apart which entailed providing them with the initial financing and office facilities, etc., in return for Jersey getting partnership and the chance to tout the project to the studios. Because Jersey Films had a 'first look' deal with TriStar and were based at that studio (i.e. TriStar would get the first option on the project), it was assumed that TriStar would more than likely pick up the film.

Tarantino and Bender had roughed up their plan of attack long ago while at Monte Hellman's house as the various components were being assembled for *Reservoir Dogs*. They had gone there for the simple reason that Hellman had a computer and they, up until that point, had been doing all their budgeting by hand.

'The plan was basically this,' explains Bender. 'We both agreed that *Dogs* was a great script and that if Quentin could direct, just do a decent job, then we thought we'd probably be able to get a second movie. Before that second movie, we wanted to win at Sundance and we were hoping that, because of that, Miramax would pick us up and we could get into Cannes and then Miramax would release *Dogs* in the fall.'

Apart from winning at Sundance, everything went according to the letter, though there was enough of a buzz created at Sundance for the deviation not to matter that much. *Reservoir Dogs* still emerged as the most-talked-about movie of that festival, even though it came away empty-handed.

'The main thing was that we get to direct a second movie and the second movie should be six to eight million dollars and a similar genre. We were gonna make a bigger movie, but we didn't want to chop off more than we could handle. We didn't want to go ahead and make a $40- or $50-million movie. That seemed kind of stupid. Not that we were being presumptuous, but the next step was to make something reasonable. We had a philosophy that we were gonna make it as inexpensive as possible because no matter what, even if it only moderately succeeded, we'd feel like a success because everyone's made their money back. And, if we received some critical acclaim, we'd be successful. You *could* have made *Pulp* for $25 million. It would still have been successful, of course, but it would be much more of a moderate success than the huge success that it is now.'

When Tarantino had finished the script in January 1993, it was kept under lock and key, the pages all code numbered. It was duly budgeted out at about eight and a half million. However, because it required an ensemble cast, this meant that there wouldn't be a great deal for the actors (whoever they may be) once the pot had been shared out. Harvey

Keitel assured them that as long as they were perceived as being fair *vis à vis* the actors, they would still get the cast they required.

Continues Bender, 'I had to come up with a way that there was an equity amongst everybody, a parity amongst thieves, so that everyone felt they were being treated fairly. Each actor got the same amount of money per week. If it was three weeks, you got three times 'x'. If it was one week, you got one times 'x', and so what I did, I took the total number of weeks that people worked and divided it by the amount of money I had left and, honestly, we could probably have got away with paying everybody half of that. They still would have been interested in doing it. That's sort of our theory about how to work with people. Within that budget we did as much as we could, but the thing is, we tried to put so much on the screen that it's hard to pay everyone a lot.'

The trick had worked with *Reservoir Dogs*, a $1.5-million movie which had been made to look like something worth five times that amount. *Pulp Fiction* by comparison, at $8.5 million (still very very modest), looks worth at least $25 million. To put it in perspective, Bruce Willis's salary for *Die Hard 2* was more than the entire budget of *Pulp Fiction*.

'This is supposed to be an epic,' said Tarantino. 'An epic in structure, an epic in scope, in intention. An epic in everything but budget.'

As *Reservoir Dogs* had already made $3 million back when it came time to sorting out the nitty-gritty on *Pulp Fiction*, things looked very shipshape. Unfortunately, in June 1993, TriStar and, subsequently, every other major studio, passed on the film (TriStar, for the record, also passed on Jersey's *Reality Bites*).

'The excuse that they gave us when we brought them the movie was that it was too violent,' says Danny De Vito, 'I always though of it as a comedy when I read it, but they'd never seen anything like it. When I read it I was laughing my head off, I said, "Either this is brilliant or I'm the sickest man you ever met in your life." '

The rights thus reverted to Tarantino and A Band Apart invited bids from the independents.

Tarantino is far less diplomatic about the reluctance of the majors.

'I had a deal with them (TriStar, via Jersey Films) and they paid me a lot of money to look at the script, but I made it into the deal that even though I got paid a lot of money to show them the script and give them first crack at it, they never owned it until the greenlight (the official go-ahead). I said, "Look, when I write this, I want to do it. I don't want it sittin' around on some fuckin' shelf, and so if they're not gonna do it, *I'm* gonna make it. They can fuckin' climb aboard or fuckin' get out of the way." They got out of the way and it actually ended up working out great for all of us.'

Amongst an independent field, which included Lumière Pictures and Majestic Film and Television, Miramax once again led the way. By this time Miramax had been bought up by Disney and so had the financial muscle to take care of business. Importantly, Richard Gladstein, who had been so instrumental in setting up *Reservoir Dogs*, had moved there from Live. Miramax, too, had had great success in distributing *The Crying Game* and *The Piano*, both small arthouse films which they had shrewdly marketed as if they were major releases. A deal was duly signed and *Pulp Fiction* became the first film to be fully financed by Miramax.

It also gained a unique distinction, passing into legend as the very first Disney film to feature anal rape.

'I think Walt'd probably get a big kick out of it, actually,' chuckles Tarantino. 'Not the anal sex *per se*, but the whole movie.'

As the summer rolled on and with shooting due to start on 20 September, casting began in earnest and an interesting ad appeared in the 25 August edition of the *Hollywood Reporter*:

Jersey Films' *Pulp Fiction*, which starts shooting in September, is looking for James Dean, Donna Reed, Elvis and M.M. lookalikes . . .

'Good actors don't intimidate me,' declared Tarantino as the process of sifting through the resumés began. 'Bad actors do because they can only be so good.'

There was never any question as to whether he'd assemble a top-notch cast.

Says Lawrence Bender, 'From *Reservoir Dogs* I think everyone saw how acting is very much part of the movie and everyone in the acting community felt that Quentin was very good with actors, so with *Pulp Fiction* we had a huge response.'

The script, with its huge chunks of meaty dialogue, again proved an incentive.

John Travolta as Vincent Vega: 'By his mid-thirties, . . . lost in Hollywood's interstellar void.'

Tarantino had actually written the script with certain actors in mind. The Young Man (who after a couple of pages becomes Pumpkin) was billed as having 'a slight working-class English accent'. This was obviously Tim Roth. Tarantino had once seen Roth and Amanda Plummer together at some function or other. Thus Pumpkin's paramour, Honey Bunny, was ordained.

More importantly, though, the lead character was written for Michael Madsen. It was to be Vic Vega once again rather than Vincent, his brother. As the summer approached, however, Madsen had opted to do Wyatt Earp instead. Tarantino subsequently flirted with the idea of Daniel Day-Lewis but passed. His solution was a bold one.

Looking at the film now it is difficult imagine anyone other than Travolta in the part of Vincent Vega, the heroin-befuddled killer – charming, philosophical, but careless enough to leave his machine gun lying around in the kitchen. A man who can accidentally blow the head off an innocent party but is worried more that the spilt brains have messed up his suit.

Pulp Fiction has since propelled Travolta to an Oscar nomination for the part, restoring his credibility and recovering his status as a film icon.

'What happened at Cannes was surprise that my performance was getting that kind of reaction,' says Travolta. 'It startled me a little bit and I was moved by it emotionally, by the journalists' reaction to my performance. I was touched by everyone's reverence towards it.'

Consider, though, that in the summer of 1993, Travolta's career was very much on the slide, a far cry from the days of *Saturday Night Fever* and *Grease* when he was *the* hot leading man in Hollywood.

As Michael Eisner, the head of Disney, described him in the late 1970s, 'He is the biggest star in the world bar none.'

Oscar-nominated in his first leading role, for *Saturday Night Fever*, he had assumed that was simply the way it was every year.

'When you're young and something big like that happens, you think, "Well, I'll do the best I can and it will be rewarded properly," and then you realize that it takes sometimes a very unique script and experience to get the attention of the critics and the Academy.'

After a series of bad career choices – he turned down the leading roles in both *An Officer and a Gentlemen* and *Splash!* – Travolta was languishing in the doldrums.

'In his early twenties Travolta was, by many magnitudes, the biggest star on earth,' says Martin Amis. 'By his mid-thirties Travolta was simply a human vacuum, lost in Hollywood's interstellar void.'

The *Look Who's Talking* films had proved big box office, his days as a serious screen actor were very much over (take a look at the gratuitous dance number he did in *Look Who's Talking Too*).

As Tarantino told *Vanity Fair*, 'As much as I like John Travolta, I couldn't bring myself to watch some fucking talking baby movie.'

Nonetheless, a big fan of Travolta Tarantino most certainly was. Tarantino always places Brian De Palma's 1981 film, *Blow Out*, of which Travolta was the star, in the top three of his (ever changing) list of top ten films of all time, along with the other two consistents, *Taxi Driver* and *Rio Bravo*.

'He is one of the very best American film actors around,' says Tarantino. 'He was awesome in *Blow Out*. I used to watch that film over and over and wonder why the other directors weren't using him.'

Tarantino had always had it in mind to approach Travolta for a part in a future project and so contacted him on the Vancouver set of *Look Who's Talking Now* with an eye to perhaps taking a part in *From Dusk Till*

Dawn, the vampire script that he still had up his sleeve. As the two got talking, he invited Travolta to Los Angeles for further discussions and by a remarkable twist of fate, it turned out that the West Hollywood apartment that Tarantino lives in was the very same one that Travolta had rented when he first arrived in Hollywood in 1974. As Tarantino said of Hollywood with regard to *True Romance*, it's a small town.

Visiting Tarantino's cramped and cluttered home, Travolta, who has a twenty-bedroom chateau in Maine, a fly-in home in Florida and three fully operational passenger jets at his disposal, found himself face-to-face with what was almost a little shrine devoted to him on the mantel-piece, including a little Vinnie Barbarino doll from *Welcome Back Kotter*, the TV series that had launched Travolta's career, and various other bits of memorabilia. Travolta indulged him by playing a couple of his extensive collection of board games – including *Grease* and *Welcome Back Kotter*. Travolta won both and Tarantino insisted he sign the boxes. Travolta was touched.

'They're very stupid games,' laughs Travolta. 'How do you *play* the *Grease* game? But there is a game, as silly as it is. It was a very funny meeting.'

Amid all the male bonding, Tarantino decided that he had now found his Vincent Vega. Tarantino carried on writing with Travolta now in mind and when it was all wrapped up, he sent him the finished piece.

'After meeting John, I kept thinking of him whenever I was writing,' reflects Tarantino. 'When I finished, I called him and said, "I'm sending you something. Look at Vincent." '

'It was an amazing script,' remembers Travolta. 'Beyond clever, it was alive and unique and real. I thought, "I would love to do this character, but there is no way in hell they're going to let me." '

He nevertheless agreed and, although Tarantino was thrilled, the decision to cast Travolta was not greeted with universal joy. In fact, it was one of the reasons that TriStar had trepidations about the movie. Even Lawrence Bender had his doubts initially.

'You can get anybody in the world, why do you want John Travolta?' he asked at the time.

Tarantino stuck by his guns and insisted that it was Travolta or nothing. He got his way.

'I didn't have to convince him of anything,' Travolta has said.

'Quentin not only remembered me from all the films he'd seen growing up, but he believed in me. But he also had to do some fast talking to get me in. Basically, he told the producers he wouldn't do the movie unless I was part of it.'

In fact, so keen to do the movie was Travolta that his fee for the film didn't even cover his expenses, choosing as he did to locate to a more pricey hotel than the one originally prescribed.

Perhaps a line that Bruce Willis's Butch Coolidge uses in the Gold Watch section of the film sums up Travolta's pre-*Pulp* predicament best of all.

'I'm an American, our names don't mean shit . . .'

The casting of Bruce Willis was again another stroke of good fortune, the celebrated action hero wonderfully sending up his image with a role as a sort of Hemingway-inspired heroic loser.

Willis, as it happens, was a big fan of *Reservoir Dogs* and would quite happily while away the hours quoting the dialogue back and forth with his brothers. More importantly, Willis also has a house on the same Malibu beach as Harvey Keitel and their kids would frequently play

Bruce Willis as Butch Coolidge: 'A sort of Hemingway-inspired heroic loser.'

153

together. Keitel had asked Tarantino and Bender over to lunch one weekend.

Explains Willis, 'Harvey said, "You know, he's getting ready to do another film. Come over to the house tomorrow and I'll introduce you." I got hold of the script, I read the script and I volunteered.'

'Quentin and Bruce took a walk on the beach and that was sort of it because Quentin is a big Bruce Willis fan, just a *big* fan,' says Bender.

The mutual admiration society paid dividends, though, as Bender stresses, in a film like *Pulp Fiction*, it's as much about chemistry and interaction – a team performance – as it is star quality.

'The thing is, there are a lot of actors who are interested in working with Quentin and we did get to talk to really a lot of wonderful actors. What we were trying to do was find the group that really made the most sense because it's an ensemble piece. It's gotta be right because John is with Sam and John is with Uma and then John is with Eric, who's with Rosanna. There is a lot of interplay.'

Other actors soon fell into place, including Sam Jackson, for whom the part of Jules had been written specifically, though, as had happened with *Reservoir Dogs*, he very nearly missed the boat. This was due to confusion over the nature of his audition. Because the part had been written for him, Jackson assumed that he was merely being called in for a reading. Head to head with another actor who *had* done his homework for the part, the odds were not in Jackson's favour, a source of professional embarrassment for both he and Bender as they were both working together on Boaz Yakin's *Fresh* at the time.

'Nobody told me I had to *audition*,' he explains, 'and so this other actor and I had to show up on a Sunday in LA and audition for the film again. Meanwhile, I did all the stuff I was supposed to do, figured out how I wanted to be and how I wanted to approach it and the rest is history . . . but I almost didn't get it.'

'Sam came in and fucking knocked us off our feet,' enthuses Bender, somewhat relieved.

The biggest problem, though, came with finding the right actress to play Mia Wallace. Tarantino, up to this point, was not noted for writing strong female characters. Women were virtually non-existent in *Reservoir Dogs* and *True Romance*'s Alabama, the fluorescent rookie hooker, never overtly dictated the course of that film. *Natural Born Killers*' Mallory was another one half of a couple, never seen beyond the context of Mickey, and, though an extremely strong personality, was far from subtle. Mia was a different dish altogether.

'Probably my favourite character I've ever written is Mia,' explains Tarantino. 'One of the things I liked about her was I didn't know where she came from, she just kind of like sprung up. She goes on that date with Vincent and she sits down in that booth. All of a sudden she starts talking and this kind of intense personality and rhythm of speech and way of talking and sense of humour and complete contradictions start coming out of her. I had a good idea where I was going with it but I'm kind of watching the movie unfold as I'm writing it. I could never write a scene and then come back to it, I have to write it in a straight line, like pac man, because everything was leading up to a point where Mia sits down on the other end of the table at Jack Rabbit Slim's and starts talking. I knew no more about Mia than Vincent did. All I knew were the rumours and the innuendo. She was Marsellus's wife and she might be a black widow. All I knew was what Vincent knew because the film was from Vincent's perspective. By the end I knew Mia backwards and forwards but I *didn't* know what she looked like.'

'We were meeting with lots of different people and Quentin didn't know if he wanted an Italian woman, an English woman, a black woman – he didn't have a clue,' remembers Bender.

Holly Hunter, Meg Ryan, Alfre Woodard and Meg Tilly were all up for the part but it was while in New York, on a recruiting drive that landed Ving Rhames (says Bender, 'He gave us one of the best auditions I've ever seen'), that Tarantino met Uma Thurman. The two of them went out to dinner.

'When we were flying back to LA I could see in his eyes it was Uma,' laughs Bender. 'It was pretty clear at that moment that Uma and Quentin wanted to work with each other, but Uma was a little gun-shy at that point in her career. Quentin was sure, but he didn't quite want to say yes. But *he* knew and *I* knew that she was the one. Between the two of them it was like who would say yes first. It was like a relationship – one was afraid to commit to the other first in case the other would say no. It was like this slow dance, the two of them.'

It is perhaps Eric Stoltz, who plays Lance the dealer, who has the best handle on Tarantino's ponderous method of casting.

Uma Thurman as Mia Wallace: 'Probably my favourite
character I've ever written.'

'We went to this little Thai restaurant and ate and talked about films.
Then we went to his apartment and played music and talked about our
past girlfriends and how we associated certain films with certain times
in our lives and *then* we talked about *Pulp*. I volunteered some ideas, he
told me where Lance came from and then showed me the great
Christopher Walken/Dennis Hopper scene from *True Romance*. We just
hung out and talked and the next day he asked me to do the role. After
he'd cast the film, he invited us all out to a great Japanese restaurant and
we all ate and hung around and told stories. It was a cool feeling. I had a
sense then that he'd assembled a wild, woolly bunch. It's really the best
way to cast a film. I'm going to try to do it that way from now on
because, basically, you want a cast and crew that you're gonna want to
hang out with and the only way to determine that is to hang out with
them.'

And, of course, the wild, woolly bunch all worked for an equal slice
of the pie.

'Everybody did. Everybody made the same grade,' chuckles Sam
Jackson. 'At least that's what they tell me . . .'

Sam Jackson, John Travolta, Bruce Willis and Uma Thurman:
'. . . a wild, woolly bunch.'

Tarantino managed to get most of the crew from *Reservoir Dogs* back together for *Pulp Fiction*.

'It was like a homecoming,' says Bender.

This time, though, it was no nervous *débutant* at the helm and the use of the same key figures, established industry names who had worked on *Reservoir Dogs* for peanuts, certainly made for a smooth ride. These included cinematographer Andrzej Sekula (who was involved in a bad car accident during production and filmed many scenes from a wheelchair), editor Sally Menke, costume designer Betsy Heimann and, once again, David and Sandy Wasco as production designer and set decorator. As with *Reservoir Dogs*, they used locations in the more unglamorous parts of LA, such as the Echo Park area where Lance's house was found. Like its predecessor, *Pulp Fiction* begins (and ends) in a diner, the Hawthorne Grill in west LA.

Diner culture is very important to Tarantino. Even when the action is not set in a coffee shop or eatery there are constant references being made to junk food – Jules and Vincent, of course, discuss the differences between burgers in America and Europe, Clarence in *True Romance* has a preference for chilli dogs and always goes for pie after a trip to the movies and, in the midst of The Gold Watch crisis, Fabienne is preoccupied with blueberry pancakes, and Marsellus goes to fetch a take-away from Teriyaki Donut. And who can forget the Kahuna burger?

There is also the extremely important matter of coffee (to wit, Mr Pink), always taken with 'lots of cream and lots of sugar' (to get particularly anal, Fabienne, the one Continental European in *Pulp Fiction*, is the only person to take it black) . . .

JULES
Goddamn Jimmie, this is some serious gourmet shit. Me an' Vincent woulda been satisfied with freeze-dried Taster's Choice. You spring this gourmet fuckin' shit on us. What flavour is this?

JIMMIE
Knock it off, Julie.

JULES
What?

JIMMIE

I'm not corn on the cob, so you can stop butterin' me up. I don't need
you to tell me how good my coffee is. I'm the one who buys it, I know
how fuckin' good it is. When Bonnie goes shoppin', she buys shit. I
buy the gourmet expensive stuff 'cause when I drink it, I wanna taste
it. But what's on my mind at this moment isn't the coffee in my
kitchen, it's the dead nigger in my garage . . .

Says Tarantino, 'The thing is in America . . . fuck America . . . in Los
Angeles, it's very much a thing where life and socialness revolves
around restaurants. Whether you're making 10,000 or 310,000 a year,
you want to get together with friends it's, "Let's get together and get
something to eat." In England they say, "Let's go get a pint." Here, it's
"Let's have breakfast, let's have lunch, let's have dinner, let's go get a
piece of pie." You know, dates happen around food, friends happen
around food. The thing is there are all these different characters, but
they're all ultimately me. They all like coffee shops and drink coffee
with cream and sugar.'

But there is one diner to eclipse them all and that is Jack Rabbit Slim's,
the one set extravagance that Tarantino allowed himself on *Pulp Fiction*.
The Wascos should take a lot of credit for this as it only cost $150,000 to
put together (it would have cost in excess of a million in a big studio picture), constructed in a warehouse in Culver City.

It was built exactly as scripted . . .

In the past six years, 50s diners have sprung up all over LA, giving
Thai restaurants a run for their money. They're all basically the same.
Décor out of an 'Archie comic book', golden oldies constantly playing,
emanating from a bubbly Wurlitzer, saucy waitresses in bobby socks,
menus with items like the Fats Domino cheeseburger or the Wolfman
Jack omelette, and over prices that pay for all this bullshit.

But then there's Jack Rabbit Slim's, the big mama of the 50s diners. Either the best or the worst, depending on your point of view . . .

Jack Rabbit Slim's was actually based on the post-war Atomic-age
Googy-style diners that are very particular to LA and was choc-full of
filmic kitsch according to Tarantino's specifications – stock footage on

the walls, cars as booths, the waiters and waitresses dressed as icons from the 1950s and a huge speedometer as the dance floor. It is also not dissimilar to an actual LA diner called Ed Debevic's.

As with all of Tarantino's references, it was citing specific movie examples that enabled the set to come together.

'That was his best way to describe what he wanted,' says Wasco. 'He'd say, "Please go and look at these two movies, *Red Line 7000* by Howard Hawks, which has a club in it, and this Elvis Presley movie *Speedway*, which also had as a club scene in it. It had automobiles that were cut in half with little tables in them. *That*'s how I want this to look." '

In addition, in accordance with Tarantino's Roger Corman fetish and as a little something for the movie buffs, the walls of Jack Rabbit Slim's were emblazoned with posters from his movies, including *Machine-Gun Kelly* (starring another favourite, Charles Bronson) and *The Young Racers* (the film on which a young Francis Ford Coppola worked as a sound man).

It is perhaps some testament to Jack Rabbit Slim's that one company actually tried to franchise it for a real-life chain of eateries.

The Culver City warehouse also housed the production offices and thus, during post-production, Tarantino could merrily stroll back and forth between his desk and a labyrinth of other sets built on the same site, such as Butch and Fabienne's motel room, the apartment room where Vincent and Jules blow away the young men, the boxing dressing room, the back room of the Mason Dixon pawn shop and its adjoining 'Russell's room' where The Gimp is kept (an in-joke, Russell being one of Quentin's friends).

The Gimp, played by Steve Hibbert, was kitted out after Sandy Reynolds-Wasco had failed to find any suitably cheap attire for him by trawling LA's sex shops. S and M, apparently, comes at a price.

'The propmaster, his sister went to an AA meeting and there was this guy there who produced bondage movies,' she remarks of a chain of coincidence that could only ever possibly happen in LA. 'So I called him up and went down to all his sets and things. He rented me all this stuff, so it was much cheaper.'

The Gimp, of course, is the ultimate nightmare after walking through a perceptibly harmless real-life pawn shop, layered with sight gags like

Southern state licence plates mounted on the wall. Wasco even wanted the Gimp's box and cage to be smaller than they were, but the end result is still one that makes Tarantino laugh every time.

'Hahaha. Well one of the fun things about watching that with an audience is like we're laughing at their expense. You're expecting the worst and, all of a sudden, they see that and they go, "Oh God, this is even worse than I thought." '

Beyond the obvious, though, it is the little customized props which give the film it own distinct style – the Fruit Brute cereal box that Lance eats from *was* real, though the line was discontinued in 1974 (he eats Fruit Loops instead) but others were created purely for the film, like Zed's keyring, the Bad Motherfucker wallet, the Red Apple cigarettes (Vincent, fresh from Amsterdam, rolls Drum), Ringside boxing gloves, the Big Kahuna Burger wrappers and Tim Roth's Hawaiian shirt, the latter two incorporating the motif from the film poster for *The Endless Summer* (a surfer standing next to his board) . . .

Tarantino, who grew up in a surfing community, openly hates anything to do with surfers or surfing (he once declared that surfers didn't

Tarantino directs Maria De Medeiros: 'Preoccupied with blueberry pancakes.'

161

deserve the film *Big Wednesday*). He does get in a dig at surfers by putting Jules and Vincent in some ridiculous beachwear ('They look like a couple of dorks,' says Jimmie), but it is strange, then, that a surfing theme runs throughout the movie – the Hawaiian-style Kahuna burgers, the shirts, the motifs and, most importantly, on the film's soundtrack. This includes the twangy guitar virtuosity of The Centurians, The Tornadoes and, most impressively in the film's buzzsaw opening number, 'Misirlou', by Dick Dale and his Del-Tones.

'It's like surf music, I've always like loved that but, for me, I don't know what surf music has to *do* with surf boards,' says Tarantino. 'To me it just sounds like rock and roll, even Morricone music. It sounds like rock and roll Spaghetti Western music, so that's how I kind of laid it in.'

The soundtrack is not that one-dimensional. The rest of it is an amalgam of funk, folk and rock and roll spanning five decades. Interestingly, one of the songs Tarantino tried to use was 'My Sharona' by The Knack, specifically as the backbeat for the anal rape scene (it was scripted as The Judds). The owners of that song preferred to have it used in *Reality Bites*. Thus, instead of the sodomization of Ving Rhames, 'My Sharona' will be remembered for Winona Ryder and Ethan Hawke bopping around a supermarket. That was probably a wise decision.

In a pattern set before it by *Good Morning Vietnam* and *The Fisher King*, the MCA albums to both *Reservoir Dogs* and *Pulp Fiction* also feature chunks of dialogue, something that is becoming an increasing trend for soundtrack releases and such has been the impact of the albums, both big sellers, that Tarantino now gets besieged with demo tapes from bands who want their songs to be used in his films. His films, too, in a strange way, have been reflected in music, the late Kurt Cobain thanking Tarantino on the sleeve notes to Nirvana's *In Utero*.

Indeed, Tarantino takes the use of music very seriously and the tracks for both films have been painstakingly selected.

As with *Reservoir Dogs*, the music is largely source. Whereas on that film, a radio station, K-BILLY's Super Sounds of the 70s, was the justification for most of it, in *Pulp Fiction*, the music comes from car stereos, radios, PA systems and records . . . but *never* CDs (another one of Tarantino's bugbears). Even Mia Wallace, in her hi-tech Hollywood Hills home, still uses a tape machine.

Explains Tarantino, 'One of the hooks that I use when I'm trying to

On the set with Bruce Willis, Maria De Medeiros and Lawrence Bender:
'As much about chemistry and interaction as it is star quality.'

find the personality of a movie, even if it's a story I might do in three years from now, is to find a song that could be a good representation of the movie. I might not end up using that song, but it really helps me find the personality of it. One of the things is in *Pulp Fiction*, I didn't use a score. I'm always intimidated by that. If I could write the score I would, but I can't. I'm always afraid I won't like what *they* write and that will just waste a lot of time and a lot of money, so I kind of like to pick the music specifically myself, like the use of "Son of a Preacher Man" when Vincent Vega comes to Mia Wallace's house. I don't know why, but that song, just from the moment I conceived the scene, I always saw him entering the house to that piece of music. And then for the twist sequence, I've always thought of Chuck Berry's "Never Can Tell". That was the whole rhythm of how I wanted them to move and how I wanted the scene to feel.'

On a trip to London in 1992, Tarantino had also visited a second-hand record store and picked up a record by a band called Urge Overkill. On the B-side was a cover of a Neil Diamond song, 'Girl You'll Be A Woman'. It was the visualization of Uma Thurman dancing to this,

163

slinking around in the manner of Anna Karina in *Vivre Sa Vie*, that convinced him ultimately to cast her.

'When you put the two together,' sighs Tarantino, 'you're *really* experiencing a movie moment.'

Tarantino wrapped *Pulp Fiction*'s movie moments on 30 November 1993 . . .

Chapter 8

The Mantelpiece

15 May 1994, the Cannes Film Festival. Another party. In a marquee on the beach of Cannes' famously opulent Carlton Hotel, hundreds of the festival faithful indulge in the nightly frenzy of hedonism that tops off the daily haze of screenings, interviews, press conferences, million dollar deals and, for a large part of the young filmmakers who've staked everything on getting a film off the ground, heartbreak. The Boulevard of Broken Dreams isn't in Hollywood, it's in the South of France – the Croisette, the broad sweep of promenade that skirts the azure blue of the Mediterranean; a catwalk for the Riviera set, whose chosen few sit behind the night lights of the yachts that twinkle in the bay. An unobtainable wealth, distanced by half a mile of sea and a great deal more of reality.

When *Reservoir Dogs* played here two years before, it came in with a whimper. *Pulp Fiction*'s bite would be even louder than its bark.

As a Euro pop dirge churns out from the speakers and a mass of bodies heaves to and fro, Tarantino and Meg Tilly, star of *Sleep with Me*, stake out their own little area of dance floor and conduct a private freeform show. Whether it's drink, jet lag or maybe something else, their self-induced trance renders their movements at odds with the relentless beat. Tarantino has only arrived in town today, but excitement at his presence is already at fever pitch. By Wednesday the full *Pulp Fiction* bandwagon will have hit town. Five days later and Tarantino will have won the Palme d'Or.

Lawrence Bender is still marked by the madness that surrounded the film's Cannes première.

'When John and Bruce and Uma and Sam and Maria flew in it was like, "Look out man." It was like *The Wild Bunch* and all of a sudden everything started becoming *very* exciting for us. And when we screened the movie, let me tell you, Quentin had never been in this much limelight, though maybe John Travolta and Bruce Willis had at points in their career. We get dressed up and we have our dinner and shit and there were twenty-five cars. They basically closed down the Croisette and it took us a half hour to get from the Carlton to the Palais and it was wild. There were thousands and thousands of people cheering Quentin and all the stars. Extraordinary. It's quite scary if you haven't seen that many people before.'

Jostled by crowds and surrounded by monkey-suited bouncers, the *Pulp Fiction* posse slowly eased their way up the grand staircase to the Palais, a French-accented chant of 'Quen-*tin*, Quen-*tin*' ringing in their ears. For John Travolta and Sam Jackson, it was the first time they had seen the movie.

'I was sitting next to Sam and I was watching his face and leaning over and looking at John's face. It was really neat to watch the movie through their eyes, and there was this huge loud ovation. Then we stepped outside and it was literally breathtaking because you get outside and there were people screaming and cameras everywhere. We were standing up there and someone was yelling, "Wave to the left . . . Wave to the right." You looked over, and as far as the eye can see there was this crowd. It was staggering. It was my five seconds of being a rock star.'

Even then, they didn't expect to win the Palme d'Or, which was presented on the Monday, the final day of the festival. With the previous two days practically having turned into *Pulp Fiction* weekend, they thought that they'd quit while the going was good. Around lunchtime on Monday, as the bags were being packed, Miramax's Harvey Weinstein went to double check with the Festival authorities that it was okay for them to leave.

'Harvey comes back and says, "Look, they said, 'don't leave,' ", that must mean *something*,' remembers Bender.

Assuming that the film must have netted one of the several critics' awards, their flight reservations were duly cancelled and they trooped off once again for the Palais. As the different awards came and went – actor, actress, the Special Jury Prize, director – *Pulp Fiction* had still won nothing, though neither had *Trois Couleurs: Rouge*, Krzysztof Kieslowki's film that had been widely expected to win. With sentiment playing such a large part in showbiz accolade, Kieslowski's decision to retire from filmmaking did not lead Tarantino and Bender to assume otherwise.

Even when the Palme d'Or was the only prize remaining, they thought that there must have been some special prize concocted for the ensemble acting. There wasn't to be one, and as jury president Clint Eastwood opened the envelope and uttered the words *Pulp Fiction*, Tarantino, Bender *et al.* leaped from their seats and bounded to the stage.

The ovation was overwhelming, yet there were still boos and hysterical catcalls from one section of the auditorium as one well-heeled madame lost her cool, upset that such a film could have triumphed over the normally tranquil fare that Cannes is famous for (or maybe she was just upset that it was the fourth American film to win in six years).

'Well there was one woman, just one, who was screaming something out,' remembers Sam Jackson who could easily have silenced her by merely reciting Ezekiel 25:17. 'She was easy to identify and yell back at. Actually, Quentin surprised them a lot, the audience that saw that film. They were totally shocked that they weren't sitting in some gorefest that was just bullets, guns and "motherfucker, motherfucker". They were looking at something that had substance, that was totally new and unique. It made them laugh in places they would normally cringe, it was invigorating and it was totally overwhelming to me because I had never seen the film until that first night. I had read it like 80, 90 times, but I was still overwhelmed sitting there, being in the presence of it.'

In his acceptance speech, Tarantino thought on his feet and silenced his critics.

'I never expect to win anything at any festival I go to with a jury, because I don't make the kind of films that bring people together. Usually I make films that split people apart.'

That night, tired with the crush of the official party scene, the *Pulp Fiction* brigade retired to their exclusive hotel along the coast, the extremely sedate Hotel du Cap. Bruce Willis fetched his ghettoblaster from his room and a box of tapes and the drinking went on till dawn.

Laughs Bender, 'It was the first time they ever had a party in the lobby . . .'

The Cannes win gave Tarantino what he describes as 'The Good Housekeeping Seal of Approval'.

'It had to do with all the people that just rejected me out of hand because of the violent quota of my films,' he says.

London Features International/David Fisher

Tarantino with the Palme d'Or, Cannes 1994: 'I never expect to win anything at any festival I go to with a jury.'

In the wake of Cannes, other awards followed, including the LA Critics' Awards (Best Picture, Best Director, Best Screenplay and Best Actor for John Travolta), the National Board of Review (Best Picture, Best Director), the New York Film Critics' Circle (Best Director, Best Screenplay), the Golden Globes (Best Screenplay), the Independent Spirit Awards (Best Feature, Best Director, Best Male Lead for Sam Jackson, and Best Screenplay) and the BAFTAs (Best Supporting Actor for Sam Jackson, Best Screenplay). More importantly, in February it received seven Oscar nominations (Best Picture, Best Actor for John Travolta, Best Director, Best Supporting Actress for Uma Thurman, Best Supporting Actor for Samuel L. Jackson, Best Original Screenplay and Best Film Editing for Sally Menke), a quite staggering endorsement.

At the 67th Annual Academy Awards, *Pulp Fiction* was ultimately the victim of a *Forrest Gump* landslide, in what was one of the most predictable Oscar races in recent memory. Nonetheless, the fact that the same body had, in the year of *Schindler's List*, awarded three major prizes to *The Piano*, encouraged the *Pulp Fiction* protagonists, particularly those lobbying for John Travolta.

It was not to be. *Pulp Fiction*'s sole Oscar, for Best Original Screenplay Award, was pretty much a formality and went with the form laid down by the Vegas bookies. On the way to the podium, Tarantino and Avary embraced, as if to publicly show that their differences had been put behind them, though to Tarantino, who again was not particularly magnanimous in his speech ('I'm just gonna improvise it like I have all my other lame acceptance speeches,' he joked on the way in to the auditorium. 'Why spoil a good thing?'), it seemed like a consolation prize. Maybe history will have us linking *Pulp Fiction* with films like *Taxi Driver*, *GoodFellas* and *JFK* which, almost criminally in retrospect, were not honoured for Best Picture by the Academy.

Nonetheless, the film was huge box office. By the time it went to video on 12 September in the US it had grossed over $107 million,

The Golden Globe: 'In the wake of Cannes,
other awards followed.'

Arriving at the 1995 Oscars: 'Ultimately the victim of a
Forrest Gump landslide.'

Miramax's highest earner ever. It also notched up over £12 million in the UK. The triumph of *Pulp Fiction* is due in no small part to the way that Miramax marketed the movie.

Pulp Fiction is, in many ways, a classic arthouse film – directed by a young cineaste, cheap, full of philosophical meanderings, a *hommage* by nature, a festival favourite, filmed in anamorphic widescreen and two and a half hours long. Because of the crowded summer schedule and the proximity to *Natural Born Killers*, the release was held back in the States until the autumn, when it premièred at the New York Film Festival, opening wide on 14 October and following in the UK a week later. Drawing on the experience of the phenomenal success that they had had in mounting another small film, *The Crying Game*, Miramax proceeded to act like a major distributor and open it on 1,300 screens across America, comparable to the release of a big studio picture. Where they had played on the key plot twist of *The Crying Game* in their marketing strategy with their 'Keep The Big Secret' campaign, this time they sought to outflank any manouevre by the anti-violence lobby with a catchy slogan: 'You won't know the facts till you've seen the fiction.'

With a budget of only $8.5 million, *Pulp Fiction* had proved to be a more than healthy investment and also gave Tarantino and Bender respect as filmmakers who could not only deliver the goods but do it cheaply.

'The thing is I could have done *Pulp* for $15 million at TriStar,' explains Tarantino. 'The thing is, it's not about "Gimme more. Gimme more money." I mean Lawrence and I were like, "Give us as little money as you can and we can still make exactly the movie we wanna make." The thing is, if we'd gone to Miramax and said we wanted ten million, twelve million to do *Pulp Fiction*, they'd have given it to us, alright, but I knew I could make the movie for eight and it would be completely profitable. Eight million, we all do okay, we're at fail safe.

'If my next movie was like *The Guns of Navarone* or something, yes, I'd want more money because I would need more money to do that, but say I came up with *Dogs* right now. Do I do *Dogs* for ten million now because I *can*? Well, the answer's No because it was perfect at what it was. I probably wouldn't do it for a million and half now, I'd probably do it for three because that would probably give me a lot more breathing room but I think the budget of the film should be determined by the

171

kind of film it is. I believe each film has an organic budget – it should cost *this* because of the kind of film it is, the audience it will attract, how it's gonna do in America, on foreign, then on video. If it costs this then everyone will be happy with it because even if it completely bombs out in America, we'll do okay on video, we won't lose anything.'

'I would have made *True Romance* for a lot less, alright,' Tarantino continues. 'The thing is, Tony did a wonderful job. He was working with really the least budget he's had since *The Hunger* and you can't tell, it doesn't look any different from *Days of Thunder*, which is a 50-million-dollar movie. But the thing is, I would have done it for six. I'm not saying that more money clouds your judgement, it's just that the less money you spend, the less money you have to make back and the more money you make . . .'

Tarantino even makes a sly reference to the profligacy of Hollywood in the original version of *Four Rooms* as comedy star Chester (Tarantino) and movie big-shot Leo (Bruce Willis) explain the profitability of one of their films to Ted the bell-hop (Tim Roth) . . .

CHESTER
What was the final take on domestic?

LEO
Well, since we're baring our souls here . . . Hold on . . . 72.1 million.

CHESTER
72.1 fucking million dollars. You know what the most-used expression is in this town, Ted?

TED
No.

CHESTER
'We'll make it back on video.' Fuck video! Fuck it! Did *Jaws* make it back on fucking video? No sir. You know why? Because there wasn't any fuckin' video when *Jaws* came out. We're talkin' asses in fuckin' seats. Same here. If video didn't fuckin' exist, we'd still be a hit, a smash, a sleeper, boffo fuckin' box office. That's because before video,

before foreign, before pay TV, before free TV, before Army, before Navy, *The Wacky Detective* made 72.1 million dollars . . .

For all the accolades, marketing and profit and loss considerations, however, it's been Tarantino's willingness to go on the road and promote his films that has been his greatest trump card. In the wake of *Reservoir Dogs* he spent the best part of a year on the road, meeting the press and key industry people, giving interviews and film lectures, and attending festivals. With *Pulp Fiction*, even though it garnered a lot of publicity by winning the Palme d'Or, he put in another five months, literally on tour. There is no greater advocate of Tarantino than Tarantino.

'He's a pretty good self-publicist,' says Philip Thomas of *Empire/UK Premiere*. 'He went half way round the world doing interviews for *Dogs* and the critics were raving about it before it opened anywhere. He's a really good interviewee with a great turn of phrase and he's got an attitude on most things, so he's perfect journalist fodder. John Dahl, after *The Last Seduction, could* have been a star, particularly in the UK, but hasn't got Quentin's self-publicity skills. That's got a lot to do with it.'

'The thing is, this hadn't come along since Spike Lee,' explains Bender. 'Spike was a huge enroller and promoter of his ideas, he would really get out there and talk with a personality. Quentin's got a big personality, his movies have a big personality, he himself has a big personality. It's almost as if he himself is becoming an icon very quickly and he's only been doing this for a couple of years.'

'One of the greatest strengths I have as far as independence as a filmmaker is that I'm known overseas, alright,' Tarantino explains. 'All over the place. I've got a tremendous amount of strength there. Miramax found out exactly how much when they went to sell *Pulp*. They made the movie for eight million and they sold it for eleven million overseas, so we were totally in the chips, alright, even before the movie opened anywhere and that was on my name. And the only reason anybody knows who I am is because I did a thousand interviews. I went to Spain, I went to Brazil, I did *all* the interviews. I went to Korea this time on *Pulp*, starting from scratch. They didn't know who I was there, so I did the interviews, I did the TV shows and it did real well in Korea, which is a really weird market. I learned very quickly on *Dogs* that when I went to a country and I banged the drum on it, it did well, or did better than it would have done. When I didn't go, it didn't do well. If you don't have somebody going over there and doing that, you just have newspaper ads, that's all you have. They don't have commercials playing all the time in all these different countries . . .'

So just how good is *Pulp Fiction*? Does it, as Owen Gleiberman of *Entertainment Weekly* claimed, represent 'nothing less than the reinvention of mainstream American cinema'? Or is the film, as Kenneth Turan of the *Los Angeles Times* put it, 'too inward-looking and self-centred in its concerns and too outward bound in the way it strives to outrage an audience?'

The critics have been overwhelmingly in its favour. 'The Greatest Story Ever Told,' according to *Empire*; 'A work of blazing originality,' said the *New York Times*; 'It hits you like a shot of adrenaline straight to the heart,' raved *Time* magazine.

A lot of that praise was reserved for the sheer innovation of the film's structure which, like *Reservoir Dogs*, cut back and forth in time. Comparisons were drawn with Robert Altman, another protagonist of the art of multifarious storytelling, though Tarantino went one better by overlapping the time frame.

'I remember the projectionist saying, "Did I get the reels mixed up?" ' laughs the film's editor Sally Menke of the first time a rough cut was screened. 'Though they were only watching it with half an eye and half an ear.'

The fact that Vincent actually dies mid-way through and then resurfaces for the finale certainly throws a lot of people.

'It has an end but, because it goes back to the beginning, you kind of realize that you've seen a complete circle,' says Tarantino, not exactly clarifying matters. 'A circle doesn't have an end, but it doesn't kind of continue either.'

In actual fact, the chronology of events goes something like this . . .

Day 1: Jules and Vincent go on their hit, cleaning up their car at Jimmie's afterwards and then going for breakfast where they interrupt Pumpkin and Honey Bunny's robbery. They then go to Marsellus' club where they see him talking to Butch.

Day 2: Vincent and Mia go out for the evening and Mia ODs.

Day 3: Butch kills his opponent and flees from the ring.

Day 4: Butch returns to retrieve his gold watch, kills Vincent and gets involved in the pawn shop incident. He and Fabienne ride off into the sunset . . .

Says Samuel Jackson, 'Quentin has an innovative mind and a unique slant on things and he's come up with this really unique film form and does strange things with time and space. That normally doesn't make sense but he knows how to make it work and he has this unique mixture of cinema and theatre. Film is basically a show-me medium and he's now turned it into an I'll-show-you-but-I've-got-something-to-tell-you-too medium. It's totally unique.'

Interestingly, the reception to *Pulp Fiction* in the States has been slightly at odds with that in Europe, or rather the UK and France, the two countries where Tarantino is most popular. *Reservoir Dogs*, though critically received in the States, was a very small release and thus it did not slip into the national consciousness the same way that it had done in Britain, where it opened on a much bigger scale. That film actually made more money in the UK than it did in the USA. For a lot of casual cinema-goers in the States, *Pulp Fiction* was their first taste of Tarantino.

'I cannot complain about the reviews for *Dogs* in America,' says Tarantino. 'But the thing is though it was treated as like a wonderful début. There were a few raves and even then with the best reviews, there were some qualifications. "He's a cool guy, but he's a new guy." In England, like France they had much less qualifications, there was a lot of press and it's like, "This movie is fucking great, and this guy, fuck me, this guy is fantastic," alright. Now, two years later, *Pulp* comes out. In America, a good majority of the reviews are like, "Wow. He has gone from here and made this big leap to here. This is like what a wonderful piece of work. What a great sense of growth. This is a masterpiece."

'Well, not *everyone*'s saying this but like, you know, in England it's like the majority of the reviews are like, "Well, it's a good movie, but he couldn't live up to *Dogs*. It's not as good as *Dogs*." That's the tone I've got from most of the reviews I've read from England. *Pulp* is being embraced with reservations in the UK and it's the same thing with other places in Europe, both *Positif* and *Cahiers du Cinema* loved *Dogs*, okay, now on *Pulp*, they drew the line. *Cahiers du Cinema* doesn't like *Pulp*,

Positif loves it. It's the same thing with Derek Malcolm and Alexander Walker, both loved *Dogs* and now Derek Malcolm has taken a strong stand against me and Alexander Walker has stood behind me.'

It is remarkable how seriously Tarantino takes film criticism.

'Oh, I follow film criticism, I'm a big fan of it,' he says. 'If I wasn't a filmmaker, I'd be a film critic. I don't have a tremendous respect for a good majority of the people who practise the profession, but as for the profession itself, I have a tremendous amount of respect. I would rather get a well-written, thoughtful review, even if it be negative than a badly-written gushy review. If they're coming from somewhere, that's interesting, it's all food for thought. You know, good writing is good writing. Pauline Kael was as much an influence on me if not more of an influence than any other filmmaker.'

While a lot of filmmakers either treat critics with utter disdain or profess not to read reviews at all, that Tarantino can sit in Los Angeles and reel off the names of film critics such as Malcolm and Walker probably explains why he is so-media friendly.

Those months on the road certainly paid off . . .

One thing is for sure is that there has been a great deal of critical conjecture.

As the *Los Angeles Times* put it, 'Not since Zapruder has a film been so thoroughly deconstructed and significance attached to the most banal details.'

Certainly, for Tarantino fans and members of the inner circle, there are enough in-jokes on display: an *Operation* board game in view while the shot is administered to Mia Wallace; Vincent Vega's initials on the syringe as he shoots up; Zed's chopper, Grace, being named after Tarantino's girlfriend and the cartoon on the side of Esmarelda's cab (Big Jerry Cab Co.), a caricature of Jerry Martinez, one of Tarantino's friends from the Video Archives days.

There is no sign, either, that these little gags will let up. Red Apple smokes are lit up again in *Four Rooms* and through the window of the hotel in that film's hotel can be glimpsed Jack Rabbit Slim's. *Pulp Fiction*'s Bonnie is even referred to in a deleted line of dialogue from *Reservoir Dogs* as the nurse called to fix up Mr Orange.

There is, too, the red Chevy Malibu, driven by Vincent Vega,

Tarantino's very own automobile. This classic car was a rare piece of indulgence, one which Tarantino has since found too much of a hassle to look after, reverting instead to his trusty Geo Metro. Thus it has become a film prop, one that doesn't cost the production any money and, as such, crops up again in *Four Rooms* as the subject of the wager between Chester and Norman.

And then there are the pop culture references: Lance watching The Three Stooges while eating his Fruit Brute; Lance wearing a Speedracer t-shirt; a young Butch Coolidge watching Clutch Cargo; Mia Wallace drawing out a square in the air as in a 1965 episode of *The Flintstones* ('No Biz Like Showbiz'); the *Kung-Fu* TV series; The Fonz from *Happy Days*; Travolta's particular Batman dance from an episode of the TV series where the Caped Crusader's drink is spiked; the burgers; the surf. Even John Travolta himself. Good old Elvis would have made it in there too, had he not been cut for brevity from Vincent and Mia's first meeting . . .

MIA

Now I'm gonna ask you a bunch of quick questions I've come up with that more or less tell me what kind of person I'm having dinner with. My theory is that when it comes to important subjects, there's only two ways a person can answer. And which way they choose tells you who that person is. For instance, there's two kind of people in this world, Elvis people and Beatles people. Now Beatles people can like Elvis. And Elvis people can like The Beatles. But nobody likes them both equally. Somewhere you have to make a choice. And that choice tells you who you are. Now I don't need to ask you that one, 'cause you're obviously a Elvis person. But you're hip to where I'm coming from? Can ya dig it . . . ?

But as pop culture seems to be part of the very fabric of a Tarantino film, so too do the references to other films. In *Pulp Fiction*, this is so much so that for the ardent cineaste, the whole thing almost comes off as an *Airplane!* style sight-gag. Even the use of Travolta dancing and Willis as a grizzled old bruiser would seem to fit into this interpretation, though it must be pointed out that these characters were scripted long before they were cast. Matt Dillon was mentioned as a possible Butch long before Willis came on the scene.

Is Tarantino really doing all this for fun or is it the logical conclusion for someone who's spent most of his life on a couch?

Neal Ascherson of the *Independent on Sunday*, while not being scathing of *Pulp Fiction*, certainly echoed Roger Avary's comment that when the time comes for Tarantino to make a film about real life rather than the one he's gleaned from the screen, he might come unstuck.

'He is, if the terms can be used as description rather than insult, a nerd and a wanker. In other words, he is entirely committed to simulating rather than doing reality, to inventing his world on a screen rather than looking at it through the window.'

So just what nods are there? An awful lot really. In fact even the script directions are loaded with movie references.

'Their dialogue is to be said in a rapid-pace *His Girl Friday* fashion' is the scripted instruction for the delivery of the dialogue between Pumpkin and Honey Bunny; 'Vincent, his one hand on the wheel, the other shifting like *RoboCop*,' comes another.

And then there are the ones onscreen. Uma Thurman not only dances a blithe little slink wearing an Anna Karina wig but her very essence is that of a classic gangster moll – Veronica Lake, Jane Greer, Gene Tierney. Jules preaches before he despatches his victims like Robert Mitchum in *The Night of the Hunter*. The boxer refuses to go down, just like Robert Ryan in the 1949 film *The Set Up*. When Butch nearly runs down Marsellus, it is a near replica of the scene in which Janet Leigh encounters her boss in *Psycho*. Winston Wolf is a send-up of Harvey Keitel's Cleaner from *Point of No Return*. Jules and Jimmie is, perhaps, a reference to Truffaut's *Jules et Jim*. The Mason Dixon pawnshop scenario has overtones of *Deliverance* and then, of course, there is the mysterious briefcase and the 'beautiful' glow from within as per *Kiss Me Deadly* and, again, in the boot of the car in *Repo Man*.

The briefcase even gave way to an interesting theory that became popular on the US Internet and was the source of much speculation on a popular LA talk radio show, namely that the opening of the case and the recitation of Ezekiel 25:17, followed by the 'miracle' of Jules and Vincent's survival, indicates some kind of religious power, as it does again in the final scene when Jules repents. Jules's discussion of 'unclean' meat, another utterance with religious overtones, precedes this. The code to the briefcase is 666, as too is the code to Mia's house, this, of course, being the mark of the devil. The devil himself 'the tyranny of evil men' supposedly has that branded on his person, in the exact same spot as the band-aid on the back of Marsellus' neck. And Butch? He rides a chopper called Grace.

Tarantino, who dismisses such theories and any Shakespeare allusions in his writing either, finds it all highly amusing.

'I heard about it on this show,' he chuckles, 'and in the briefcase was hope and Jules is not just a gangster, he's a serf of the devil who's turning over. It's a good theory, hahaha.'

Rod Lurie, the jovial host of that show, had a far more original take on what glowed from within the Samsonite.

'An Oscar for John Travolta,' he mused at the time.

Maybe it was Tarantino's instead. Maybe it was the head of Alfredo Garcia.

In many ways *Pulp Fiction* represented film criticism at its worst, the critics smugly lapping up the filmic minutiae and straying from their primary function of informing the consumers, the people who buy the tickets, as to whether *Pulp Fiction*, as opposed to say, *The Specialist*, was a better bet for their trip to the mutliplex at the weekend. While the critics may have been wetting themselves at the ultimate in-joke, Vincent Vega ordering a Douglas Sirk steak, for example, the fact is, not everyone gets it, especially outside of the States (Sirk was a director whose films were laced with ironies about American culture).

One disgruntled Internetter had clearly had enough of it all.

'Do you really think that Quentin Tarantino filled every scene or line of dialogue of his movie with some hidden meaning or homage to some other film? Give it up. Sometimes a cigar is just a cigar . . .'

'I think that aspect of his work is vastly overstated,' says Gleiberman. 'In the two and half hours of *Pulp Fiction* there are plenty of scenes that recall other movies, but the bulk of the movie does not. The whole idea is that we watch these movies in a kind of post-modern way, ticking off the references. Anyone who watches a Tarantino film like that is a phoney, he is not admitting the true narrative drive that Tarantino creates. What you see there is the underlying jealousy of film critics and their wanting to cut him down. They're wanting to acknowledge what a well made film it is but not what a visionary he is. One of the reasons that critics can't deal with Tarantino is that although he's an artist, he's such a down and dirty entertainer. He's like Howard Hawks. His films are not pretentious. Even at the height of their artistry, they make their statements by entertaining. A lot of critics see that as less reputable than what an artist like Kieslowski does. Tarantino does not allow you to separate the art and the vision from the sheer fun of his films. In a sense the vision is in the fun that the characters are having . . .'

Another *hommage* aspect is that Jules is very much modelled on a blaxploitation stereotype, as evident in such films as *The Mack*, the film playing in the background at Drexl's place in *True Romance*. Even then, Jules's distinct hairdo – 'Jheri Kurls' – was an accident, the wrong wig being brought to the set when they were finalizing the costumes. He should have been sporting a huge Afro.

On reflection, *Pulp Fiction* is very much Jules's story for, even though Vincent has more screen time, it is Jules's conversion which provides the coda. In *Reservoir Dogs*, the only black character, Holdaway, was marginal. In *True Romance*, there were stereotypical characters – black crooks, Italian gangsters, a Jewish movie producer and a curious Waspafarian. In *Pulp Fiction*, the two most powerful characters are Winston Wolf, Jewish, and Marsellus, black. Mia, too, could very nearly have been played by the black actress Alfre Woodard.

Has Tarantino really delved that deeply into the concerns of race in *Pulp Fiction*? Probably not consciously. Part of the success of *Reservoir Dogs* has been attributed to the fact that he'd simply given white boys the kind of movies that black boys have, in the vein of *Juice*, *Boyz N The Hood* and *Menace II Society*. Screenwriter Kit Carson, one of Tarantino's favourites, even congratulated him after *Reservoir Dogs* for producing a real 'White Guy Movie'. The truth is, the casting of *Pulp Fiction* has well and truly dispelled any notion of racism . . .

Pulp Fiction once again resurrected the question of violence, not so much for the acts of brutality *per se* (though, predictably, conservative papers like the *Daily Mail* howled their indignation), but for the overall malevolent tone.

Under a headline that ran 'Nasty, Brutish and Stupid', the *Sunday Times* commented that, 'The hitman seems to have superseded the serial killer as the emblematic protagonist of modern cinema. What a comment on a once great art form.'

Fintan O'Toole, writing in the otherwise favourable *Guardian*, still found the film sadistic.

'His film should be studies as Exhibit A in the museum of moral vacuity. What Tarantino lingers on is not the actual despatch of his victims, which is casual and off-hand, but the long moments of absolute power beforehand.'

And the *Los Angeles Times* once again talked about the far-reaching consequences of violent films generally.

'Like contemporary tobacco chiefs who deny any link between cigarettes and cancer,' it wrote, 'Hollywood executives will be sitting before congressional courts ten years from now in adamant denial.'

While promoting the film, Tarantino refused to comment on the violence aspect, stating that he'd answered all those questions on *Reservoir Dogs*.

Surprisingly, drugs were never really an issue, even though the film does contain a quite graphic image of Vincent shooting up. As an amusing corollary to each film's budget, the low rent *Reservoir Dogs* had yielded marijuana, the hi-tech Hollywood gloss of *True Romance* meant cocaine and the drug *du jour* in *Pulp Fiction* is heroin . . .

LANCE

This ain't Amsterdam, Vince. This is a seller's market. Coke is fuckin'
dead as disco. Heroin's comin' back in a big fuckin' way. It's this
whole 70s retro. Bell bottoms, heroin, they're as hot as hell . . .

And, anyway, the drug users get their comeuppance (certainly Vincent does). If ever there was a good warning to stay away from smack, it's the sight of Mia when she overdoses.

The original plan had been for Vincent and Lance to inject Mia with salt water, to try and revive her, an old junkie trick. For greater dramatic impact, Tarantino decided to opt for an adrenaline shot instead. Interestingly, there is a discussion of how to administer such a thing in the Martin Scorsese short film *American Boy*. Tarantino's old friend Craig Hamann, who's had a brush with this sort of thing in the past, was called in to advise John Travolta and Uma Thurman on exactly how their characters would behave in the lead up to this scene, particularly Travolta, who was having a little difficulty identifying with a heroin addict.

Hamann and Tarantino joked around about the nature of the credit that Hamann would receive – 'consultant drugs expert' that sort of thing, but 'at the end of Pulp Fiction there wasn't even a special thank you or a bottle of wine or anything,' says Hamann. '. . . He's pretty busy, though.'

Eric Stoltz recalls how frantic it was shooting that scene.

'The thing I remember was the medical kit and how on earth I was going to assemble it in less than thirty seconds because we wanted that scene to play like wildfire. That scene was a blast to shoot because a lot of it was shot in one take, hand held. At one point we did about four or five pages of dialogue without a cut and that made *our* adrenaline start pumping. I remember Quentin even grabbing the camera and shooting some stuff with John and I bickering on the front lawn. It was also great fun slinging Uma around like a sack of potatoes.'

The only noticeable reaction to the drug abuse came at the New York première of *Pulp Fiction* when someone fainted, not at Mia overdosing but at that adrenaline shot. The lights came on at the Lincoln Centre and the film was actually held up for nine minutes as the plaintive plea, 'Is there a doctor in the house?' went up.

'I never even thought about that when I was doing it because I don't even have a fear of needles,' says Tarantino, 'so it never worked into the equation until I saw people diving under the seats . . .'

There are many Lances in Los Angeles, the congenial dope dealer for whom a sale is not merely a transaction but a social occasion. Even after a few lines, we feel we know him, as we do Winston Wolf (this Cleaner using soap and sponges rather than acid baths). Tarantino has, once again drawn even the minor characters extremely well.

Of course, by the same token, we know the lead characters intimately.

'Of late Hollywood films have concentrated on all the aspects other than the characters,' says Philip Thomas. 'The characters are completely cardboard. Tarantino has gone back to the character-driven drama. You know more about Mia Wallace in five minutes than you do about Juliette Lewis' character in *Natural Born Killers* after the entire movie.'

Says Owen Gleiberman, 'There's a certain anger and nihilism in Tarantino's films but he doesn't push it. That nihilism fills all of the characters. Each of them are individuals. They are interacting, but their bonds are shaky. These are people who are just defined by being who they are, but he has such a playful sense of that, it allows him to do what Preston Sturges does, create a gallery of characters that are each entertaining. What he gets you thinking in each scene is what is the connection between each of these characters together. That was the whole theme of *Reservoir Dogs*, the theme of loyalty and what it culminates in is that finally someone does something that's loyal and he's killed.'

As John Travolta has claimed. 'I said, "Either this is going to be the best move of my career or the worst," because I have never seen an actor filmed on the toilet, especially somebody who's supposedly a superstar. Is that a low for me?'

As Tarantino has been at great pains to point out, the characters are all very complex and beneath the façade one tends to overlook the subtleties of the performances, especially Travolta, who as a cold-blooded killer and heroin user must not only engender sympathy but must also not let us forget that he can turn in an instant. Travolta's favourite scene is where he is in the bathroom at Mia's house, talking to himself in the mirror.

'It's my favourite situation in the whole movie because what an opportunity to have something to play,' he says. 'Imagine an actor who has four or five different levels to play at once – being in fear of his death, being attractive. It's what you live for as an actor to have these scenes to play.'

And then there is the deliberately understated dance routine.

'That's how he danced, because he had too much going on,' he says. 'There's too many problems for him to be "Woooo". He had to do his job with her. He had too much to worry about to be like fancy free.'

As Tarantino says, each major character goes through a sort of a transformation.

'If you are going to look at a character as far as a theme, it has to be the spiritual journey that Jules takes, and even though a lot of things happen in the movie that don't have to do with Jules, they still kind of add up in their own way to Jules' epiphany. Mia takes Vincent on an emotional ride, not just the fact that he's got to save her, but it's conceivable that, in a small way, Vincent's not quite the same guy after having lived through that night.'

And then there is Butch.

TARANTINO

'Butch, when he's not with Fabienne, he's a jerk, he's a cold-hearted bastard. Before he meets Fabienne. He lived in a shitty world and he was a shitty guy. Marsellus is not saying, "Take the money or I'm gonna kill you," he's saying, "I'm gonna *offer* you this money to throw the fight, you might as well, you're never going to become champion, you've only got another couple of fights in you." Butch is thinking, "I'm taking your money and I'm still going to win. I'm screwing you." He kills the guy in the ring and doesn't give a damn. He takes out Vincent, doesn't think two things about it. If it wasn't for the hillbillies, he would have killed Marsellus right there. He found Fabienne and she's such a breath of fresh air into his fucked up world that he's, "Okay, I can get rid of all this, so I'm going to have to do one more dirty trick in order to get the money that's going to allow me to be a good person." When he walks into that hotel room and closes that door, he's closing it on Butch forever, but she leaves that watch and it's like, "I've got to be Butch one more time." '

The depth of these characters and, once again, the opportunity to sink their teeth into some huge chunks of dialogue, was an obvious attraction for the actors.

'I think perhaps he is the greatest American screenwriter since Preston Sturges,' says Owen Gleiberman, 'in that he gives in to his wildest impulses. He takes the dialogue and he lets the language fly in that it will take him wherever it will. He takes pop culture references and he seems to mirror what's going on in the modern mind and his dialogue really does contain ideas. The dialogue between Samuel L. Jackson and John Travolta is really a series of debates but it's done in such a playful way it manages to camouflage the fact. The thing is that hitmen talk 'bout the same stuff we do and that's Tarantino's way of humanizing them.'

Says Willis. "It's never happened to me in twenty-three films. I've never been in a film that we've shot the script that we've started out to shoot. Quentin's dialogue makes an actor look better. Frankly, and I think all the actors would agree, we worked very hard to try to serve the original script, which is the complete opposite of what normally happens in films. Actors always try and change their lines.'

Having said that, Travolta did suggest one script amendment that was followed through, tidying up a still messy exercise. Originally, when Vincent accidentally shot Marvin in the car, he didn't kill him out-right . . .

JULES
  What the fuck's happening?

VINCENT
  I just accidentally shot Marvin in the throat.

JULES
  Why the fuck did you do that?

VINCENT
  I didn't mean to do it. I just said it was an accident.

JULES
  I've seen a lot of crazy ass shit in my time.

VINCENT
  Chill out, man, it was an accident, okay? You hit a bump or somethin'
  and the gun went off.

JULES
  The car didn't hit no motherfuckin' bump!

VINCENT
  Look! I didn't mean to shoot this son-of-a-bitch, the gun just went off,
  don't ask me how! Now I think the humane thing to do is put him out
  of his misery.

JULES (*can't believe it*)
  You wanna shoot 'im again?

VINCENT
  The guy's sufferin'. It's the right thing to do.

(*Marvin, suffering though he is, is listening to this debate, not believing what
he's hearing.*)

JULES
This is really uncool.

(*Vincent turns to the backseat, places the barrel of the .45 against Marvin's forehead. Marvin's eyes are as big as saucers. He tries to talk Vince out of this, but when he opens his mouth, only gurgles come out.*)

JULES
Marvin, I just want to apologize. I got nothin' to do with this shit. And I want you to know I think it's fucked up.

VINCENT
Okay, Pontius Pilate, when I count to three, honk your horn. One . . . two . . . three.

(*Jules presses down hard on the horn: Honk! and Bang!*)

Amongst all the juicy exchanges, probably one of the most impressive uses of dialogue is in the Jack Rabbit Slim's scene where Vincent and Mia are getting to know each other for the first time, though its significance has more to do with the 'uncomfortable silences' that punctuate proceedings than the actual lines themselves.

The success of this scene is a good example of the work of the film's Oscar-nominated editor Sally Menke, whose juxtaposition of long-drawn-out dialogue and fast action did so much to make *Reservoir Dogs* a success.

'Quentin wanted it to be as drawn out as if you were meeting someone for the first time,' she explains. 'There's a lot of dialogue that's been taken out in this scene. I actually lobbied very hard to take out even more dialogue, but Quentin really stuck by his guns for it to remain as long as it is, especially the silence when they're not talking to each other.'

Adam Mars-Jones of the *Independent* may have had a valid point, that the inane dialogue in *Reservoir Dogs* came out because the characters were unable to discuss their identities and had little else to talk about. In *Pulp Fiction*, the rationale seems to be that it's there because 'they lapped it up last time'. Nonetheless, regardless of motive, the verbal tradings are still extremely funny (interestingly, gaffe spotters will notice that there is a slight mismatch between the dialogue that Amanda Plummer spouts at the beginning and end of the film).

As Lawrence Bender explains, 'There are two reasons why actors like to work with Quentin and that's number one, his dialogue, and two, actors never really get to *work* with a director. There are lots of great directors out there, but very few of them understand the process of acting. Quentin understands the process of acting and so you can feel comfortable about going places that you don't normally go, and trusting that the guy out there who's watching you and make you look good (for that reason, Tarantino never directs from a monitor because it acts as a barrier between director and actor). That's why all those performances on *Dogs* and *Pulp Fiction*, all those guys, it's some of the best performances they've had in years.'

Although Chris Penn, who plays Nice Guy Eddie, may have told the *Independent* in December 1992, 'When I first met him, I didn't think he could direct traffic,' the actors who have worked with him are all full of praise for their helmsman.

'Quentin is a great collaborationist,' says Uma Thurman. 'He is extremely clear about what he wants, but he's not closed-minded – he's no bully.'

A good example of this was in the preparation for the Twist scene. Travolta, obviously, knew how to take care of himself on the dance floor, but Thurman was extremely nervous, assuming that she would actually have to dance *well* to pull it off (they do, after all, win a trophy). To allay her fears, Tarantino simply took her and Travolta to a trailer and showed them a video of Jean-Luc Godard's *Bande À Part*, with Anna Karina, Sami Frey and Claude Brasseur doing a little synchronized jig to the juke box in a French café. Tarantino liked that scene, not because of how well they danced, but because the characters simply *enjoyed* doing it.

Thurman got the picture and got stuck into her routine, even finding time to stretch out her hand and point a finger at her partner *à la* Olivia Newton-John.

'It was something so camp it was not to be missed,' she laughs. 'I'm quite shy physically in a certain way, so I was a bit embarrassed about the idea of it."

And as Travolta has said, 'For whatever reason, people get so excited when I dance. I'm a heroin-addicted hitman with a gut. It never ceases to amaze me, but at least I didn't have to wear white polyester . . . I'll tell you what, it's been fun. The 90s, from *Look Who's Talking* on, there's a new thing that happened. I think a generation denied loving me, meaning they secretly loved and were afraid to admit it.'

As Julie Birchill wrote in the *Sunday Times*, 'Tarantino makes us marvel that John Travolta, teen icon of the 70s, abandoned like a human hula-hoop when his three minutes on the dance floor were up, is now playing a leading role in the latest film of the most accomplished filmmaker of his decade . . .'

In the original script, Travolta's Vincent still dies, but in the final scene as the characteristic Mexican stand-off ensues there is a segment in which Jules actually blows Tim Roth's Pumpkin away, shooting him up through the table before turning his gun on Honey Bunny. We then cut back to the conventional ending as it is revealed that this scenario has existed purely in Jules's mind.

Tarantino explains why he chose not to film that.

'I started thinking about it and I go, "You know what, it actually will fuck it up if we do it because once we have this big dream sequence, you *know* it's not going to end in a gunfight and part of the fun of that scene is not knowing what's going to happen, that he *could* blow them away. Once you've seen it, you know that that's as bad as it's gonna get, so if you *don't* have it, you've got the tension up until the very last moment when he forgives them and says, 'Get out of here.' " I've heard audiences considering that he could blow 'em away right up until the very last moment.'

And so Jules is released, to walk the earth, 'like Caine in *Kung-Fu*'.

'I want to know what happens to Jules on his walk,' muses Sam Jackson. 'I wanna take a little walk around the world with him and see what happens.'

People tend to talk about just how cool Tarantino's films are, an unquantifiable term if ever there was one. In a sense the religious epiphany of Jules suggests otherwise.

'I think that is the biggest bunch of bullshit said about Tarantino,' says Gleiberman. 'His films play off coolness and heat. There's a certain

coolness in the style, but the heat is in the acting, the heat is in the performances. Look at Samuel Jackson's speech at the end, or the Bible
speech. Are you telling me that's cool? That's pure heat. If people are
saying his films are cool they're missing the alchemy between cool and
heat and hip.'

Tarantino has actually kept a copyright on all the characters, and
although it's extremely unlikely that there will ever be a *Pulp 2*, the possibilities exist for the characters' resurrection.

I like the idea of keeping the characters and just bringing them in and
out,' he says. 'To tell the truth, I actually think that all those characters in
Pulp deserve a movie of their own. You know, *The Further Adventures of
Butch and Fabienne, Pumpkin and Honey Bunny.*

'The two characters that I would really like to explore more are Jules
and Vincent. When we were mixing the movie, the guy who's the mixer
laughed so much at Jules and Vincent – "They're so fuckin' funny." It's
really rare when you find people who work good together and actually
the last time I saw two actors who were just a ripping comedy team was
Tim (Roth) and Gary (Oldman) in *Rosencrantz and Guildenstern are Dead.*
They fucking played like a house on fire, and I was telling Tim, "You
guys should do a comedy. Don't do a fuckin' drama. I don't wanna see
Murder in the First, I wanna see you guys as a great comedy team." I
actually think that Sam and John could actually become a *great* comedy
team – *Jules and Vincent Meet Frankentstein*. I even thought about the idea
of doing a Vega Brothers movie. Vic visiting Vincent in Amsterdam
when Vincent is running his club.'

He has even joked about doing a genuine TV version of *Fox Force Five*.

'Oh actually, I'd be into that to tell you the truth, I love that show.
When I was doing Margaret Cho's TV show I bumped into Ellen De
Generes. She came in and read for *Pulp*, she read for the part Rosanna
Arquette plays. She said it's just so funny when Jules is explaining to
Vincent what a pilot is. The thing is that it's a very Los Angeles thing
because like even people here who have nothing to do with the industry
whatsoever are semi aware of at least that much of how it works, they
know what a pilot is. That's still not knowing that much but it's probably still more than they know in Wichita.'

That such characters can exist so vividly is an uncommon thing in the
world of modern cinema and beyond anything else – beyond the

structure, the acting, the dialogue, the pop culture, the filmic references or anything else, it is, in the opinion of this author, the overriding reason why Tarantino as a filmmaker has achieved such remarkable success. On that we will leave the final word to Lawrence Bender.

'The context that he writes in, is that he takes the dark, the quintessential hitman Harvey Keitel in *Reservoir Dogs*, Sam Jackson in *Pulp Fiction* and he imbues them with goodness. Harvey Keitel killed Tim Roth out of complete love. Samuel Jackson recited the Bible. So there's light and dark and what Quentin really deals in is in the twilight of it, in this grey area which is so intriguing to people.

'People are so used to looking at people as black or white, good or bad, it's dark, it's light. Quentin really deals in this grey area and it sort of makes you uncomfortable or intrigued. These are nasty people, hitmen who kill people or rob but what makes them interesting is that they talk about a foot massage on the way to a hit. Something that Lee Srasberg taught is that you take a character and what you, as an actor, have to do is take a very specific part of your personality and that's what you've got to bring to that character. Don't play a general character. The more specific about what you are *in* that character, the more universal that character becomes.

'Quentin does that with his writing. He gets really really specific, about, say, tipping a waitress – anyone who watched that scene will think this is a fucking ridiculous conversation. Quentin does that with everything, whether it's about sex or violence or love or comedy, he gets really specific. It can be scary, it can be embarrassing, it can be awkward and it becomes messy . . . which is sort of what life is . . .'

Chapter 9

Four Rooms and Beyond

Saturday, 21 January 1994 – Barney's Beanery, a West Hollywood bar/diner. One of the few places in LA that actually still looks and feels like a genuine honest-to-goodness drinking hole, not the interior-designed chic beloved of the Beverly Hills set – dollar bills and licence plates pinned up behind the bar, a ball game playing on the TV, pool tables, homely waitresses and, more importantly, a place where you can still get a generous plateful of full-fat food with cholesterol on the side, anathema to most Californians. It had been a frantic evening filming *All American Girl* the night before and, with the Golden Globes to look forward to tonight, Tarantino chows down with gusto on a good ole American breakfast – scrambled eggs, mashed potatoes, chicken gravy, rye toast and, of course, coffee . . . lots of cream, lots of sugar.

There is art and there is food.

But Tarantino is in a state of considerable anguish. Not over anything of consequence but due to one of those bar-room conceptual conundrums we're mulling over – you're about to be executed and you have to choose your last meal, last film to watch, last album to listen to (no greatest hits compilations) and an eminent person with whom you would choose to spend your final fifteen minutes (no girlfriends, family or any such cop-out) – sex is optional.

It's not a debate in the 'Elvis Person' vs 'Beatles Person' league of *Pulp Fiction*, but a good teaser nonetheless and Tarantino thinks long and hard about his answers.

The Meal?

'Probably Pizza and I'd have one of those ice-cold Coca-Colas, but in one of those 16 ounce bottles, the kind they don't make any more. You know, the deposit bottles, they always taste better out of that,' he offers, though not without advocating the merits of what a good burger might do for a dying man's spirits.

The Film?

'I'd have to say *Rio Bravo*,' he states, remaining loyal to his favourite director, Howard Hawks.

The Album?

'I'd listen to Dylan's *Blood On The Tracks*. Definitely, definitely.'

And the Eminent Person?

'I'm trying to thing of some mystery that I've always wanted to know the answer to,' he muses. 'I'd talk to Orson Welles and say, "Was it you or Herman J. Mankiewicz?" '

(Welles and Mankiewicz co-wrote *Citizen Kane*. Welles took all the credit, though it has since been claimed that Mankiewicz was the originator of the story. Some would say this is quite poignant.)

After a while the coffee becomes beer – Killian's Red, one of the house specials. Tarantino knows the TV ad for that brew by heart and proceeds with a somewhat careless rendition of Christopher Plummer's cod-Irish voice-over (this, after all, is the mind that produced a Palme d'Or-worthy piece of art). The consequences of this early drink, the first of several throughout the day, will manifest itself in his acceptance speech for the Golden Globe he will win later on for Best Screenplay at the nearby Beverly Hilton.

'I've just been sitting here getting hammered . . .' a bemused Tarantino announced to the evening's hosts, the Hollywood Foreign Press Association. 'Waiters! More red wine at this table . . .'

Even though *Pulp Fiction* has won a hatful of awards (especially where the critics have been involved) and ultimately landed Tarantino with the greatest prize in showbiz, he is still ambivalent about the whole process, a legacy of the embarrassment at coming away with empty hands from Sundance '92. Not that he begrudged *In the Soup* winning the big prize on that occasion, but he thought *Reservoir Dogs* might have won at least something.

'It's not a big fuckin' deal. It's not gonna change my life one way or the other,' he shouts over a juke box that begins pumping out some quintessential American sounds – from The Eagles to Pearl Jam.

'It doesn't change the movie one iota. I won the Cannes Film Festival and *Pulp* wouldn't be any different if I'd lost it either.

'This is how I feel about awards. I like think about it like this. We *all* have our sexual pride, alright. There's a girl over there that you're not attracted to one iota. You're not *repelled* by her, but she's just not your type. But if you start talking to somebody who knows her and somebody says, "Georgina over there, she really kind of likes you," even though you're not attracted to her, you like the *idea* that she's attracted to you, you feel kind of cool. And you know what, if a guy says, "I was talking to Georgina the other day and she's really attracted to Tony, but she's *not* attracted to *you*, there's just nothing there," you feel a little weird. What's wrong with her? It doesn't matter that you feel the same way. It's kind of how awards are. If you win, it's fucking great, but if you lose, it's kind of a bummer and you can't help but take it personally a little bit. At the end of the day, it's not a big deal because nobody's going to remember a few years from now what you won and it doesn't affect the work. The work is the work, especially if, like me, you're making films that aren't for everybody. They are what they are.'

As if by magic, a small man appears at the side of the table. He shakes Tarantino's hand, tells him he loves his movies and gives him a business card.

'Next time, you call *me*, man,' he urges, while a somewhat embarrassed Tarantino politely thanks him and puts the card in his pocket. A producer or a plumber, we will never know.

Tarantino continues.

'The funny thing that happens, though, you spend your whole life watching the Academy Awards and it's, "Oh, they don't know what they're talking about, they're always giving it to the wrong movie. Always wrong, always wrong." But the night you've got your tuxedo on and you're at the ceremony it's the fairest thing in the world. The right movie will be honoured and we'll see the right recognition and it ends up the same old blackjack that you've always watched your whole life . . . '

Awards are not uppermost in Tarantino's mind. He's still in the editing process of *Four Rooms*, shot in December and scheduled for release in autumn 1995, the next official directorial offering. It's another ensemble piece, this time of directors – Allison Anders, Robert Rodriguez, Alexandre Rockwell and Tarantino (or 'the Class of '92,' as Anders calls them). There was going to be Richard Linklater, too, making it *Five Rooms*, but he was off shooting *Before Sunrise* in Vienna.

'Me, Allison and Alex were all in Sundance '92,' explains Tarantino. 'And then about three months later, me and Alex met Robert at Toronto and then Allison met Robert. Basically, in '92, there was this big explosion of independent filmmakers and we wanted to showcase that. In its own silly way it's like a piece of time and, you know, it's kind of a document of where we are right now, three years after.'

The deal, however, for a $4 million picture with Miramax, was signed before *Pulp Fiction* was released and the four directors have all subsequently met with varying degrees of success

'The hardest thing on producing *Pulp Fiction* was getting all twelve stars in the one place at the same time,' says Lawrence Bender. 'Everyone was off shooting a movie somewhere. Because of their schedules, man it was a feat. Well the only thing harder than that was getting these four directors together. We had to force the circle into the square.'

'The Quentin phenomenon is like making a film with Elvis Presley,' joked Rockwell.

The idea was actually kicked off three years ago by Rockwell, the idea being to produce an anthology of four short films, each set in a different room of a Los Angeles hotel on New Year's Eve, the fictitious Monsignor (modelled on LA's Château Marmont and London's Blake's), with a central character, Ted the bell-hop (Tim Roth) who links the four stories.

'He's left in control of the hotel and he's not ready for it,' says Tarantino of Ted. 'And then it was, "Okay, we've got that . . . Go off, go to it," and then we went off and wrote our separate stories.'

The end result makes for an eclectic mix: Anders' story, *Strange Brew* – about a coven of witches (Valeria Golino, Madonna, Alicia Witt, Lili Taylor, Ione Skye and Sammi Davis) who try to resurrect their goddess, a 1950s stripper called Diana (Amanda De Cadenet); Rockwell's *Two Sides To A Plate* – Ted is embroiled in a domestic dispute between Sigfried (David Proval) and his wife Angela (Jennifer Beals); Rodriguez's *The Misbehavers* – in which a hotel room is trashed by two kids while their parents (Antonio Banderas and Tamlyn Tomita) go out on the town.

And then there is Tarantino's – *Thrill Of The Bet* – which again draws on an old source, this time from TV and an episode of the *Alfred Hitchcock Show*. In a story entitled *The Man From Rio* (which, interestingly, Tarantino has never seen, although he did see a TV remake

194

starring Melanie Griffith), Peter Lorre makes a bet with Steve McQueen that he can't light his cigarette lighter ten times in a row. If McQueen succeeds, he wins Lorre's new sports car. If he can't, Lorre gets to chop McQueen's little finger off.

Tarantino has kept the original premise, altering the details to fit in with the hotel setting and new characters – comedy star Chester Rush (Tarantino) and his friend Norman (Paul Calderon) make the same wager, overseen by Chester's manager Leo (Bruce Willis).

Like the original, Norman stands to win the perennial red Chevy Malibu but lose his finger if his Zippo won't do the business. And thus Ted is summoned to their penthouse suite bearing on his trolley a chopping block, hatchet, a bucket of ice, a roll of twine and three nails and is offered $1000 to be the hatchet man. Of course, there is a classic left turn, the finger being swiftly severed on the very first click of the lighter, our cinematic training having taught us that it would at least be left to the final go, or more commonly that something would happen to resolve the issue. Not in this. The lighter fails on the first attempt, Ted instantly hacks off the finger, scoops up the money and runs out the door, catching you unawares.

'It was just like, you know, that's such an old time-worn device,' chuckles Tarantino. 'You know, counting it down and everything, the way to make it fresh is to let real life get into it. It could just as easily not happen on the first one as the last one. It's like the whole idea, the whole story is the build-up to an event and you think you're getting on the ride and then there *is* no ride . . . Boom, it's over.'

The star of his own show, Tarantino as per the script, almost seems to have written his part in self-parody . . .

INTERIOR PENTHOUSE – NIGHT
The penthouse is huge, far and away the best suite in the house. And standing in the middle of the biggest room in the hotel is the hottest, newest comedy star to burst onto the Hollywood scene in nearly a decade, Chester Rush. At this moment in time he's the king and he has the swagger of a new king. After only one movie he pulled the sword out of the stone. And the look on his face says, 'King's good'. . . .

In accordance with both *Reservoir Dogs* and *Pulp Fiction*, in which the drama follows an early-established moment of terror, the fact that Norman *could* lose his finger provides a tense backdrop against which the drama is played out. Perversely, the potential loss of a finger, beyond exploding heads and severed ears, seems the most gruesome act of the Tarantino canon so far.

Tarantino agrees.

'Well, in its own weird way, it's identifiable. You can relate to it more. If you see a movie and someone gets decapitated, you can say, "Oh, that was a neat special effect," and everything, but can you really relate to it? In a movie, if you see someone get a paper cut, you go, "Oooohh," because you *can* relate to it. Little things like cutting off fingers, we could accidentally do that at any point during the day. I'm not gonna accidentally cut off your head.'

During the shoot, however, there were rumours of in-fighting.

'Any kind of collaboration, you're gonna have arguments and fighting and all that kind of stuff, but there's no bad blood there,' says Tarantino.

The only rift, though, seems to have been over the actual name of the bell-hop. The part was originally written for Steve Buscemi, who declined the role as it was too similar to that of the part of Chet he played in *Barton Fink*. Rockwell had lobbied for the name Benny, Tarantino wanted him to be Larry, while Anders really didn't care, as in her story he was only required to provide a sperm donation.

When Buscemi was about to decline the part, Tarantino allegedly offered him a part in his 'room' as an alternative. Seen as an undiplomatic move by the others, the offer was rescinded apologetically.

Thus, we now have Tim Roth. And Tim Roth is called Ted.

Tarantino admits that part of the fun of doing such a buddy movie was that it gave the four directors, all good friends, the opportunity to once again play the festival circuit *en masse* in the autumn of 1995, with the film scheduled to play at the Venice Film Festival and then open in the US in September.

Doing the festival thing may be the intention, though, but it's not as easy as it used to be and Tarantino, by his own admission, admits that it's often 'too big of a deal'.

However, one shindig that Tarantino *has* managed to frequent annually is the UK's annual Shots in the Dark Festival in Nottingham, dealing

principally with the crime, mystery and thriller genre. He likes this festival, not generally regarded as a major stopover on the festival circuit,
because he can go and hang out in pubs (such as Ye Olde Trip to
Jerusalem) and go for fish and chips without the bother that accompan-
ies his presence at one of the more established jamborees. As a mark of
gratitude to that particular festival, of which he is the honorary patron,
he even unveiled *Pulp Fiction* (with French subtitles) as the event's 'surprise film' in June 1994 – the first time it had been seen in the UK . . .

While promoting *Four Rooms* will remain a serious occupation, there are
other forthcoming assignments with which Tarantino is currently associated. There still exists the possibility that he may direct a feature-length
version of the TV series *The Man From UNCLE* for Turner Pictures. In
April 1995, press rumours were rife that this was a distinct possibility
though, at the time of going to print, Tarantino had never met or been
officially approached by anyone to make the film. 'The chances are pretty
distant and remote' is the official response. And then *From Dusk Till
Dawn*, the script he penned back in the early days for $1500, is at last
going to see the light of day. Based on a story by Robert Kurtzman of
KNB-EFX and redrafted by Tarantino, it went before the cameras in June
1995 in LA with Tarantino and Bender producing under the auspices of
Rodriguez's Los Hooligans Productions. George Clooney and Tarantino
are the leads, with Harvey Keitel and Juliette Lewis also starring.
Wrapping in August, it has again been picked up by Miramax and will
get a Christmas release in the US.

Plus there is *Crimson Tide*, Tony Scott's big buck tale of
derring-do and treachery on a US nuclear submarine, starring Denzel
Washington and Gene Hackman, which came out in May in the US,
proving to be extraordinarily successful. Scott invited Tarantino to give
the script a dialogue polish, which he duly did as a favour and without
screen credit, a legacy of the good relationship they struck up with *True
Romance*.

'I thought the story worked really well and all the stuff about the
workings of a nuclear submarine, which I knew nothing about, was very
very interesting,' he explains. 'The one thing is some of the dialogue was
just a little like "normal" movie dialogue. It had its brain, it just needed a
bit more of a heart, so I took it and did a rewrite on it, although I actually

didn't change any scenes. I just changed the dialogue, just tried to bring more characterization out. I told them, "We're not gonna fuck around with the plot at all," because I *couldn't*, 'cause I don't know enough about a submarine to fuck around with it. I just beefed up some characters and had a little fun with the dialogue.

'The big mutiny scene is my scene and I wrote a scene over a dinner table in the officers' mess. Now I really like the scene, but for some reason or other Tony didn't really get into it and he had Robert Towne rewrite it. He did a really great job and you can *tell* Robert Towne wrote it. There is this other scene that I wrote that I liked and Tony didn't like, and then Robert Towne came up with an idea and he didn't like that one, either, and so they talked Steve Zaillian, who wrote *Schindler's List*, into writing the scene, so actually there's kinda like a lot of heavy duty talent involved.'

Though he would probably prefer to forget it, Tarantino also managed to fit in a script polish on *It's Pat*, the comedy vehicle for close friend Julia Sweeney (who appears as Racquel in *Pulp Fiction*). Pat, an androgynous oddball portrayed by Sweeney on the swiftly deteriorating *Saturday Night Live*, is yet another character culled from that show and given the big-screen treatment. Not even Tarantino could save the film from bombing.

A regular player at the stand-up comedy nights at The Groundlings Theatre on LA's Melrose, Sweeney, along with Phil Lamarr (*Pulp Fiction*'s Marvin) and Steve Hibbert (The Gimp) are part of a comedy crowd who have cropped up in minor roles in Tarantino's work. Tarantino occasionally appears there on stage himself for a spot of improv.

He has also taken time out to direct an episode of the TV series *ER*, entitled 'Motherhood', which aired on US TV on 11 May 1995, and there is, too, an alternative cut of *Reservoir Dogs*, released in the US in August – an extended edition for the fans, the original release still being the definitive director's version. But, over and above these diversions, Miramax have optioned for Tarantino and Bender four Elmore Leonard novels – *Rum Punch*, *Killshot*, *Bandits* and *Freaky Deaky*. These will be adapted and filmed over the next few years with Tarantino possibly holding back one to direct himself, perhaps *Killshot* . . .

Beyond all this, Tarantino has achieved a personal ambition. He is now a movie actor. And not just an actor but a star. *Four Rooms* doesn't exactly count as that's one of his own creations, but this notwithstanding, the parts are coming in.

His first role, albeit a cameo, is still memorable and the one that got the ball rolling, as Sid, the wallflower movie geek in the party scene in Rory Kelly's 1994 film *Sleep With Me* – a day's filming squeezed in while Tarantino was location scouting for *Pulp Fiction*.

'That was a favour and it was funny how it worked out because originally I said, "No, I can't do it." And the reason that I didn't want to do it because it was written in there that it was *me*, Quentin Tarantino, and I go, "I don't want to play me, I want to be taken seriously as an actor, I don't want to be like some cheesy celebrity fucking around. I'll do it, but I won't be me and I'm not gonna say what you had me saying about myself." '

'In the script we just wrote, "Quentin enters the party and says something funny," and we cut him loose,' says Eric Stoltz, who starred in and was one of the producers of that movie. 'We shot four or five mags of him just going on and on until we couldn't shoot anymore because it was a handheld shot and Andrzej (Sekula)'s arms were getting tired. Quentin and Todd Field (who plays Duane) worked out a few basic points they wanted to hit and figured out the ending and then just basically winged it and it turned out to be one of the best moments in the film. I think Quentin is a fantastic actor and I hope that he does the John Huston thing, alternates making great films with acting jobs.'

The resultant spiel, the *Top Gun* speech, was, in actual fact, a routine that Tarantino and Avary used to do as a stand-up turn back in the old Video Archives days . . .

SID

You know what one of the greatest scripts ever written in the history of Hollywood is? . . . *Top Gun*.

DUANE

Oh, c'mon!

SID

Top Gun is fucking great. What is *Top Gun*? You think it's a story about a bunch of fighter pilots.

DUANE

It's about a bunch of guys waving their dicks around.

SID

It's a story about a man's struggle with his own homosexuality . . .

(*Duane laughs in disbelief*)

SID

That's it. That is what *Top Gun* is about, man. You've got Maverick, he's on the edge, man. He's right on the fucking line, alright, and you got Ice Man and all his crew.

DUANE

Right.

SID

They're gay and they represent gay man.

DUANE

Right.

SID

Alright, and they're saying, 'Go! Go the gay way! Go the gay way!' He could go both ways . . .

DUANE

Like Kelly McGillis, right?

SID

Kelly McGillis, right, she's heterosexuality. She's saying, 'No, no, no, no. Go the normal way, play by the rules, go the normal way.' And they're saying, '*No*. Go the gay way. Be the gay way. Go for the gay way.'

DUANE

Right.

SID

That's what's going on throughout that whole movie.

SID

He goes to her house, right.

DUANE

Alright.

SID

It looks like they're going to have sex, yeah. They're just kind of sit-
ting back. He's taking a shower and everything. They don't have sex.
He gets on the motorcycle, drives away. She's like, 'What the fuck?
What the fuck is going on here?'

DUANE

Right.

SID

Next scene you see her, she is in the elevator. She is dressed like a
guy. She's got the aviator glasses. She's wearing the same jacket the
Ice Men wear. She is like, 'Okay, how can I get this guy? This guy is
going towards the gay way. I've got to bring him back. I've got to
bring him back from the gay way so I'm going to dress like a man' . . .
Alright, but the real ending of the movie, right, is when they fight the
Migs because he has passed over into the gay way. They are this gay
fighting, fucking force alright. Alright, the gays are beating the
Russians, alright. And it's over. And they fucking land, and Ice Man's
been trying to get Maverick the entire time. Finally he's got him,
alright. And what is the last fucking line they have together after
they're all happy and hugging and kissing with each other? Ice
comes up to Maverick and he says . . .

BOTH IN CHORUS

'Man, you can ride my tail . . .'

SID

'*Anytime!*' . . . Yeah, and what does Maverick say?

CHORUS

'You can ride mine . . . !'

'Yeah, yeah we used to do that at parties all the time,' chuckles Tarantino. 'We would do it at the drop of a hat. Roger came up with the original theory about it and then the two of us proceeded to perfect it. Like a comedy team, kept expanding on it.'

Tarantino's claim to authorship is, however, not something that sits well with Avary.

'That was a routine that I came up with,' he states. 'I spent hours trying to convince everybody that it's true. If you shut your eyes during the flying sequences, it's two guys having sex, it's "Good, get it in, get it in higher." And Kelly McGillis, her name is Charlie. There are many more themes than were laid out in *Sleep With Me*.

'When I was doing rewrites on *True Romance*, I brought it up to Tony Scott. Now Tony is a man's man and that's his worst nightmare, the fact that there's a homoerotic subtext. I would love to do a commentary for a special edition laserdisc.'

Nonetheless, he is still obviously rankled by Tarantino's usurping of the shtick as his own.

'It annoyed me the way I found out about it more than anything,' says Avary. 'I was in a restaurant with Eric Stoltz and I was telling him about it and he goes, "Oh my God, Quentin just improvised that."

'Quentin isn't ever very eager to hand out credit and that's something that's a little bit of a bummer. Look, Quentin did it well, but it would be nice if he gave credit where credit's due.'

'I figured out what I was going to do that driving to the set that day. But what's odd about it, is that it was so successful and people liked it so much that the exact reversal of what I was scared of happened, not that people didn't take me seriously because I was doing that scene, but that I've gotten all these acting offers. It was because of *Sleep With Me* that I got *Destiny Turns on the Radio* in Cannes.'

Destiny Turns on the Radio was a script that had been kicking around for a while and had been brought to Tarantino's attention through Kit Carson, one of his favourite screenwriters.

'He was telling me about his script two years ago, the producers gave me the script and they go, "We've got a part for you," and I thought they were giving me *Red Scorpion 2* or something and I said, "*Destiny Turns on the Radio*, I hear that's a really wonderful script." I had dinner with Bridget Fonda and Eric Stoltz and Bridget was like, "Really, you're doing that? God, I read that four years ago," so like the script's really been around for a long time. The producers gave it to me in Cannes and I took it to my hotel room and I read it that night and it's like, "I'm aboard, I'm the guy." ' Unfortunately, the film was a critical and commercial disaster.

Another acting job, *Hands Up*, directed by Virginie Thevenet, came to Tarantino under different circumstances but was again sealed at the same festival. In it, Tarantino is to play a criminal who falls in love with a young singer-cum-prostitute (Charlotte Gainsbourg) and a sort of road trip adventure ensues. This part was actually written specifically for Tarantino.

'I actually met Virginie at a festival workshop right after Cannes (1992), the Avignon French-American workshop,' he explains. 'We became really good friends and then when I was in France I visited her and then when she was in America she'd visit me. We wrote to each other and stuff. I said I wanted to do more acting and I was a big fan because I'd seen a couple of her films after I'd met her. She said, "I'm gonna write something for you," and then, sure enough, having worked on it all through '93, just before Cannes '94 she called me up and said, "I have it, but it's in French and I have to translate it to English." She gave it to me at Cannes and then we got together to talk about it in Paris.'

This project has since been put on hold, though Tarantino redeems himself from the *Destiny* venture with a memorable cameo, in Robert Rodriguez's quite brilliant *Desperado*, the sequel to 1992's *El Mariachi*.

'That was fun. He wrote it for me,' Tarantino grins. 'I'm like this guest bad guy and like I have the most dialogue of anybody in the movie because I come in the bar with some other guy, this gangster, this drug-dealin' mule kind of guy, but I tell this real long joke. According to Robert, it's the fastest talking and the longest stretch of dialogue in the whole film.

'They made it so I could like get in and get out and they cut all my stuff down to one day. It's like the only day of the whole shoot that Antonio Banderas had the day off because I didn't have any scenes with him, so it was like I was the star for that day. It was really wild because I showed up in Mexico and had a beautiful trailer, the nicest trailer I've ever had in my life, but I was never in because Robert shoots so fast you know it was just like working my fucking ass off all day long.'

In all honesty, he probably wouldn't have agreed to do *Destiny and Desperado* if he'd known what a storm *Pulp Fiction* was going to cause, but for a trained actor, it was a difficult temptation to resist.

'I was a little freaked out when I first started *Destiny* but it all worked out just fine. We had a really good time just doing it. I mean it's the only thing that would have given me pause.'

Even now the possibility exists that he might be acting in a further feature for Kit Carson opposite Richard Gere, star of Tarantino's beloved *Breathless* . . .

Beyond that, who knows? His brief foray into producing, as with Roger Avary's *Killing Zoe*, would seem to be pretty much over. After *From Dusk Till Dawn* comes *Curdled*, going before the cameras in Florida in October, starring Billy Baldwin and Angela Jones (the taxi driver from *Pulp Fiction*) with Reb Braddock directing and John Maas producing – the pair were film students, Tarantino saw a short film of theirs at a festival and encouraged them to write it into a feature version. Angela Jones starred in the original short and Tarantino borrowed her for *Pulp Fiction* as a consequence. But after that, that's it.

'If I had another Quentin, he could do those things, it'd be a lot of fun, but my feeling is when I'm *not* doing a movie now, I don't want to *do* a movie. You know, I give up a year and a half of my life when I do a film. I don't mind giving up a year and a half of my life, but I want at least a year back in return and so when I'm not working, I don't want to fuckin' work.'

Tarantino has often talked about doing a film about 'a bunch of guys on a mission', and has made quips about doing a 'swashbuckler', but if the procuring of the rights to the Leonard novels is anything to go by, he may well adapt something further down the line, though this would perhaps mark a change for someone with a penchant for directing his own material, one good reason why *The Man From UNCLE* seems unlikely.

'I would think it would always have to be *my* thing if I'm going to do a good job with it,' he says. 'And if I was hired by someone else to do something, it would have to be my thing too, hiring me to take it over and do what I do. But I'd like to adapt a novel, very much so. It's much different to like doing somebody else's screenplay. Adapting a novel you can totally make that your own. Stanley Kubrick has basically only adapted novels . . .'

Unfortunately, whatever he does, Tarantino is now a marked man, for as with anyone who succeeds at so much, so soon, the critics, fickle beasts that they are, will be keen to catch him out as a one-trick pony, a spent force.

'The Tarantino Backlash: *Pulp Fiction* Pulped,' trumpeted the *Modern Review* in October 1994, almost as if it was the clarion call for some new popular movement.

'Well people were saying that after *Dogs*,' says Tarantino. 'Will they stop asking after I make a big flop, a bomb, a complete piece of shit? *Pulp Fiction* may be the best movie I ever made twenty years down the line, but like I'm not in that game of, "I've got to top this." '

David Thomson, writing in the *Independent on Sunday*, even warned Tarantino of falling into the Godard syndrome.

'Tarantino loves to take old American genres and give them a shot of hip and mannered adrenaline: elegant camera moves adorning gutter talk. Godard excelled at that for seven or eight years. He revolutionized film, and he showed us how the old stories might be camp. Then he went cold, reclusive and academic and gave up making films. Can Tarantino change? Hollywood may tempt him to remain the same, the perfect modern moviemaker – brilliant so long as he stays in the dark.'

But while Tarantino should afford himself a quiet chuckle at such intellectual dissection, the urge to change, or 'develop' as they patronizingly call it in Hollywood, will inevitably become a pressure. Tarantino, after all, has admitted on occasion that he doesn't just want to be known as 'the gun guy'.

'Well it's not so much that I don't want be "the gun guy", I just don't want to be limited by the genre,' he differs. 'But then I've kind of gone back and forth on it because it's just like, you know, wait a minute. For instance, when I was doing *Pulp* I was thinking that the next movie I do definitely won't be in the crime genre. Then I started thinking, "What the fuck are you saying? You've done *two* movies, not *six* movies that were about gangsters."

'When you're coming up with a story, there are all these tunnels you can go down. I'm gonna put out a roadblock now in front of one of the

205

tunnels on my *third film*? Who gives a fuck, alright. I've got my whole life. I can go anywhere I want to go. It's like saying, "I will not fall in love with a blonde this time. A redhead, a brunette – but not a blonde." You know what, you can't fuckin' say that. What I would like to do is like Howard Hawks and work in a whole load of different genres. I'd like to do a Western, I'd like to do a war film . . .'

We finish breakfast and head out into the bright LA sun, stopping on the way for Tarantino to pick up some enthusuastic praise from admirers, including one gooey-eyed gamine who turns to jelly in his presence (Tarantino once joked that he should write a guide about how to get laid at film festivals). And, as we walk up the road, he ponders the day ahead, so much so that he is almost hit by a dawdling motorist as he crosses the road.

'Gotta look both ways, buddy,' he yells in mock anger, tapping on the bonnet of said vehicle, driven by an overly apologetic middle-aged gay man.

If he can survive the perils of modern traffic, Tarantino will go a long way, trailing in his wake a whole army of young filmmakers who have suddenly realized that if you have unswerving faith in your script, then that's a damn fine place to start. And though the impact may not be immediately apparent, already the references are there (*Shallow Grave* soundbites: 'The Scottish *Reservoir Dogs*,' 'Fans of *Pulp Fiction* will love it').

To pursue a musical analogy, when the Sex Pistols burst on the scene in 1976, the years following were filled with the sounds of amateur bands thrashing away in garages. They weren't all necessarily any good, but they'd thrown away their inhibitions. More importantly, they realized that creativity isn't the preserve of a cosy private élite.

In filmic terms, Tarantino has achieved an equivalent. He whetted the appetites of grass-roots filmmakers who now understand that you don't have to go through the film school route – if you believe in your talent and know your stuff, nothing can stop you. Filmmaking belongs to Everyman.

'I don't know anybody so far who's actually *made* a film and said, "Oh, it was *Dogs* that inspired me," ' says Tarantino. 'But I meet a lot of film *students*, you know, who say that *Dogs* was a big inspiration for them and that's great because in a way that was always my dream when

I was younger, before I'd ever made a film, was to make movies that would inspire other people the way other people's work has inspired me. And now, one of the things that's cool is this attitude of kinda, "Fuck it. I'm not gonna wait until I get everything. I'm just gonna do it." The best advice to anyone who ever wants to make a movie is, "Stop fucking thinking about it. Stop trying to make everything perfect. Just fuckin' *do* it. Get the film and just start shooting." '

'Filmmaking used to be this sacred thing that was impossible to break into,' says Roger Avary. 'If Quentin has done anything, he's brought back a little bit of excitement into independent films and he's proven that somebody can come from nowhere and just with love and passion make a movie.'

Only time will tell, but according to Jon Ronson, writing in the *Independent*, the movement has already begun.

'Recently, I went to see Hal Hartley's *Amateur* in which two hitmen discuss the relative merits of mobile phones before blowing away their target. The next day I attended the National Film School's end-of-term screenings. Out of the five student movies I watched, four incorporated violent shoot-outs over a soundtrack of iconoclastic 70s pop hits, two climaxed with all the main characters shooting each other at once, and one had two hitmen discussing the idiosyncrasies of *The Brady Bunch* before offing their victim. Not since *Citizen Kane* has one man appeared from relative obscurity to redefine the art of moviemaking.'

Quentin Tarantino as Orson Welles? That's a hell of a compliment.

Or was it Herman J. Mankiewicz . . . ?

Index

Characters are indexed by their first name (followed by surname and film in parentheses).

INDEX